Michael Baigent was born in New Zealand in 1948. He obtained a degree in Psychology from Canterbury University, Christchurch. Since 1976 he has lived in England with his wife and children in order to research and write. His book, *From the Omens of Babylon*, is published by Penguin Arkana.

Richard Leigh followed up his degree from Tufts University, Boston, with MA and Ph.D. studies in comparative literature at the University of Chicago and the State University of New York at Stony Brook respectively. Despite his success in non-fiction he regards himself primarily as a novelist and short-story writer. He has recently completed a volume of short stories and has a long and ambitious novel in progress.

Michael Baigent and Richard Leigh have also co-authored a number of other investigative books. These include *The Temple and the Lodge*, *The Dead Sea Scrolls Deception* and, with Henry Lincoln, *The Holy Blood and the Holy Grail* and *The Messianic Legacy*. Their work has received much critical acclaim: *The Dead Sea Scrolls Deception* was described as 'absolutely stunning' by Douglas Adams; while the late Anthony Burgess, writing about *The Holy Blood and the Holy Grail* in the *Observer*, said, 'These young men are no fools; they have learning, energy [and] enthusiasm tempered by scepticism.'

# MICHAEL BAIGENT AND
# RICHARD LEIGH

―――――

## SECRET GERMANY

### CLAUS VON STAUFFENBERG AND THE
### MYSTICAL CRUSADE AGAINST HITLER

To Fergie
from
Rosemary & Jilia

Sept. 1995

PENGUIN BOOKS

PENGUIN BOOKS

Published by the Penguin Group
Penguin Books Ltd, 27 Wrights Lane, London W8 5TZ, England
Penguin Books USA Inc., 375 Hudson Street, New York, New York 10014, USA
Penguin Books Australia Ltd, Ringwood, Victoria, Australia
Penguin Books Canada Ltd, 10 Alcorn Avenue, Toronto, Ontario, Canada M4V 3B2
Penguin Books (NZ) Ltd, 182–190 Wairau Road, Auckland 10, New Zealand

Penguin Books Ltd, Registered Offices: Harmondsworth, Middlesex, England

First published by Jonathan Cape 1994
Published in Penguin Books 1995
1 3 5 7 9 10 8 6 4 2

The acknowledgements on p. xiii constitute an extension of this copyright page

Printed in England by Clays Ltd, St Ives plc

# Contents

# Illustrations

Maps and Charts

# Acknowledgements

Although this book revolves around the charismatic figure of Colonel Count Claus von Stauffenberg, Chief of Staff of the Reich Reserve Army, it is not intended to be a conventional biography. Neither is it merely an account of the plot he conceived with a group of conspirators to kill Adolf Hitler in July 1944. Some say that had he succeeded he would have become the de Gaulle of Germany and saviour of the national soul, but even in failure he stands as an atonement for the Third Reich and a resolution of the conflicting myths of German culture. If Stauffenberg occupies centre stage in our story, it is because he throws such a clear light on the troubled past of the German-speaking people and explains the dilemma of their search for national identity.

A conventional biography of all three Stauffenberg brothers was published recently in German by Peter Hoffmann, whose book we acknowledge as a useful source of information. But our enquiry has taken us far beyond its parameters. We have viewed Stauffenberg as a reflecting medium, a lens through which we could focus the forces and circumstances that fostered the phenomenon of National Socialism and, not least, the meaning of heroism in the twentieth century.

Any approach to a corpus of historical data demands an element of selectivity. In addressing ourselves to the wider trends, we were obliged to omit some of the more detailed material we encountered in our research. We have not attempted to do full justice to the

*Widerstand* (the German resistance to Hitler) and have deliberately avoided certain aspects of it, such as the diplomatic activities of Adam von Trott zu Solz and the civilians of Helmuth James von Moltke's 'Kreisau Circle'. In some cases we derive a measure of consolation from the knowledge that we have deferred to the wishes of those who agreed to talk to us. Some of the people we interviewed were reluctant to see the events of the 'Bomb Plot', or the *Widerstand*, exposed and raked over again. They were prepared to recall painful memories for us, and to re-open old wounds, precisely because they endorsed the broader issues we wanted to explore. For these people, the details of what happened were less important than the interest we showed in the tradition, the heritage, the mentality and the code of honour that made resistance to the Third Reich a moral and spiritual imperative.

Among the officers directly involved in Stauffenberg's conspiracy we must cite the late Axel von dem Bussche who, in 1944, was prepared to sacrifice his own life in an attempt to eliminate Hitler. In the months preceding his death in 1992, Freiherr von dem Bussche displayed immense generosity in making available to us both his time and his memories. We are equally indebted to Ewald von Kleist, who was also prepared to sacrifice himself and who was actually present in the War Office on 20 July 1944. Ludwig von Hammerstein was another officer present at the scene, and we owe our thanks to him for sharing his recollections. The exploits of these men and their seemingly miraculous escape from Nazi retribution would constitute a gripping and self-contained narrative of its own.

We must thank Otto John, another eyewitness of the events at the War Office and subsequently, during the 1950s, head of West Germany's security services. We must also thank Angela zu Solms and Nona von Haeften, whose network of friends and relations made themselves available to us – in particular Jan von Haeften, Barbara von Haeften, Gottliebe von Lehndorff and Vera von Lehndorff. Some of their accounts proved as poignant and harrowing as those of active participants in the conspiracy.

We are especially grateful to General-Major Berthold von Stauffenberg, who took time from his official duties to talk to us about his father and his family's tradition of service. For their comments on Stefan George, we would also like to thank Harold-Victor Koch and Hans-Dietrich Fühlendorf.

An enormous debt is owed to Nadia Shah, who undertook a daunting job of translation for us, and for additional help with translation our thanks go to Belinda Hunt, Dörte McCourt and Anne Westholm.

Among others who have helped in a variety of ways, we wish to thank Sacha Abercorn, Jane Baigent, Peter and Christabel Bielenberg, Karl Blessing, Brie Burkeman, Pascal Cariss, Jonathan Clowes, Tony Colwell, Rolf Cyriax, Ann Evans, Patrick Janson-Smith, Sir George Kennard, Claudia Limmer, Tom Maschler, Michael and Brigitta von Preussen, Caroline Michel, Ulrike Netenjakob, Ute Oelmann and John Saul.

All extracts from the works of Stefan George are reprinted from *The Works of Stefan George*, translated by Olga Marx and Ernst Morwitz. Copyright © 1974 by University of North Carolina Studies in Germanic Languages and Literatures, Chapel Hill, North Carolina, USA. All rights reserved.

For permission to reproduce photographs we thank Archiv für Kunst und Geschichte (1, 15, 16); Bilderdienst, Süddeutscher Verlag (3, 4, 7, 8, 18, 26, 33); Gedenkstätte Deutscher Widerstand Berlin (6); Gehlen-Memoirs 'Der Dienst' published 1971 by von Hase & Koehler Verlag, Mainz (21); Stefan George-Archiv, Stuttgart (32, 34, 36, 37); Barbara von Haeften (5); Sir George Kennard (24); Ullstein Bilderdienst (2, 9, 10, 11, 12, 13, 17, 19, 20, 22, 23, 25, 27, 35). Other photographs were taken for this book by Michael Baigent.

We also wish to acknowledge Lori Keenan, who contributed appreciably to the work's original inspiration. And we would like to acknowledge the memory of Hauptmann Jaspers, who helped bring something of significant worth into the world.

M.B. and R.L.
February 1994

# *Introduction*

By the spring of 1943, the Second World War was careening towards its fourth year of conflict. It would still have another two years to run, and some of the bloodiest and most bitter fighting had yet to occur. Nevertheless, the tide, in Churchill's phrase, had at last begun to turn. In three of the most important theatres of operations, the Allies – the British Empire, the Soviet Union and the United States – had forced the Axis on to the defensive, and were just beginning to take the offensive themselves.

During the previous year, three decisive engagements had transformed the course of the war, dramatically reversing the flow of its momentum. The first of these was the Battle of Midway, in June 1942, when Japan's seemingly inexorable sweep across the Pacific had been abruptly halted, and the loss of four aircraft carriers left Japanese air and sea power irreparably impaired.

On the Russian front, where Hitler's advancing forces were locked in a titanic struggle with those of the Soviet Union, the German 6th Army's assault on Stalingrad had ground to a halt. By the last week of November, the army was entirely encircled by the Russian counter-offensive. On 31 January 1943, the 6th Army surrendered with its surviving 91,000 men, having already suffered nearly 200,000 casualties. Germany had previously undergone reverses, of course – in the Battle of Britain, for example, and at sea – but Stalingrad was the German war machine's first major setback on land. It was a decisive defeat and led to the series of Russian counter-thrusts that carried the Red Army across the whole of Eastern Europe, into the pulverised ruins of Berlin.

In North Africa, the progress of the war had see-sawed almost since the outbreak of hostilities in 1939. After being repeatedly thrashed by British forces, Italy's battered and demoralised troops were reinforced by the Afrika Korps under General (later Field Marshal) Erwin Rommel, known respectfully even by his adversaries as the 'Desert Fox'. For more than a year, Rommel and a succession of British commanders fenced with each other across the sands of Egypt and Libya. The situation was at its worst for the British in March 1942, when Tobruk, the last bastion before Alexandria and the Suez Canal, finally fell. Rommel seemed unstoppable: he had only to smash his way through the exhausted British 8th Army, and Alexandria and the canal would be his for the taking. Loss of the canal would have been a fatal blow for Britain, permanently depriving her of a crucial sea route to such distant parts of the empire as India, Australia and New Zealand. It would have allowed the Afrika Korps to fulfil Hitler's grand design – to advance eastwards, up through Palestine, into the vital oil fields of modern-day Iraq and Iran. From here, they could have linked up with the German armies already striking down through the Ukraine and the southern regions of the Soviet Union.

Such was the daunting prospect confronting the Allies in mid-1942. But in July, Rommel's thrust towards the Suez Canal was parried by the 8th Army under General (later Field Marshal) Sir Claude Auchinleck at the first Battle of El Alamein. Shortly thereafter, Auchinleck was replaced by a new commander, the then little-known General Bernard Law Montgomery, and during the summer and early autumn, 8th Army was massively reinforced. At last, on the night of 23–4 October, Montgomery launched his counter-offensive with the famous artillery barrage of more than eight hundred heavy guns, the most ferocious and concentrated such barrage of the war. After eleven days of sustained fighting, 8th Army broke through the German and Italian defences, and Rommel began a retreat which was to carry him westwards across Egypt and Libya into Tunisia – fifteen hundred miles back across the desert with Montgomery in hot pursuit.

Five days after Montgomery's breakthrough at Alamein on 3

November, British, American and Free French forces had landed at the opposite end of the North African coast – at Algiers, Casablanca and Oran. According to the language employed at the time, they were to constitute the anvil on which the hammer of Montgomery's 8th Army smashed the retreating Germans. But things did not go entirely to plan. German reinforcements were rushed into Tunisia. The soldiers of the American II Corps, moreover, were green, their discipline was lax and they offered an enticingly vulnerable soft spot on the Allied front.

On 4 February 1943, the Staff Officer in charge of operations for the German 10th Panzer Division had been seriously injured by a mine. Ten days later he was replaced by a 36-year-old aristocrat from an 800-year-old Swabian family, Oberstleutnant (Lieutenant-Colonel) Claus Philipp Maria Schenk, Graf (Count) von Stauffenberg. On that same day, 10th Panzer Division attacked the American II Corps at Sidi Bou Zid. For the Americans, it was their baptism of fire, and their nominal commander, General Fredendall, was nowhere near the front – he had queasily ensconced himself in an underground bunker more than sixty miles away. Daunted by the German onslaught, most of the Americans abandoned their weapons and fled.

A much larger and even more ignominious humiliation followed five days later, at the Battle of Kasserine Pass. Held in reserve for the first day of the engagement, 10th Panzer Division joined the German assault on 20 February. Again, the Americans panicked and fled, losing nearly 2,700 killed and wounded and another 2,500 prisoners. Eisenhower, the supreme Allied commander, had been reluctant to call on British support, hoping his troops would acquit themselves honourably on their own. The urgency of the situation, however, took precedence over national pride. General Fredendall was relieved of command (and packed off to the United States with a face-saving promotion). While his successor, George Patton, undertook to rebuild the tattered American morale, help was invoked and a counter-attack launched by the British 6th Armoured Division. By 22 February, the Germans had been driven back to their former positions at Mareth.

Two weeks later, 10th Panzer Division was in action again, this time striking east from Mareth in an audacious but futile attempt

to halt Montgomery's advancing 8th Army at Medenine. When
Montgomery counter-attacked on 20 March, 10th Panzer offered
particularly fierce resistance, and it was not until six days later that
the Germans were forced to abandon their positions at Mareth. In
both of these engagements, 10th Panzer's new Staff Officer
(Operations) made a dramatic impression on subordinates, colleagues and superiors alike.

> In spite of all his office work, the Staff Officer (Operations)
> invariably found time to keep in touch with the troops. He would
> frequently visit regiments and battalions to discuss personal or
> official problems with commanding officers. By informal discus-
> sion on the spot, he would deal with a whole mass of business
> which would otherwise have had to be cleared up through official
> channels. His conversation was not, however, limited solely to
> official matters; he would range over history, geography,
> literature, and, of course, politics. Though he was clearly
> opposed to the existing system, he never tried to persuade or
> influence anybody. He did not seem to me to be in any sense
> fanatical, impetuous or a go-getter trying to change everything at
> once . . . He had the natural charm of the Swabian, which
> everybody found irresistible.[1]

One of the new Staff Officer's subordinates offers a particularly
eloquent testimony:

> Although I was only a twenty-two-year-old subaltern . . . I was
> extraordinarily impressed by Stauffenberg's personality. He
> seemed to me the ideal of an officer. His manner was so frank and
> friendly that one did not get the impression of being a subordi-
> nate. His thoughtfulness inspired one with confidence. On the
> other hand, the incision with which he spoke drew respect; he
> was a man possessed of natural authority. It was typical of
> Stauffenberg's way of going about things that he was determined
> to get to know personally all officers in the division, down to
> company commander, as soon as he could – which was why I was
> ordered to report to him. This was not normal procedure. He was
> determined that there should be close contact between the staff
> and the troops.[2]

On 7 April, two weeks after the German retreat from Mareth, the Allied pincers closed – the Anglo-American forces that had landed in November linked up with Montgomery's 8th Army advancing from the east. This determined the fate of the Africa Korps and its Italian allies, now boxed in amid Tunisia's rocky hills and flat barren passes. On 12 May, 250,000 German and Italian troops surrendered, thereby paving the way for the invasion of Sicily and then the Italian mainland – the first Allied foothold on the continent of Europe since the evacuation at Dunkirk three years before.

With the Allies enjoying air supremacy, as well as control of the Mediterranean, no German equivalent of Dunkirk could even have been contemplated. But while the army itself could not be saved, it was still possible for individual commanders, senior officers and other important personnel to be rescued. An ill and depressed Rommel was invalided home shortly after his withdrawal from Mareth. Claus von Stauffenberg was booked for a flight back to Italy, whence he would be re-assigned to a new posting. He himself had recognised that the North African campaign was irretrievably lost. Not caring to spend the duration of the war as a prisoner, he had requested a transfer, maintaining he could be of greater use elsewhere. No one disagreed with him, for Stauffenberg was universally recognised as the single most brilliant and promising young officer in the entire Wehrmacht. There seemed little question that he was destined for high command, eventually for a field marshal's baton. It was said that he had the capacity 'to inspire the Army and the General Staff with a new spirit and to compete with the narrow military point of view'.[3] One of his colleagues observed: 'What surprised me was the manner in which those who surpassed him in rank recognised his natural superiority and yielded to it.'[4] In the view of one of his commanders, he was 'the only German Staff officer of genius'.[5] Heinz Guderian, the mastermind of German armoured warfare and architect of Panzer formations and the 'Blitzkrieg', was soon to put Stauffenberg's name forward as most likely candidate for Chief of the General Staff.[6]

On the day that the Anglo-American forces advancing from the west joined up with the 8th Army, Stauffenberg was helping to organise the German retreat towards the Tunisian coastal town of Sfax. His staff car was manoeuvring through a lengthy file of other vehicles and demoralised soldiers on foot when the entire column came under strafing attack from a squadron of American P-40 fighter-bombers.[7] The road was at once transformed into an inferno of blazing vehicles, each of which, as it burst into flames, provided another easily discernible marker for the low-flying aircraft. As his driver threaded a path between the gutted hulks, Stauffenberg stood upright in his staff car, issuing orders and directing such lorries as still remained mobile. Then, he himself became a target for one of the P-40s' .50 calibre machine-guns. Hands covering his head, he hurled himself out of the car as the bullets struck home.

He was found, half-conscious, beside his overturned, burnt out and shell-pocked vehicle. His injuries were appalling. His left eye had been hit by a bullet, his right seriously damaged as well. His right forearm and hand had been virtually shot away, as had two fingers on his left. One knee was badly wounded and his back and legs were pitted with shrapnel. In this condition, he was rushed to the nearest field hospital, at Sfax. Here, he received emergency treatment. The remnants of his right hand were amputated above the wrist. The little finger and ring finger of his left hand, and what remained of his left eye, were removed.

Three days later, as Montgomery's troops advanced on Sfax, Stauffenberg was transferred to another hospital at Carthage – a difficult and extremely painful journey, with the ambulance under constant attack by Allied aircraft. From Carthage, he was flown to Munich. He was running an alarmingly high temperature, and most of the doctors concluded he was unlikely to live. If, by some miracle, he did, he was unlikely to walk again. He would probably be permanently crippled, an invalid for the rest of his life. He might also be blind.

His head, arms and legs swathed like a mummy's in bandages, he was visited in hospital by an array of distinguished officers, who, during the previous years of both peace and war, had come to esteem him. They included the Chief of the General Staff, Kurt Zeitzler, who brought him a decoration, the Golden Badge for the Wounded, and a personal gift of wine. 'The large number of high-ranking visitors calling on the lieutenant-colonel caused astonishment at the military hospital.'[8]

Stauffenberg was also visited by his mother, by his wife, Nina, and by his uncle, Nikolaus, Graf (Count) von Üxküll-Gyllenband, as well as by other relatives. To Üxküll he confided that he felt his survival had not been coincidental; his life, mutilated though it might now be, had been spared for some specific purpose, some ordained design.

'You know,' he said to Nina on one occasion, 'I have a feeling I've now got to do something to save the Reich. As General Staff officers, we all share the responsibility.'[9]

To a friend, the son of his surgeon, he stated: 'I could never look the wives and children of the fallen in the eye if I did not do something to stop this senseless slaughter.'[10]

To Üxküll and a number of others, he was even more incisively determined: 'Since the generals have so far done nothing, the colonels must now go into action.'[11]

From childhood, Stauffenberg had cultivated self-discipline and a tenacious application of will – a fierce concentration of inner resources, psychological or spiritual, whereby, as he saw it, flesh could be mastered and transcended. These resources were now to be augmented by a consuming sense of mission. The first step for Stauffenberg was to rehabilitate himself. He set about establishing a personal supremacy over physical pain, affirming what he regarded as his spiritual identity in defiance of the body's ordeals. While the surgeons laboured over him, he adamantly refused all pain-killing drugs, all soporifics, anaesthetics and sedatives. Even the official Gestapo report speaks admiringly of the 'great will-power' with which he embarked on his recovery.

Grievous though his injuries had been, Stauffenberg remained hospitalised in Munich for no more than two and a half months, from 21 April until 3 July. As early as the end of April, his recovery was being pronounced 'remarkable', and he wrote to a friend, General Friedrich Olbricht, that he hoped to be ready for duty again by August. Despite the dire prognostications to the contrary, he recovered the use of his right eye. With the two fingers and thumb of his left hand, he taught himself laboriously to write. In the sleeping compartment of a train, shortly after he had discharged himself from hospital, a fellow officer, pitying his condition, offered to help him change clothes. Stauffenberg chuckled and, in a matter of moments, had undressed and dressed himself again, employing three fingers and his teeth. When the hospital asked him to return to have an artificial limb fitted, he replied that he had no time for such matters. When an artificial limb was suggested by a friend, he laughed and again dismissed the idea. He could scarcely remember, he said, what he'd done with all ten fingers when he still possessed them. He insisted on regarding his injuries as no more than a minor inconvenience, training himself to function as normally as possible, even to ride horseback – and, when later circumstances so required, to activate a bomb.

Stauffenberg would not let himself be demobilised either. He declared his intention not only to remain in the army, but to resume active duty and even to get posted to the front. Almost at once, he was besieged by senior commanders seeking to woo him to their staff. He chose a position as Chief of Staff in the Allgemeine Heeresamt, the General Army Office, one of the departments of the Reserve Army based in Berlin. The Reserve Army consisted of all troops stationed on German soil, within the precincts of the Reich itself. The task of the General Army Office was to supply matériel, as well as trained replacements, to the Reserve Army, which could then transfer them to the appropriate theatre of operations. Such replacements consisted of new recruits, wounded who had recovered, workers withdrawn from industry, over-age and under-age volunteers.

Stauffenberg's immediate superior at the General Army Office was Colonel-General Friedrich Olbricht, with whom he had corresponded in April; and it has been suggested that he and Olbricht had already come to a secret understanding. In any case, there were reasons for Stauffenberg wanting to be attached to Olbricht's department. Through his own network of connections, he knew it to be a clandestine hotbed of officers militantly opposed to Hitler and the National Socialist régime. These officers had begun to act in close concert with another cadre, led by one of the most dynamic young commanders on the Eastern Front, Major-General Henning von Tresckow, whom Stauffenberg had known since at least the summer of 1941. Under Tresckow's auspices, an embryonic plan had been formulated for using the Reserve Army as the nucleus of a coup. The General Army Office was the vital connecting link between the Reserve Army and Tresckow's circle on the Eastern Front.

By mid-August 1943, some five weeks after discharging himself from hospital, Stauffenberg was in Berlin. Here, he began actively conspiring with Tresckow, then on leave; and when Tresckow returned to the Eastern Front, leadership of the conspiracy in Germany devolved almost entirely upon Stauffenberg. The pace of events quickened when, on 1 October, he officially assumed his post as Chief of Staff at the General Army Office. He was now based at the building on the Bendlerstrasse which served as headquarters for the Reserve Army.

Energy, resourcefulness, determination, eloquence, charisma, an irresistible magnetic charm and an infectious sense of humour – all the qualities Stauffenberg had previously employed in his wartime tasks were now directed towards conspiracy. From his house in a Berlin suburb, shared with his brother Berthold, he proceeded to consolidate the requisite network of contacts, as well as to familiarise himself with the civil and military measures which seizure of power would entail: proclamation of a state of emergency, arrest of Party officials along with SS and Gestapo personnel, occupation of ministries, railway depots, communications centres, strategic installations and access roads. It was a dauntingly arduous and complex undertaking, yet Stauffenberg's unflagging stamina – especially in a man so recently and terribly wounded – seemed to his colleagues almost superhuman. Tirelessly, he moved through the upper military and administrative echelons of the Reich, screening prospective supporters, probing, evaluating, interrogating, arguing, recruiting – always with a ready laugh, an apparently slapdash cavalier insoucience, a mesmerising force of character and will that seldom failed to win people over.

'Let me be blunt,' he declared to one young officer whose services he wished to recruit. 'With all the resources at my disposal, I'm committing high treason.'[12]

In meeting with co-conspirators, he would often recite fragments from the work of Stefan George, his former mentor, who had died in 1933 and is, after Rilke, probably the greatest German-language poet of the century. In particular, he would quote from a poem entitled 'Der Widercrist' ('The Antichrist'), which George had published – with what now seemed uncanny foresight – in 1907:

The high Prince of Vermin extends his domains;
No pleasure eludes him, no treasure or gain.
And down with the dregs of rebellion!

You cheer, mesmerised by demoniac sheen,
Exhaust what remains of the honey of dawn,
And only then sense the débâcle.

You then stretch your tongues to the now arid trough,
Mill witless as kine through a pasture aflame,
While fearfully brazens the trumpet.[13]

On 6 June 1944, history's most ambitious seaborne invasion swept half a million British, American and Canadian soldiers ashore in Normandy. The repercussions were soon to give Stauffenberg his long-sought opportunity. Colonel-General Fritz Fromm, Commander-in-Chief of the Reserve Army, had been out of favour with Hitler for some two years. Now, on 7 June, owing to a particularly impressive report Stauffenberg had composed for him, Fromm was summoned to the Führer's headquarters above Berchtesgaden, at the Berghof in the Bavarian Alps, and Stauffenberg accompanied him.

It is often assumed or asserted by historians that the meeting at the Berghof was Stauffenberg's first personal contact with Hitler. A photograph published for the first time in this book proves they had met previously – at least as early as the summer of 1942, at Vinnitsa, German headquarters in the Ukraine. There Hitler, as always on encountering a new face, endeavoured to stare Stauffenberg down. In the past, his stare had always dominated others, forcing their eyes down or aside, but Stauffenberg remained uncowed, his eyes locking and holding the Führer's. For the first time in the experience of those present, Hitler's own gaze is said to have given way, growing veiled, jellied, then flicking furtively away – as if intimidated by a charisma, a magnetism, a force of will comparable to his own. Stauffenberg is said to have commented afterwards on this silent contest with typical self-confidence: 'The man is a magician. He almost hypnotised *me*!'

Two years later, all vestiges of Hitler's hypnotic power had evaporated for Stauffenberg. His own accounts of the meeting at

Berchtesgaden reflect, above everything else, an overwhelming revulsion. To his wife, when asked whether Hitler's eyes had been impressive or exerted any spell, he replied contemptuously: 'Not at all. Nothing.' They had only been 'veiled'. Goering had been wearing make-up, and the whole atmosphere of the Führer's headquarters had been 'stale', 'paralysing', 'rotten and degenerate'. Only Albert Speer, the Minister for Armaments, had seemed normal. All the other members of the National Socialist hierarchy had been 'patent psychopaths'. According to eyewitness reports:

> Hitler, his right hand trembling, looking worried, suddenly cast a searching glance at Stauffenberg across the long table; then, after quickly reassuring himself that there was no danger, he again turned his attention to the reporting officer.[14]

From that day on, the Führer ordered a tightening of his personal security, and emphasised that all briefcases carried to conferences should be closely watched.

Whatever Hitler's suspicions, the record of the dashing, one-handed and one-eyed officer was impeccable, his brilliance could not be disputed and endorsements from such senior commanders as Guderian could hardly be dismissed. On 20 June, he was seconded by Olbricht from the General Army Office to a position as Fromm's deputy: he became Chief of Staff of the Reserve Army. Promoted to full colonel, he officially assumed his new post on 1 July. He would now have access to the Führer's headquarters and to Hitler personally.

# Part One

———

## THE BOMB PLOT

# 1

# *The German Resistance*

Istory has been kind to the anti-German resistance in most of Nazi-occupied Europe. In part, of course, this is a consequence of Allied propaganda during the war itself. In the struggle for 'hearts and minds', much was to be gained by stressing the rôles of Free French, Free Polish, Free Czech and other forces fighting alongside those of Britain, the Empire as it then existed, and the United States. There were also vested interests, both during the war and afterwards, in stressing the activities of partisan organisations in occupied France, Holland, Belgium, Denmark, Norway, Czechoslovakia, Yugoslavia, Poland, Greece and, after September 1943, northern Italy – activities ranging from smuggling Allied airmen to safety and transmitting messages to co-ordinating air raids, engaging in sabotage and conducting large-scale guerrilla operations. In the English-speaking world, even the most cursory account of the war will accord some notice to the work of the underground resistance; and there can scarcely be a cinema-goer or television viewer who has not seen at least one film revolving around resistance activities, from Scandinavia to the Balkans and Greece. Nor must one forget the actions of partisans within the former Soviet sphere of influence, and within the former Soviet Union itself.

The German Resistance, or '*Widerstand*', has received altogether less attention from serious historians, and virtually no popular attention whatever. For most people, the Third Reich looms as a

*The Bomb Plot*

single sinister monolithic entity – the entire German population standing mesmerised, in docile thrall to Hitler's spell. In some quarters, it may even come as a surprise that a German resistance existed at all. Although there will generally be a vague awareness of the abortive plot to assassinate Hitler on 20 July 1944, for most non-historians, this will figure only as it was depicted at the time by the Nazis themselves and by Allied propaganda – a single doomed flash-in-the-pan attempt at a coup d'état improvised, in slapdash and amateurish fashion, by a few disgruntled high-ranking officers. Even among the better-informed, the plot of 20 July is seen as nothing more than an ad hoc and bungled endeavour to remove Hitler personally, rather than a manifestation of a coherent, long-standing, widespread and well-organised resistance movement.

In fact, a subterranean and organised German resistance had existed since before 1938 – before Hitler's invasion of Czechoslovakia and the notorious conference in Munich which, according to Neville Chamberlain, promised 'peace in our time'. This resistance consisted of senior military officers and civil servants, and international diplomats, jurists, intellectuals and men of letters. Some of these were among the most august and influential names in Germany. Hjalmar Schacht, President of the Reichsbank and former Minister of Economics, was involved, as well as Julius Leber, refugee of concentration camps and chief spokesman for German socialism. There were Carl Gördeler, former Mayor of Leipzig, Ulrich von Hassell, former German ambassador to Italy, and Adam von Trott zu Solz, one-time Rhodes Scholar at Oxford and probably the most brilliant mind in the German Foreign Office. Eminent jurists like Counts Peter Yorck von Wartenburg and Helmuth James von Moltke – cousins of the Stauffenberg family and founders of the intellectual 'Kreisau Circle' – took part, as did Pastor Dietrich Bonhöffer, the internationally distinguished teacher, lecturer, scholar and theologian.

Among the military, the list is equally impressive. It starts with Colonel-General Ludwig Beck, beloved former Chief of the General Staff, and Admiral Wilhelm Canaris, Chief of Military Intelligence, and goes on to involve at least eight senior commanders, including two other former Chiefs of the General Staff, two field marshals and the military governor of France, as well as numerous junior officers.

16

Although the true number can never be known, one historian records at least forty-six significant attempts on Hitler's life between 1921 and 1945.[1] In 1933 alone, there were ten which the police regarded as both genuine and serious. Some of the projected assassination schemes were wildly flamboyant and romantically dramatic – a battalion of German and Cossack paratroops, for example, dropping into the airport near Berchtesgaden, storming the headquarters and capturing the Führer, who would no doubt have been shot while trying to escape. Others were more realistic and, in other circumstances, might well have succeeded. And quite apart from plans to remove Hitler by violent means, there were numerous other plots for deposing the National Socialist régime and seizing power.[2] A few of these are worthy of note.

On 11 March 1938, the 'Anschluss' of Austria occurred. German troops marched into Vienna, and the original domains of the once-proud 600-year-old Habsburg empire were annexed to the Greater German Reich. Hitler then turned his designs to Czechoslovakia, a country which, unlike Austria, was not going to submit peaceably. Under its Chief of Staff, Ludwig Beck, the German high command was alarmed at the prospect of a major European war. Even apart from the moral issues, and the guilt Germany would incur for such aggression, the country was militarily unprepared for a large-scale conflict. If at first Beck's opposition was based on simple expediency, it soon became a matter of duty and honour:

> History will indict these commanders of blood guilt if, in the light of their professional and political knowledge, they do not obey the dictates of their conscience. The soldier's duty to obey ends when his knowledge, his conscience and his sense of responsibility forbid him to carry out a certain order.[3]

Towards the end of July 1938, Beck prepared a statement to Hitler:

> The Commander-in-Chief of the Army, together with his most senior commanding generals, regret that they cannot assume responsibility for the conduct of a war of this nature without carrying a share of the guilt for it in face of the people and of history. Should the Führer, therefore, insist on the prosecution of this war, they hereby resign from their posts.[4]

While most of the high command shared Beck's objections to war, few of them possessed his integrity and preparedness to act on his principles. Lacking the requisite unanimity of support from his subordinates, Beck resigned alone on 18 August, to be succeeded by General Fritz Halder. Halder was no more cordial to Hitler, whom he described as a 'criminal', a 'madman' and a 'blood-sucker'.[5] At the same time, he worried that any attempted coup might rend the whole of Germany and culminate in outright civil war. Despite the risk, he proceeded to plot a coup with other highly placed individuals, including Beck and Ernst von Weizsäcker, the father of Germany's present-day president.

Any premature movement or re-deployment of the army would, it was recognised, attract attention and give the game away, but if Hitler actually ordered the invasion of Czechoslovakia, the army would have to move in any case. Hitler's own orders, it was therefore decided, would set the army into motion – not towards an advance into Czechoslovakia, but towards an overthrow of the régime and a seizure of power. Among the units assigned to a key rôle in the projected enterprise was the 1st (Light) Division under Lieutenant-General Erich Hoepner, who had been initiated into the clandestine plans. One of Hoepner's most trusted subordinates, and friends, was the 31-year-old Captain Claus von Stauffenberg. Among the others associated with the undertaking were Stauffenberg's brother, Berthold, his uncle, Nikolaus von Üxküll, and two of his cousins, Cäsar von Hofacker and Peter Yorck von Wartenburg. When Stauffenberg emerged from hospital in 1943, he was no stranger to anti-Hitler conspiracy; he had been privy to the network of opposition within the military for five years.

The 'cover story' for the coup in 1938 – the official reason or 'excuse' for the army's seizure of power – was to be an alleged plot by the SS to usurp control of the country. This, it was felt, would ensure the allegiance of military personnel of all ranks. Such, already, was the animosity felt towards the SS by the army, and that animosity was only to intensify.

Many of the 1938 plotters wanted only to arrest Hitler and place him on trial. This would have precluded his being transformed into a martyr, and would also have pre-empted any accusations of a 'stab in the back'. Since 1933, one of the conspirators had secretly been collecting and collating material for a legal indictment. But there was also talk of having the Führer officially declared insane by a panel of doctors. And despite a number of objections, there evolved a contingency plan for assassination, on the grounds that 'tyrannicide had always been looked upon as a moral commandment'. According to Hans-Bernd Gisevius, then serving in the Ministry of the Interior:

> Not every attempt at a coup d'état can be judged by the same ethical standards. I am speaking of a situation in domestic and foreign politics which already was rife with murder and injustice, which was moving towards the bloodbath of a war. At stake was much more than the peace and security of one single country. The interests of millions of innocent people were more imperative than the requirements of justice – requirements which the tyrant himself had unfailingly violated.[6]

A 'raiding party' of armed officers was accordingly formed, quietly assembled and 'held ready in certain Berlin apartments'. When the coup was launched, this 'raiding party' was to descend on the Chancellery, ostensibly to arrest the Führer. In fact, 'more drastic measures' had been prepared: the 'raiding party' was 'determined to provoke an incident and shoot Hitler in the process'.[7] A new German government would then be formed and a democratic constitutional monarchy established, the crown being conferred on one of two grandsons of the former Kaiser Wilhelm II.

In the meantime, high-level diplomatic moves had been initiated through the Foreign Office. Secret emissaries were dispatched to France and to Britain, whose support was deemed to be of paramount importance. Throughout the autumn, consultations were conducted in secret with British officials.[8]

On 15 September, Britain's Prime Minister, Neville Chamberlain, arrived at Berchtesgaden to discuss the escalating Czech crisis with Hitler. So far as the projected coup was concerned, everything was in place: Chamberlain would remain adamant in the face of Hitler's voracious demands, Hitler would in turn refuse to back down and, with the prospect of war looming, the conspirators would have grounds on which to act. Instead Chamberlain gave way to Hitler, accepting that the Sudetenland – the German-speaking enclave of Czechoslovakia – should be ceded to the Reich. The conspirators were thrown into 'consternation' and 'confusion'. 'In their view the British statesman had been doing homage to a gangster and thus had let them down.'[9]

For the moment there was still hope. In his statements, Chamberlain had said more than he was authorised to say and had to return to London for Parliamentary ratification. Under clandestine pressure from the conspirators themselves, Britain placed her fleet on alert – though it is hard to see how this can have been much consolation to a landlocked Czechoslovakia. Czechoslovakia herself mobilised. France recalled her reservists. International tension intensified, and it looked as if the renewed threat of war would at last give the conspirators the sanction they required.

On 27 September, Hitler mobilised certain divisions near the Czech border. On the 28th, the 'raiding party' bent on Hitler's removal readied themselves for their assault on the Chancellery, the doors of which, in accordance with their plan, had been left open. But on the very next day, there occurred the infamous Munich Conference, in which Chamberlain and the French Premier Daladier capitulated to Hitler's demands, thereby removing the last obstacle to his advance, unchallenged and unmolested, into Czechoslovakia. Without the threat of war to validate their undertaking, the conspirators were stripped of all justification for action. 'So,' the historian Peter Hoffmann observed, 'the ground was cut from under the feet of the most promising attempt to overthrow Hitler', and, 'The Munich Conference and the abandonment of Czechoslovakia by the Western powers administered to the anti-Hitler opposition a blow from which it could not recover.'[10] At the Nuremberg trials after the war, General Halder was asked directly: 'If Chamberlain had not come to Munich, would the plan have been executed and Hitler deposed?' He replied that the plan would indeed have been carried out.[11]

It is, of course, easy to second-guess history, but it is difficult to imagine a moment of indecision and irresolution with more tragic consequences. Had Chamberlain remained firm at Munich, it is often asserted, Hitler would have backed down. In fact, Hitler would *not* have backed down, but, by virtue of not doing so, he would almost certainly have been deposed and very probably eliminated – and this would have been even more beneficial to humanity and to twentieth-century history. In their policy of 'appeasement', Chamberlain and Daladier have more to answer for than is generally believed.

Of all the plots against Hitler, that of 1938 stood probably the greatest chance of success and came closest to effective realisation. It was also the last occasion on which senior officers of the high command, including a presiding Chief of the General Staff, would have the willpower, the unanimity and the opportunity to work in such close concert. After the invasion of Czechoslovakia, German successes in the field, and the stranglehold of the SS and Gestapo at home, ensured a support and a docility among the populace that made a full-scale coup increasingly difficult to contemplate. Yet even before Stauffenberg's appearance on the scene, attempts on the Führer's life continued.

In September 1939, immediately after the outbreak of war, Colonel-General Kurt von Hammerstein tried desperately to engineer one such assassination. Hammerstein was a former Commander-in-Chief of the army, who, on the inauguration of hostilities, was entrusted with one of the German armies on the French front. He was involved in no organised conspiracy, gave no thought to wider political repercussions; but his hatred for Hitler was more than a decade old, pre-dating even the Nazis' rise to power. Acting virtually alone, he tried repeatedly – and unsuccessfully – to lure Hitler to his headquarters. 'I would have rendered him harmless once and for all,' Hammerstein subsequently said, 'and even without judicial proceedings.'[12] The military historian Sir John Wheeler-Bennett writes that, had Hitler only come within Hammerstein's reach, the general 'would have dealt faithfully and adequately with him'.[13] Shortly before his death from cancer in 1943, Hammerstein stated: 'A nation that has lost every feeling for right and wrong, good and evil, that commits such crimes, deserves to be destroyed . . .'[14]

The following month, after the successful conclusion of the Polish campaign, General Halder himself tried again, hoping to neutralise the Führer before shooting actually started with Britain and France. The speed and one-sidedness of the victory in Poland had made it more difficult to muster support than in 1938.

Nevertheless, Halder was able to draw on most of the individuals involved in the previous year's plot. Among his new co-conspirators were the Panzer commander Heinz Guderian and the young Henning von Tresckow (later to become one of Stauffenberg's closest associates and colleagues). Plans were laid to arrest and, in all likelihood, assassinate not just Hitler, but most of the Nazi Party hierarchy as well. The Kaiser's grandson, Prince Louis-Ferdinand, secretly declared his readiness, if called upon, to serve.[15] Clandestine links were established with the Vatican. The 9th Infantry Regiment of Potsdam – among whose young officers were Axel von dem Bussche and Ewald von Kleist, two of Stauffenberg's subsequent collaborators – was placed on alert and assigned a key rôle in the undertaking.

Almost immediately, things began to go wrong. A bomb which had nothing to do with the conspiracy was planted in a Munich beer hall on 8 November. There followed a clampdown on the availability of explosives, making it impossible for the conspirators to obtain the supplies they needed. Worse still, they were unable to obtain the support of Field Marshal Walter von Brauchitsch, Commander-in-Chief of the army, who had just had a row with Hitler and been badly intimidated. Without Brauchitsch's co-operation, action was unthinkable. Halder panicked, called off the projected coup and ordered the destruction of all records. For the next few weeks, he carried a loaded revolver in his pocket on every visit to the Chancellery, intending to shoot Hitler personally, but he could never muster the resolve to perform the act. At one point, he even talked about employing a contract killer, but it was too late for that.

One of Halder's co-conspirators in the plots of 1938 and 1939 was Field Marshal Erwin von Witzleben. As Commander-in-Chief in the West, Witzleben devised elaborate plans for assassinating Hitler in Paris in 1941. The Führer was to be invited to the French capital. A parade would be organised down the Champs Elysées, and Hitler would take the salute at the Place de la Concorde. Here he was to be shot by two officers on Witzleben's staff; and, in case anything went wrong, another officer was entrusted with a bomb to throw.[16] But after his unannounced visit at the end of the French campaign, on 23 June 1940, Hitler was never again to visit Paris.

He repeatedly declined Witzleben's invitations; and in March 1942, while in hospital for an operation, Witzleben was relieved of command and forced into retirement.

In January 1943, Major-General Henning von Tresckow was stationed with Army Group Centre on the Russian front. Tresckow had set about assembling more than fifteen prominent staff officers into a cadre that would turn the entire army group 'into an instrument for a coup'. Among the troops on whom Tresckow counted was a highly mobile cavalry unit: two battalions of 1,100 men each, 650 of them Russian Cossacks. Once a coup was set into motion, this unit would have quickly been flown to Berlin. According to Tresckow's original plan, Hitler was to be invited to the army group's headquarters at Smolensk. During a meal in the mess, some two dozen officers would simultaneously draw their pistols and shoot him – thus making the responsibility collective and, at the same time, ensuring that at least one bullet elude the security entourage of SS to find its target. Unfortunately, the army group commander, Field Marshal Günther von Kluge, had to be informed, if only to prevent his getting into the line of fire. Kluge scotched the plan not because he objected to assassinating Hitler, but because, by the tenets of the German Officer Corps, 'it was not seemly to shoot a man at lunch'.[17]

On 13 March 1943, Hitler did visit Army Group Centre at Smolensk, and Tresckow tried again. As Hitler returned to his aircraft from the army group's headquarters, troops lining the route were to open fire with their submachine-guns. But Hitler, seized by a sudden whim, decided to take another, apparently more scenic, route.[18]

Tresckow had a contingency plan which depended on the help of one of his friends from before the war, Lieutenant Fabian von Schlabrendorff, a former lawyer attached to Army Group Centre as an aide-de-camp. In 1939, Schlabrendorff had met secretly with Churchill, hoping to make the British government aware of the strength of the German opposition to Hitler. Now, Schlabrendorff had prepared a lethal package. He had used British explosives – dropped for Special Operations Executive agents and captured – because British fuses were silent, whereas German fuses made a slight hissing sound that might give them away. The principle governing Schlabrendorff's devices was simple. A wire held the firing pin of the detonator in place against a spring. At the opposite end of this wire, there was positioned a small glass phial of acid. Once the phial was broken, the acid would eat its way through the wire. After a calculated interval, it would release the detonator's firing pin.

Tresckow and Schlabrendorff had constructed their explosive devices carefully, packed so as to resemble two square bottles of Cointreau. During lunch at army group headquarters, Tresckow casually asked a member of Hitler's entourage if he could take two bottles of liqueur to a friend at Hitler's headquarters in Rastenburg, whence the Führer's aircraft was bound. The request appeared innocent enough and was unthinkingly granted.

Schlabrendorff took the parcel to the airstrip and waited to see which aircraft Hitler would board. He then activated the bomb by breaking the phial of acid and handed the parcel to an aide. The aircraft took off, accompanied by a fighter escort. Back at army group headquarters, Tresckow and Schlabrendorff telephoned a codeword to their co-conspirators in Berlin to indicate that the assassination attempt was under way. According to their calculations, the package would explode when Hitler's aircraft was more or less over Minsk. 'With mounting tension,' Schlabrendorff subsequently wrote, 'we waited for news of the "accident" . . .'

> After waiting more than two hours, we received the shattering news that Hitler's plane had landed without incident at the airstrip at Rastenburg, in East Prussia, and Hitler himself had safely reached Headquarters.[19]

The projected coup had to be cancelled immediately, and Tresckow and his collaborators were in despair. In the meantime, the explosive device had urgently to be retrieved before it was discovered. Tresckow telephoned the aide who had carried it and nonchalantly asked if it had yet been delivered to its intended recipient. On being told it had not, Tresckow feigned embarrassment and said he had mistakenly sent the wrong package. He would undertake to get it exchanged for the right one. The following day, Schlabrendorff flew to Rastenburg with two bottles of genuine Cointreau.

As I exchanged parcels . . . I felt my blood running cold, for Hitler's aide, serenely unaware of what he was holding, handed me the bomb with a grin, juggling it back and forth in a way which made me fear a belated explosion.[20]

Schlabrendorff took his deadly package to the nearby railway station, where he caught a night train for Berlin. Locking himself into a compartment, he proceeded to dismantle the device to see what had gone wrong. The glass phial had broken according to plan. The acid had spilled out and eaten its way through the wire. The firing pin had been released, but for some reason, the detonator had not triggered the desired explosion. At the time, Schlabrendorff guessed the detonator had perhaps been a dud, but it was blackened, which indicated that it had indeed gone off. It now seems most likely that, in the extreme cold over Russia in March, the explosive had simply failed to ignite.

Eight days later Tresckow and Schlabrendorff made another desperate attempt on Hitler's life. As part of the ceremonies of the annual 'Heroes Memorial Day', 21 March 1943, Hitler was to tour an exhibition of captured arms mounted in the Berlin Arsenal on Unter den Linden. Field Marshal Model was to direct Hitler through the display and, to answer any queries, an officer from Army Group Centre was detailed to accompany them.

This officer, Colonel (later General) Freiherr Christophe von Gersdorff, was chief of Intelligence at Army Group Centre and a close colleague of Tresckow and Schlabrendorff. On 20 March Schlabrendorff had delivered to him another cache of British explosives, but he could only obtain ten-minute fuses. Gersdorff was to pack his clothes with these explosives and blow up Hitler and himself.

The dignitaries were present at 1 pm when the official ceremonies began, all of which were broadcast live on German radio. Hitler made a short speech and then moved towards the entrance to the exhibition hall. Here the Führer was greeted by Gersdorff who saluted with his right hand, while setting off the chemical fuse with his left.

As the acid ate through the wire Gersdorff tried to keep as close to Hitler as possible. But Hitler apparently had some presentiment of

Gersdorff's plan: he refused to stop and view any of the exhibits. He almost ran straight through the hall and, despite the attempts of both Model and Gersdorff to interest him in the captured material, within two minutes emerged from the building. This threw the schedule into a confusion noted even by the BBC which was monitoring the radio broadcast.

With only minutes left, Gersdorff rushed to a nearby toilet to disarm himself. Back at his HQ, listening to the radio broadcast with a stop-watch in his hand, Tresckow knew that this attempt, too, had failed.

Gersdorff survived the war.[21]

# 2

# Operation Valkyrie

After the 'appeasement' of Munich in 1938, opportunities to involve the army's entire high command in Hitler's overthrow began to recede. Following Germany's military successes in Poland, Norway, Denmark, Holland, Belgium and France, such opportunities receded even further. While younger commanders like Tresckow remained ready to act, they had few chances to do so, being too far removed from Berlin and other crucial centres of power. When a rare chance did come their way, it was invariably dogged by bad luck. Although they had a network of associates in Berlin and other strategic locations, these associates were too often vacillating, indecisive, imperfectly united, lacking in the requisite initiative and, perhaps most important, lacking in authority. By 1943, Germany's armed forces were stretched from the Atlantic to the Russian heartland, from the Barents Sea to the Mediterranean – and, at almost every point of the compass, fully engaged. As long as this remained the case, the prospects were inauspicious for a coup originating on the periphery and radiating inwards. Any such undertaking would have to originate from the centre, from Berlin and from other internal concentrations of power; and the centre remained 'soft'.

The men in Berlin, for example, were not, for the most part, senior military officers, but figures of lesser rank and influence. They were also seldom, if ever, wholly united, either about their objectives or the means of attaining those objectives. For many of the individuals involved, there were serious questions – of both expediency and morality – to be considered. In the moral sphere, prominent members of the 'Kreisau Circle' were steeped in law, and questioned whether political assassination, even of Adolf Hitler and his colleagues, could ever be legitimate. Opponents of murder and terror found it understandably difficult to have recourse to murder and terror themselves. Were they to do so, would they not be guilty of transgressions as grievous as those they sought to redress? 'They were, to their credit, too conscious of their responsibilities, too torn by moral qualms to achieve the necessary degree of ruthlessness.'[1] Helmuth James von Moltke, founder of the 'Kreisau Circle' and one of Stauffenberg's cousins, is reported to have said to a member of the Stauffenberg family: 'We're not conspirators, we're not capable of being, we've not learnt how to do it, we shouldn't try to make a start now, it would go wrong, we should make an amateur job of it . . .'[2]

If violence were repudiated, what were the alternatives? In certain quarters, there was talk of 'impeaching' Hitler and putting him on trial, but such ideas, however theoretically valid, could, in the context of circumstances, hardly have been implemented. Yet even if violence were adopted, what then? It would not be sufficient simply to assassinate Hitler – or even Hitler and his immediate entourage of Party officials. Such action might produce a traumatic effect, as did the assassinations that have characterised our own era – those of John and Robert Kennedy, or Martin Luther King, or Anwar Sadat, or Indira and Rajiv Gandhi – but the machinery of the state, manifested particularly through the SS, would have remained immovably in place. And there were other repercussions to be considered. Most German soldiers and lower-echelon officers had been thoroughly indoctrinated in National Socialism, receiving their formative intellectual ideological training through the Hitler Youth Movement. Apart from those at the front, they were fervent supporters of the régime. To topple the régime would thus be to risk full-scale civil war. It would disastrously divide the army, or plunge the army into open and armed conflict with the SS. And while the army's upper echelons vehemently despised the SS, such conflict between the two institutions was too terrifying to contemplate.

In order to succeed, any prospective coup would somehow have to neutralise the SS. It would also have to neutralise, if not wholly dismantle, the entire machinery of the state. This was a rather more daunting prospect than just eliminating Hitler and his immediate cohorts. It was made more daunting still by the fact that Germany was fighting a major war at the time – a war that was no longer a struggle for conquest, but for survival, against adversaries little disposed to give quarter. So further complication confronted the conspirators, especially the military men. Although they felt it increasingly urgent to remove Hitler and his entourage from power, they also felt obliged – and this became an ever more pressing consideration as the war turned against Germany – to protect their country, their homes and families from being overrun.

Had the Western Allies been prepared to negotiate a peace, the conspirators – and, for that matter, most of the German military machine – would have been only too eager to comply. Serious proposals were made for collapsing the entire Western front, or for allowing an unopposed Allied landing near Hamburg. Such actions would at least have ensured that Germany, if the Fatherland had to be overrun at all, would be occupied by Western rather than Russian soldiers. Unfortunately, the Western Allies, believing victory within their grasp, refused to settle for anything less than unconditional surrender; and they had, moreover, negotiated their own accords with Stalin, on which they could not feasibly renege. In consequence, Germany lay vulnerable to the onslaughts of the Red Army and the 'Communist menace', a prospect as terrifying for the country's population as it was later to become for Americans during the immediate post-war period and the McCarthy years. The need to remove Hitler and the National Socialist hierarchy was becoming ever more obvious, and not just to the conspirators, but if doing so would render Germany susceptible to total conquest and occupation by the Soviet Union, where did duty lie? If only to protect their homeland and their families, many Germans, who would otherwise have readily laid down their arms, felt they had no choice but to continue fighting.

Haunted by questions such as these, conspirators in Berlin and other focal points of power were paralysed. They talked, they debated, they quarrelled among themselves, they often worked at cross-purposes to each other, they agonised over prospects and implications, they explored ways and means, they devised feasibility studies, they complained, hoped and, not infrequently, prayed. They remained, however, incapable of action.

'Freedom', Stauffenberg asserted, 'can only be won by action.'[3] It was with this passionate commitment that he joined the ranks of the conspirators, and he passed among them like an electric current, jolting and galvanising them out of their inertia, infusing them with his own fiery fixity of purpose, and welding their often nebulous and ineffectual decency into a coherent and dynamic movement. Men twice his age and far superior in rank were suddenly kindled by the energy of the 36-year-old colonel and, at last, animated with a will to act. Previously irreconcilable differences between soldiers and civilians, radicals and conservatives, republicans and monarchists, plebeians and patricians, dissolved in the intensity of a focused resolution and fused in a new sense of direction. For the first time, the German resistance became a positive *force*, a force rooted not in caste or in calling, in sociology or in politics, but in ethics, morality and the lofty imperatives of 'the spirit'. To designate this force, Stauffenberg again had recourse to the work of Stefan George, invoking one of his last and most apocalyptic poems: 'Geheimes Deutschland' ('Secret Germany').[4]

Under Stauffenberg's auspices, activities against the régime proceeded on a number of fronts. In reprisal for bombs dropped on German cities, Hitler had decreed mass executions of captured Allied airmen, and lists of those killed were to be sent to him. In a ploy reminiscent of Gogol's *Dead Souls*, Stauffenberg and his colleagues obtained from POW camps the names of men who had already died. These were then forwarded to his cousin, Helmuth James von Moltke, then serving with OKW (High Command of the Armed Forces) Intelligence. Each Allied prisoner slated for execution was, on paper, assigned the name of a dead or fictitious comrade, and reported to the Führer as recently shot. Many British and American airmen thus officially died twice, while a great many other pilots, gunners, navigators and bombardiers owed their lives to the deception.[5]

But the newly revitalised resistance could not confine itself simply to thwarting Hitler's perverse and vindictive whims; and even if he and his entourage were eliminated by violence, there remained the question of what would happen next. Plans had to be evolved for wresting control of the entire nation, for dismantling its existing institutions, for bringing the war to an end and creating a new democratic Germany out of the ashes of the Third Reich. This was made all the more difficult because there was no single central point, no building or office or headquarters, that could be seized. Hitler had created a labyrinthine network of overlapping authorities for exercising command and control, each with its own hierarchy and its own, often secret, lines of communication. There was OKW (Oberkommando der Wehrmacht), the High Command of the Armed Forces. There was OKH (Oberkommando des Heeres), the High Command of the Army. There was OKM (Oberkommando der Kriegsmarine), the High Command of the Navy. There was RSH(A) (Reichssicherheits-Hauptamt), the Central Reich Security Office which, under Himmler, ran the SD (Security Service), the Gestapo and the Criminal Police. And, of course, there was the SS itself, also under Himmler.

As it happened, a blueprint already existed which could be adapted for wresting control of Germany – a blueprint endorsed, ironically, by Hitler himself. It was code-named 'Valkyrie'. In the event of emergency within the Reich (an uprising of foreign workers, for instance), Operation Valkyrie was to be activated. This entailed the mobilisation and deployment of the Reserve Army, which, by 1944, numbered more than four million. Troops were to occupy the cities, martial law would be imposed and the army would wield supreme authority. Politicians, civil servants and Party officials would all be subordinate to military commanders. The plans for Valkyrie and its activation were entirely in the hands of the army: neither the Nazi Party nor the SS knew anything about them.

Stauffenberg and his colleagues resolved to avail themselves of the administrative machinery already in place. At the appropriate moment, Operation Valkyrie would be set in motion – on behalf of purposes very different from those for which it had originally been designed. To ensure the unwitting co-operation of pro-Nazi younger officers, troops loyal to the régime and any civilians who might be able to affect the situation, a 'cover story' would be released. It would be the same as that planned for the abortive 1938 conspiracy: an attempted or intended *Putsch* by the SS (which was, in 1944, a not implausible possibility). To counter this alleged

*Putsch*, the Reserve Army would be mobilised and deployed throughout the Reich. SS and Party Officials would be arrested, and only then would the operation unmask itself as a full-scale coup d'état. Valkyrie would thus be double-edged, with a 'legitimate' façade to screen its real clandestine purpose. Many of the secret orders were typed by Tresckow's secretary, Margarethe von Oven.[6] He instructed her always to wear gloves, even when typing, so that any documents, if found, could not be identified. She said later in an interview that she vividly remembered typing the primary order for the first time. It began: 'The Führer, Adolf Hitler, is dead . . .'

Much of the ground had still to be prepared. Timetables had to be synchronised, not only within the Reich itself, but in occupied territory as well. The allegiance of numerous local commanders and subordinate officers had to be enlisted – and was, in Berlin, in Königsberg, in Stettin, in Dresden, Münster, Munich, Kassel, Hamburg, Wiesbaden and Nuremberg, as well as in Danzig, Vienna, Salzburg, Paris, on the Eastern Front and elsewhere in the field. Programmes had to be prepared for the future, and policies had to be formulated, including an immediate peace settlement with the Western Allies. A provisional government would have to be established to negotiate a ceasefire, preserve order within Germany, and avert a national collapse or civil war.

Had he wished to do so, Stauffenberg might have presided over this provisional government and named himself undisputed ruler of the projected new Germany. Instead, shunning all positions of personal power, he assigned himself the relatively modest post of Under-Secretary of State for War. The new President or head of state was to be the beloved old soldier Field Marshal Ludwig Beck. The Chancellor was to be either Julius Leber, the Socialist spokesman, or Carl Goerdeler, Mayor of Leipzig. Stauffenberg's superior as Minister of War was to be either his current commander, General Olbricht, or his former commander, General Hoepner. Field Marshal von Witzleben was to be Commander-in-Chief of the armed forces. Tresckow was to take charge of the police.

Before anything of this ambitious project could be implemented, however, some means had to be devised for neutralising Adolf Hitler. So far as Stauffenberg was concerned, there was no point whatever in trying to remove the Führer by non-violent or legal means – impeaching him, for example, or forcing him voluntarily to abdicate. And if merely arrested, his survival would continue to command allegiance from fanatics in the Party, from the SS and from much of the population, thereby increasing the risk of civil war. Although numerous in theory, the options in practice were few – and only one was likely to be effective.

Although it contravened his principles, his code of honour, the oath of allegiance he had sworn as an officer and his personal code of moral and spiritual values, Stauffenberg saw that Hitler had to die. There was no alternative to political assassination. For a man of his chivalric background, who saw himself as a loyal German, a Catholic, an officer and a nobleman, there could scarcely have been a more onerous, more painful conclusion. Unflinchingly, Stauffenberg was prepared to reconcile this conclusion with his own conscience. He also undertook to incur, as he recognised he would, the most terrible of stigmas – that of high treason.

> I know that he who acts will go down in German history as a traitor; but he who can and does not will be a traitor to his conscience. If I did not act to stop this senseless killing, I should never be able to face the war's widows and orphans . . .[7]

Assassination entailed problems of its own. Stauffenberg quickly discovered that while Hitler's whereabouts at any given moment were easy enough to establish, it was seldom possible to know his movements in advance. Prompted perhaps by his own acute and highly developed sense of self-preservation, Hitler avoided fixed schedules and, insofar as he could, travelled only on the shortest possible notice. He wore a bullet-proof waistcoat and a metal-plated bullet-proof cap. When he did travel, it was invariably with a large entourage, which included his personal cook, driver, doctor and SD (Security Service) personnel, as well as a heavy SS escort armed with submachine-guns. His private aircraft, a Focke-Wulf Condor, was equipped with a thickly armoured cabin, and a parachute was attached to his seat. He always used his own cars, and during the war four separate motorcades were kept in perpetual readiness for him at different quarters of Germany. The cars themselves had bullet-proof tyres and windows, and extensive armour plating.[8]

Since the fall of Stalingrad at the beginning of 1943, moreover,

Hitler had taken to travelling less and less. He adamantly refused to visit hospitals or bombed cities, fearing such sights might make him give way to pity and, in his own eyes, weaken. He now shunned the crowds on which he had formerly sustained himself. He made almost no public appearances and became virtually invisible, save to his personal entourage and staff. Even Goebbels grew concerned:

> It is tragic that the Führer has become such a recluse and leads such an unhealthy life. He never gets out into the fresh air. He does not relax. He sits in his bunker, worries and broods . . . The loneliness of General Headquarters and the whole method of working there naturally have a depressing effect upon the Führer.[9]

For some time, Hitler had not even visited Berlin. The Berghof too, with the 'Eagle's Nest' in the Bavarian Alps, was now used far less, except for extra-marital dalliances by the oafish Martin Bormann. It was as if Hitler's carefully cultivated pre-war persona – associated quite deliberately with light, with altitude, with loftiness, with vastness, with soaring and sweeping vistas – had now contracted along with Germany's war effort and successes in the field. As the country's military machine shrivelled, so did Hitler. A tremor developed in his hands. He stooped. His left foot dragged behind him as he walked. His face grew gaunt and haggard. If he had previously identified himself with the eagle, he now had more in common with the wolf.

The '*Wolfsschanze*' or 'Wolf's Lair', Hitler's headquarters at Rastenburg, was admirably in harmony with Hitler's state of mind from 1943 on. Now in Poland and called Ketrzyn, it lies amid the Masurian Lakes, the low-lying marshes, swamps and forests of what was then East Prussia, some fifty miles east of the old Teutonic Knights' capital at Königsberg (now Kaliningrad). The soil around Rastenburg was compounded of centuries of corpses. Here, in 1410, the Battle of Tannenburg had been fought, and the Teutonic Knights, then at the apex of their power, had suffered a shattering defeat at the hands of a combined Polish and Lithuanian host. At the outbreak of the First World War in 1914, two complete Russian armies had been outfought, outmanoeuvred, encircled and forced to surrender by the ingenuity of Hindenburg and Ludendorff. They had christened the engagement 'Tannenburg' to ensure that their triumph, rather than the 1410 débâcle, would be permanently associated with the name. But whatever echoes or residues of former victory remained, Rastenburg was a dark, bleak and forbidding place. The austere headquarters compound consisted of 'a gloomy camp of huts' and underground concrete bunkers scattered about the depths of the sombre forest. Visitors spoke repeatedly of an atmosphere of brooding and oppressive isolation, of a dank clamminess rank with perversity, decay and death. This was hardly surprising. Beyond the wooded low hills surrounding the place, smoke rose from the chimneys of the ovens at Stutthof and Treblinka and, not too much further to the south, at Chelmno, Sobibor and Maidanek.

Unless he could be caught on one of his increasingly rare forays into the outside world, the conspirators, in order to strike Hitler, would have to reach into Rastenburg itself. In either case, the undertaking would not be easy. Someone had to be found who enjoyed at least some access to the Führer and could circumvent his elaborate security precautions or penetrate to him in the isolation of his headquarters. Although the conspirators' network did have individuals placed within the 'Wolf's Lair', none of them was suitable or prepared to assume the task of committing the assassination personally.

Although his access to the Führer was at first not much greater than most other officers', Stauffenberg announced his readiness to do the job himself. There were obvious disadvantages to his performing that rôle, and urgent objections from his colleagues. In the first place, he was severely handicapped. However impressively he had managed to surmount his injuries, he would, inevitably, be lacking in dexterity. More important still, Stauffenberg was the acknowledged leader of the conspiracy, the figure to whom everyone else turned for guiding force and strength of resolve. His qualities had imparted cohesion and momentum to the enterprise; and except perhaps for Tresckow, then a thousand miles away on the Eastern Front, there was no one of sufficiently authoritative rank to fill his shoes. He might indeed succeed in assassinating the Führer, but if he himself died in the process, the conspiracy would be left headless, bereft of impetus, morale and presiding spirit. In his absence, the conspiracy itself might fragment, and the consequences would then be disastrous – a backlash, anarchy or civil war.

Volunteers had therefore to be found for what would undoubtedly be a suicide mission. Stauffenberg accordingly turned to the 9th Infantry Regiment of Potsdam, which had been assigned a crucial rôle in the aborted coup of 1939. The man chosen to exterminate the Führer was a young captain, Axel, Freiherr (Baron) von dem Bussche.[10] Among his many decorations was the Ritterkreuz (Knight's Cross), the highest German military honour. Having been wounded in action, Bussche was unfit for further front-line duty and had been attached as adjutant to his regiment's reserve at Potsdam. Himself a passionate opponent of the régime, he had been asked by the conspirators to ensure that his unit, insofar as possible, contained no Nazis and no supporters of the Party.

During the summer and early autumn of 1943, new uniforms – particularly winter clothing for the Eastern Front – had been designed and produced for the army. Stauffenberg undertook to arrange a demonstration at which the new kit would be modelled for Hitler personally. Bussche would serve as model – with explosives strapped around his waist and, should a *coup de grâce* be required, a long thin knife in his boot. At the appropriate moment, he would clasp the Führer in an embrace and both would be blown up.

Hitler assented in principle to attending a display of the new uniforms, but refused to be pinned down to a specific date. Until the end of November, Bussche held himself in readiness for self-immolation and martyrdom. Before he could be called upon, an Allied air raid destroyed the specimen kit he was to model. Before replacements could be produced, Bussche himself was returned to active duty and was again badly wounded, losing a leg. Unable conveniently to dispose of them, he was forced to carry his explosives around with him from hospital to hospital. Only towards the end of 1944 did he find an opportunity to discard them into a lake.

With Bussche no longer available, the suicide mission he had undertaken to perform devolved on another young officer from the 9th Infantry, Lieutenant Ewald Heinrich von Kleist.[11] Descended from the great Prussian playwright and story-writer, as well as from a long line of military commanders, Kleist was fervently anti-Nazi. His father had been a long-standing opponent of the régime, marked down to be murdered on the Night of the Long Knives in 1934 and escaping only by virtue of advance warning.

Towards the end of January 1944, the stock of new uniforms had been replenished and Stauffenberg made the requisite preparations with Kleist. The lethal fashion show was re-scheduled for the second week of February, and the conspirators, from the Eastern Front to the Atlantic Wall, again put themselves on alert, awaiting the codeword signifying the Führer's death. At the last minute, for reasons that remain unknown to this day, Hitler ordered the demonstration postponed.

Another attempt, this time to shoot Hitler, was undertaken on 11 March. It, too, was thwarted by chance. And by now Germany's situation was becoming increasingly desperate. An Allied invasion of France was imminent, the only uncertainty about it being when and where it would take place. Allied columns were racing each other, almost unimpeded now, towards Rome, and the juggernaut of the Red Army was advancing from the east. If Hitler had been inaccessible before, he became even more so now. Given his failure to come within range of the conspirators, they, it was clear, would have to go to him. Assassination would have to be attempted at his headquarters in Berchtesgaden, or in Rastenburg, but no outsider could hope for access to either sanctuary.

On 5 July, Julius Leber – one of the conspirators' two candidates for future Chancellor – was arrested by the Gestapo. The authorities had got wind of something and were beginning to close in. Stauffenberg had visited Rastenburg a month before, on the day following the Allied invasion of Normandy. He had now been promoted and, as Chief of Staff of the Reserve Army, could expect to be summoned at frequent intervals to the Führer's headquarters. It was becoming daily more apparent that he would have to carry out the assassination himself, and that he would have to do so quickly. Stauffenberg said, 'Now it is not the Führer or the country or my wife and four children which are at stake; it is the entire German people.'[12] He would also have to preserve himself intact, escape from the scene of his deed and contrive somehow to return safely to Berlin, there to preside over the details attending activation of Operation Valkyrie.

Again his colleagues protested, insisting that 'the Chief of the General Staff could not at the same time lead the assault party'.[13] Even more than before, Stauffenberg was now recognised as the incendiary soul of the entire German resistance.

These objections were not without validity. If human error doomed the conspiracy to failure, the error was a simple and understandable one. Everything depended too entirely, too exclusively, too absolutely on the power of a single man. The will to act, the capacity to improvise and deal with contingencies, impetus, tenacity and resourcefulness – all rested with Stauffenberg. He was the catalyst, the binding and solidifying agent that held disparate components together, making them cohere. In his absence, concerted decision would disintegrate into uncertainty, panic, hysteria, inertia; and the machinery he had set in motion would falter, then stall.

By July 1944, it had become clear that the assassination – the key to everything else – would not be carried out at all unless Stauffenberg himself acted as assassin. But the odds against Stauffenberg were staggering . . . From a military standpoint, Stauffenberg's plan to act in both rôles was absurd. A commander was to carry out his own orders at the front; then, three hours would elapse between the assassination and the return of the assassin to Berlin – if he did return. He had to try to survive the assassination attempt and return to the coup d'état centre, because no one could lead the coup in his absence.[14]

Stauffenberg had no illusions about the difficulties of the task he had taken upon himself. He and his colleagues were dubious about any prospect of success:

Stauffenberg and his friends knew that their chance of success was as good as naught. They acted in the face of overwhelming odds, without substantial hope of succeeding in killing Hitler or in seizing control of Germany. They had even less hope of surviving politically more than a few days or weeks, no hope therefore of putting into effect their reconstruction ideas, for they saw no way of avoiding the occupation, amputation and division of Germany by enemy forces. But General Beck, Brigadier von Tresckow,

Dietrich Bonhoeffer, Claus and Berthold von Stauffenberg all agreed: The assassination had to be attempted at all cost.[15]

Statements by the conspirators themselves would seem to support this contention, reflecting a resigned scepticism. Lieutenant-Colonel Cäsar von Hofacker, Stauffenberg's cousin and one of the leaders of the conspiracy in Paris, when asked the odds in his favour, replied coolly: 'Ten per cent.'[16] When asked by his wife if he thought the coup could succeed, Julius Leber answered: 'I don't know. I have only one head, and I can't use it for anything better than this cause.'[17] According to Tresckow:

> The assassination must be attempted at all costs. Even if it should not succeed, an attempt to seize power in Berlin must be undertaken. What matters now is no longer the practical purpose of the coup, but to prove to the world and for the records of history that the men of the resistance movement dared to take this decisive step. Compared to this objective, nothing else is of consequence.[18]

Stauffenberg's uncle, Graf von Üxküll, felt that 'even though I believe that it has in fact no chance of success, it at least has the advantage that we shall have shown the world that some attempt has been made by Germans to rid themselves of these criminals.'[19] And Stauffenberg's brother, Berthold, stated: 'The most terrible thing is knowing that it cannot succeed and that we must still do it for our country and our children.'[20]

Yet it is clear that for Stauffenberg and his colleagues, the enterprise was much more than just a poetic symbolic gesture. If their intention was simply to demonstrate to the world that there were 'good Germans', it would have been easy enough, after all, to martyr themselves. A head-on suicidal attack on the Führer, on one of his headquarters, on the SS or on some crucial installation would have served that purpose, and spared the conspirators the complexities of organising a coup extending from the Eastern Front to the Atlantic wall. Even a kamikaze-style attack on Hitler alone would have stood a greater chance of success. The point is that, whatever their misgivings about its outcome, the conspirators went about their undertaking quite as if they expected it to succeed, and they were to continue doing so even after the last hope of success had been extinguished. This requires greater courage and tenacity than simple martyrdom; and it means more than any poetic symbolic gesture, such as those one finds, for example, in the history of Irish republicanism.

In the days following the Normandy invasion, Stauffenberg would again rally his co-conspirators with the poetry of Stefan George. He would recite 'The Antichrist' and the prophetic 'Verses for the Dead':[21]

When men of the future are purged of dishonour,
Their shoulders released from the shackles of bondage,
Their vitals alive with the hunger for virtue,
Then flashes of blood will illumine the millions
Of graves of the fallen, then thundering armies
Will ride over clouds, and the terror of terrors,
The third of the tempests will sweep through the country:
        The dead are returning.

When men of this nation no longer are cowards,
Or weaklings, but feel their vocation and mission,
Their hearts will decipher in untold disaster
A message from heaven, their hands will be lifted,
Their lips will be tuned to the homage of honour,
The flag of the king, the legitimate symbol,
Will fly through the dawn and be lowered in praise to
        The highest of heroes.[22]

And at the prospect of enjoying access to the Führer's headquarters, even though it meant performing the act of assassination personally, Stauffenberg said: 'This is more than we dared hope for; fate has offered us this opportunity, and I would not refuse it for anything in the world. I have searched my conscience, before God and before myself. This man is evil incarnate.'[23]

Although precise details are vague and confused, Stauffenberg is reported to have taken a bomb with him to a briefing at Berchtesgaden on 6 July. It is unclear whether he actually intended to use it, or was simply testing his own courage in a sort of 'dress rehearsal'.

There has been one plausible suggestion that it was indeed a test of some kind, of security, if not of his own courage, and that he did not expect to encounter Hitler personally. It is also possible that somebody else was actually supposed to take charge within Berchtesgaden proper and activate the bomb. In any case, nothing happened and Stauffenberg returned to Berlin in a state of intense exasperation: 'he talked with noticeable emotion and fiery impatience about the situation at Berchtesgaden and declared that now he would have to take charge of that as well'.[24] He is even reported to have snapped irritably: 'I'll do it myself with my three fingers!'[25]

He tried again, on 11 July, once more smuggling a bomb into Berchtesgaden. Everything was in place, and cars and aircraft were ready to get him back to Berlin as quickly as possible. But the conspirators had agreed that it was essential to eliminate not just the Führer, but Himmler as well. Himmler, it transpired, was not present, and Stauffenberg returned to Berlin with the bomb intact. By the 14th, Hitler had left Berchtesgaden and installed himself at Rastenburg.

On 15 July, Stauffenberg flew to the 'Wolf's Lair' at Rastenburg and smuggled his bomb into the Führer's East Prussian headquarters. On this occasion, the initial order to activate Operation Valkyrie was given. Again, however, Himmler was not present, and the assassination was postponed. Such delays could clearly not be allowed to continue: it was agreed among the conspirators that on 20 July, Stauffenberg would strike, regardless of whether Himmler was there or not. That week a friend told Stauffenberg of rumours which had surfaced in Berlin, claiming that the Führer's Headquarters were soon to be blown up. Stauffenberg commented. 'So there is no longer a choice. We have crossed the Rubicon.'[26]

In the early evening of 19 July, he stopped at a small church in a Berlin suburb where a service was in progress. For some time, he stood alone at the back, then had himself driven home and spent the rest of the evening with his brother Berthold.

# 3

# In the Wolf's Lair

At seven in the morning, on Thursday 20 July 1944, Stauffenberg boarded a courier aircraft at a military aerodrome south of Berlin. He was accompanied by his aide-de-camp, Lieutenant Werner von Haeften, and by another officer, also privy to the conspiracy. Even at this early hour, the day was hot and sultry, promising to become more oppressive as it wore on.

The flight to Rastenburg was ordinarily of some two hours' duration. Today, however, it was delayed, and did not land until ten-fifteen. At the airstrip, a car awaited Stauffenberg and his fellow officers, to convey them to the Führer's compound. For four miles, the road ran tunnel-like through the sombre gloom of pagan fir forests dank with the stench of mould. The trees then gave way to a camouflaged perimeter of minefields, networks of festooned barbed wire, checkpoints manned by hand-picked SS who demanded precise passwords. The temperature was now in the upper eighties, the air was stifling with humidity and Stauffenberg, like everyone else, was sweating profusely. This very discomfort, however, would work in his favour.

At a table laid under an oak tree outside the mess, he breakfasted. At eleven o'clock, he met with two general officers. At eleven-thirty, there followed a forty-five minute conference with Field Marshal Wilhelm Keitel, Chief of the General Staff and one of Hitler's most contemptibly abject subordinates. To Stauffenberg and the other conspirators, Keitel was known as 'Lakeitel', a play on

the German word 'Lakei', meaning 'lackey' or 'toady', and with
effeminate connotations as well.

The conference with the Führer, scheduled originally for one
o'clock, had been moved forward by half an hour. With fifteen
minutes to spare, Stauffenberg, blaming the heat and humidity of
the day, requested premises in which he might wash, and change his
sodden shirt. A deferential officer directed him to a washroom. On
the way he was joined by Haeften, carrying a suitcase with two
bombs. The bombs were not unlike the one employed by
Tresckow's subordinate, Fabian von Schlabrendorff, in the abortive
assassination attempt of 1942. Detonation depended on acid eating
its way through a length of wire. In order to rupture the container of
acid, Stauffenberg had equipped himself with a specially modified
pair of pliers which enabled him to perform the operation with the
three fingers of his left hand. The remains of these pliers are today on
display in Berlin, in the building that once housed the Reserve
Army's headquarters on the Bendlerstrasse, now the Stauffenbergstrasse.

Once the bombs were activated, there would be a time delay of
ten minutes before they exploded. This delay, however, was only
approximate. The speed with which the acid consumed the wire
would be, to some degree, affected by temperature, atmospheric
pressure and other indeterminate factors. The hotter the day, the
more quickly the explosion would occur; but there was no way of
predicting precisely how quickly.

In the washroom, Stauffenberg changed his shirt and, assisted by
his aide, began to arrange and activate the bombs in his briefcase.
Using the specially modified pliers, he had already activated the first
when he was interrupted by a sergeant-major, who – since the
briefing with Hitler was about to begin – had been sent to hurry him
up. The sergeant-major waited until Stauffenberg and Haeften had
finished what they were doing. He was later to testify that he saw
them busy with a wrapped parcel. It was undoubtedly the incom-
modious presence of this intruder that prevented Stauffenberg from
arming both bombs. The device that remained inert was left with
Haeften, who slipped it into his briefcase. With the activated bomb
now in his own briefcase, Stauffenberg left the washroom. Within
ten minutes, the blast would occur.

Emerging into a corridor, Stauffenberg again encountered Field Marshal Keitel. It was now twelve-thirty, and the field marshal, huffy and flustered as usual, begged him to hurry. Tardiness was not seemly for a German officer and might provoke the Führer's wrath. Another officer, standing nearby, offered to help Stauffenberg with his briefcase. When Stauffenberg declined the courtesy, it aroused no suspicion. He was known and respected for his fierce self-sufficiency.

Presumably he had hoped to be conducted to the visitors' bunker, where Hitler was staying at the time and where conferences usually occurred. The concrete walls of this structure would contain and maximise the effects of the blast. But since 15 July, conferences had been held in the adjacent map room, which had now become a separate briefing hut. It was a wooden structure of some sixteen by forty feet, with three large windows in the north wall. A blast here would be significantly less lethal.

As Stauffenberg approached the hut, another officer volunteered to help him with his briefcase. This time he accepted and added a request: 'Could you please put me as near as possible to the Führer so that I can catch everything I need for my briefing afterwards.'[1] It has been plausibly suggested that this was a reference to his hearing, which had been adversely affected by his injuries.

When he entered, the conference had already begun. General Heusinger, Assistant Chief of Staff, was reporting on the situation on the Eastern Front. Most of the two dozen men present, including Hitler, were clustered around a heavy oblong table, bent over maps which littered its surface. Stauffenberg joined them, edging his way to a position on the Führer's right, some six feet distant. Keitel introduced him. He and Hitler shook hands. Placing his briefcase on the floor, Stauffenberg nudged it under the table with his boot. General Heusinger paused for breath. Taking advantage of this intermission, Keitel suggested that when Heusinger had finished speaking, Stauffenberg might report on the status of the Reserve Army. The Führer nodded approval, not deigning to say anything. General Heusinger then resumed his exegesis. There could now be no more than seven minutes before the bomb exploded.

Turning to the officer beside him, Stauffenberg excused himself. He had to telephone Berlin, he explained. It was urgent. He would return at once. Leaving his briefcase under the table, he threaded his way to the door. No one paid any attention to his departure except the fussy Keitel, who made a half-hearted attempt to go after him, then gave it up.

Once outside the briefing hut, Stauffenberg, in accordance with pre-arranged plans, hurried to a shelter across the compound. Here, General Erich Fellgiebel, Chief of Signals at Rastenburg, awaited him. Fellgiebel was a colleague, a fellow conspirator and integral component of the plot. When the explosion occurred, he was to telephone the other conspirators in Berlin, who would activate Operation Valkyrie, the mobilisation and deployment of the Reserve Army. Fellgiebel was then to cut all communications from Rastenburg, thus truncating the chain of command and thwarting all interference. The 'Wolf's Lair' would be altogether isolated, severed from events unfolding elsewhere.

For three minutes, Stauffenberg and Fellgiebel waited in the shelter, concealing their tension. A subordinate signals officer happened to be present, and this compelled them to sustain an anodyne conversation about which car Stauffenberg should take to the landing strip. Then, at twelve-forty-two, a single shattering detonation ruptured the humid summer somnolence, followed by a stunned stillness. Stauffenberg contrived to give 'a violent start' and Fellgiebel feigned alarm. The signals officer dismissed the matter irritably. It must have been a mine, he said. Given the defences at Rastenburg, such things often occurred. Atmospheric pressure, defective mechanisms, stray wildlife were constantly triggering explosions in the minefields. There was no cause for concern. From the briefing hut across the compound, a plume of sulphurous smoke boiled upwards, staining the sky.

Outside the signals shelter, Haeften appeared in a requisitioned car. Fellgiebel accompanied Stauffenberg to the vehicle, which lurched quickly into motion. It was necessary to escape from Rastenburg before the compound was sealed off. On the way from the signals shelter, the car passed within fifty yards of the briefing hut. Security personnel were rushing about in great disorder, like wasps from a disturbed nest. Figures were being carried out, though it could not be determined whether they were dead or only injured. The hut itself appeared gutted, and rubble littered the grass for some distance. Greasy smoke gushed from the windows, together with fitful flickers of flame. Stauffenberg was absolutely convinced that no one could possibly have survived the blast.

By now, klaxons were braying and Rastenburg's former torpor had been supplanted by frenzy. A full security alert had galvanised the compound, internal telephones were ringing, guards being reinforced. At the first two checkpoints, Stauffenberg knew the sentries, who, after a moment's chatter, waved him through the barriers. At the last and southernmost checkpoint, the car was halted by an officious sergeant-major. No one, he announced, was permitted to enter or leave the premises. Stauffenberg snapped at him impatiently, 'in a parade-ground tone'. The sergeant-major was cowed but stolidly insisted on adhering to orders. Stauffenberg got out of the car, snatched up the telephone and personally rang the aide-de-camp of Rastenburg's commandant.

'Colonel Count Stauffenberg speaking, from outer checkpoint South. Captain, you'll remember we had breakfast together this morning. Because of the explosion, the guard refuses to let me pass. I'm in a hurry. Colonel-General Fromm is waiting for me at the airfield.'[2]

Without waiting for a reply, he replaced the receiver, but the obstinate sergeant-major insisted on receiving the order personally and telephoned the commandant's aide himself. On being told that Stauffenberg could pass, he raised the barrier. The car set off for the landing strip, Stauffenberg ordering the driver to hurry. Haeften tossed the second and unused bomb from the window.

By one-fifteen, Stauffenberg was airborne, and on his way back to Berlin. He could not yet confirm definitely the Führer's death, of course. There was no means of doing that if he intended to get out of Rastenburg. Nevertheless, he was confident. With his own eyes, he had seen the devastation caused by the explosion. It seemed inconceivable that Hitler could have survived it.

In the briefing hut, an unwitting colonel, taking Stauffenberg's vacated place at the table, had barked his shin against a briefcase. Cramped for space, he had pushed it further under the table, behind one of the heavy oak supports on which the tabletop rested. These supports were not just legs. They were solid slabs of wood extending the width of the table – tantamount, in effect, to sturdy waist-high partitions. The tabletop, too, was of solid oak, four inches thick. Hitler was thus shielded from the bomb by both the table's top and its supports, which deflected the impact of the blast. The unwitting colonel, two generals and a stenographer were to die from their injuries. Nine other men had to be hospitalised, and everyone else present suffered at least minor wounds. Hitler's hair was set aflame and his right arm was temporarily paralysed, his eardrums were pierced and he was badly dazed. The tremor he had begun to display, symptom of a nervous disorder, was to become exacerbated and remain acute for the duration of his life. It has been suggested that he may have suffered a form of breakdown. Certainly he was never again to appear in public. But he was very much alive; and the relieved lackeys attending him could see only minor burns and the indignity of shredded trousers.

In the signals shelter, General Fellgiebel had waited expectantly, ready to telephone Berlin and start Operation Valkyrie, then cut all communications to and from Rastenburg. To his horror, Fellgiebel saw the dazed and bewildered Führer being led shakily from the smouldering débris of the briefing hut. Despite this unexpected development, the general showed great presence of mind, anticipating what he knew would have been Stauffenberg's own decision – the coup must proceed anyway. Shortly before one o'clock, he telephoned Berlin and activated Valkyrie. He then rang a contact at OKH (Army) Headquarters not far away.

'Something fearful has happened,' he announced. 'The Führer is alive.' When asked what had now to be done, Fellgiebel replied, 'Block everything.'[3]

In other words, news of Hitler's survival had to be kept from the outside world. As for cutting communications from Rastenburg proper, Fellgiebel had no need to do so: the compound's security authorities had already ordered a total blackout. At the same time, it was impossible to isolate Rastenburg completely. Although the telephone and teleprinter exchanges could be cut, there were still radio transmitters; and both the Ministry of Propaganda and the German News Agency had their own private teleprinter lines which did not pass through the main exchange. No provision had been made, or could have been made, for dealing with these. In any case, despite whatever its planners had overlooked or been forced to omit, Operation Valkyrie was now in progress.

In Berlin, the conspirators had thronged the War Office in the Bendlerstrasse, anxiously awaiting Fellgiebel's call. When it came, it implemented Valkyrie but made no mention of Hitler's survival. By one-thirty at the latest, however, news of the Führer's escape would have filtered through, if only via OKH Headquarters, but no one was able to consult with Stauffenberg. He, of course, was airborne at the time, and out of communication, still wholly convinced everything was going according to plan. In his absence, no one in any position of authority dared make a decision or determine what to do next. Some of the younger officers, Stauffenberg's contemporaries, tried desperately to coax things into motion. An old friend of Stauffenberg, Colonel Albrecht Merz von Quirnheim, deserves special mention for his resolute insistence. But General Olbricht, from whom all orders had ultimately to issue, remained paralysed. Two hours passed. Tension intensified, nerves grew strained and the telephones remained silent. The conspirators hung suspended in a vacuum, the lack of information as painful and stifling as a lack of air. Immobilised by uncertainty, Olbricht continued to hesitate. And the minutes during which the coup might yet have succeeded slipped away.

In Rastenburg, there was no doubt by now who had been responsible for the bomb. Stauffenberg's rapid and unauthorised departure – he had left behind his cap, his belt and other accoutrements – had made that clear enough. Even so, no one as yet suspected an organised conspiracy, and the maimed colonel was thought to have acted alone, a solitary depraved assassin. It was assumed he would attempt to flee the country, seeking refuge on neutral soil. An order was issued to the Luftwaffe, to intercept and shoot down a Heinkel bound for Switzerland or Sweden. The officer charged with transmitting this order, however, was one of Stauffenberg's collaborators, and left it unimplemented on his desk.

Shortly after three-thirty, Merz von Quirnheim at last managed to goad Olbricht into action. Senior officers were summoned. Hitler, they were told, had been assassinated. The army was now under the supreme command of Field Marshal von Witzleben. The new head of state was General Beck. An officer was dispatched to Berlin Military Headquarters carrying orders for the further implementation of Operation Valkyrie. The same orders were issued by telephone and teleprinter to all military districts in the Reich.

Shortly before four o'clock, Olbricht and Merz von Quirnheim went to see General Fromm, Commander-in-Chief of the Reserve Army and Stauffenberg's immediate superior. Throughout the previous months of planning, Fromm had vacillated abjectly. Although he had never been a committed member of the conspiracy, his co-operation had been deemed essential. The conspirators, albeit reluctantly, had therefore made him privy to their designs. Intent on nothing more than self-preservation, Fromm had tepidly aligned himself with them, as long as their enterprise promised some measure of success. Now, in the absence of any official information, he began to dither anew. As Olbricht and Merz von Quirnheim argued with him, a call came from the airport. Stauffenberg and Haeften had just arrived. They had no reason to assume that everything was not already well under way. In fact, scarcely had anything begun, and more than three valuable hours had elapsed since the explosion at Rastenburg.

The driver awaiting Stauffenberg and Haeften at the airport somehow contrived to miss them. The absence of any other car – and of petrol as well – meant further delay. In the meantime, Olbricht continued to dispute with Fromm. At four-ten, Fromm attempted to ring Keitel at Rastenburg. To everyone's surprise, he got through. What, Fromm asked, was happening? A bomb had exploded, Keitel replied, but the Führer was alive. Keitel then enquired as to Stauffenberg's whereabouts. Stauffenberg, Fromm reported, had not yet returned.

Olbricht had listened to this exchange. It was clear to him that Fromm's co-operation could no longer be relied upon – if, indeed, it ever could have been. After resisting for so long, Olbricht was now thoroughly determined, as if steeled by Stauffenberg's imminent return. Leaving Fromm, he hurried back to his own office and, at four-thirty, issued new orders. These were the first to offer the agreed 'cover story' for the coup.

The Führer, Adolf Hitler, is dead . . . An unscrupulous clique of non-combatant party leaders has tried to exploit the situation to stab the deeply committed front in the back, and to seize power for selfish purposes.[4]

A state of martial law was declared. All Waffen-SS (combat SS) units were immediately to be incorporated into the army and rendered subject to military authority. All Party officials were similarly subordinated to military control. The security service, the SD, was dissolved. The statement was signed by Field Marshal von Witzleben.

As these orders were going out, Stauffenberg and Haeften arrived back at the Bendlerstrasse. Stauffenberg went directly to his office, where four officers were waiting, and, without any greeting, said simply:

'He's dead. I saw how he was carried out.'[5]

In Olbricht's office a few minutes later, Stauffenberg gave a more detailed report:

'I saw the whole thing from the outside. I was standing outside the hut with General Fellgiebel. There was an explosion inside the hut and then I saw large numbers of medical personnel come running up and cars being brought along. The explosion was as if the hut had been hit by a six-inch shell. It is hardly possible that anyone could be alive.'[6]

By this time more reports had come in from Rastenburg. Although nothing as yet could be substantiated definitely, there was increasing evidence to suggest that Hitler was indeed still alive. Stauffenberg refused to believe it. Having personally witnessed the effects of the explosion, he could not accept that it had failed to kill everyone in the briefing hut, the Führer included.

With Stauffenberg attending him, Olbricht returned to Fromm's office. Stauffenberg, he reported, had confirmed that the Führer was dead.

'That is impossible,' Fromm replied. 'Keitel has assured me to the contrary.'[7]

It must have been at this moment that Stauffenberg first seriously began to suspect the truth. Keitel, after all, had also been in the briefing hut. If Fromm had just spoken to him, Keitel had obviously survived; and if Keitel had survived, the Führer might have done so as well. At the same time it is also possible that Stauffenberg's conviction remained unshaken. In an interview with the authors of this book, Otto John, one of the few conspirators to survive, made an interesting and revealing statement. As late as 22 July, Otto John declared, two days after the event, he personally continued to believe that Stauffenberg had been telling the truth and that Hitler was indeed dead. 'All we heard over the radio was Hitler's voice, and we all knew that there was a double.'[8] The belief that Hitler had a double was widely held in the Third Reich, and this belief would clearly have contributed to the conspirators' confusion. Stauffenberg may well have wondered whether the Party hierarchy, and the authorities at Rastenburg, were not attempting a sort of bluff. Whatever might be the case, he recognised the necessity, even more urgent now, of proceeding with Operation Valkyrie according to plan, even if that required a bluff of his own to prevent demoralisation from setting in among the conspirators. Accordingly, Stauffenberg retorted to Fromm, 'Field Marshal Keitel is lying as usual. I myself saw Hitler's body being carried away.' And a little later he repeated what he had said to Olbricht, 'General, I myself set off the bomb during the conference with Hitler. There was an explosion as though a six-inch shell had hit the room. No one who was in that room can still be alive.'[9]

Before Fromm could reply, Olbricht announced that the orders for Operation Valkyrie had already been issued. At this news, Fromm exploded with rage, banging his fist on the desk. Was he not in command here? He would not tolerate his subordinates doing what they liked. They were guilty of insubordination, revolution, high treason. The penalty for all of them would be death. Who, he demanded, had actually issued the orders to activate Valkyrie? When Olbricht replied that Merz von Quirnheim had issued them, Merz was summoned to confirm the assertion. When Merz did so, Fromm declared that he, Olbricht and Stauffenberg were all under arrest. Merz was then commanded to go to the teleprinter and cancel the orders. Merz simply sat down in the nearest chair.

'Colonel-General,' he replied drily, 'you've just put me under arrest. My freedom of movement is therefore restricted.'[10]

Fromm then turned on Stauffenberg. The attempted assassination had miscarried, he shouted. Stauffenberg now had no alternative but to shoot himself.

'I have no intention of shooting myself,' Stauffenberg answered coldly.

Olbricht added to Fromm, 'You are deluding yourself about who actually has the power. It is we who are arresting you.'[11]

Lurching up from his desk, Fromm lunged forward with fists flailing – at Stauffenberg according to some reports, at Olbricht according to others. Junior officers, who by now had gathered in the room, intervened. Haeften drew his pistol. So, too, did Lieutenant Ewald von Kleist, the man who, earlier that year, had volunteered to model a new uniform for the Führer with explosives strapped around his waist. With the muzzle of Kleist's pistol pressing into his stomach, Fromm subsided back into his chair. Stauffenberg told him he had five minutes in which to think things over, and, accompanied by Olbricht, left the room. When Olbricht returned and asked Fromm for his decision, he replied, 'Under the circumstances, I regard myself as under constraint.' Without any further protest, he allowed himself and his aide to be locked in an adjacent office. The telephone was disconnected and sentries were placed at both exits. By five o'clock, the coup had begun to show the momentum it should have had four hours earlier.

Olbricht reported to Stauffenberg that all requisite Valkyrie orders had been issued. It was now a matter of waiting for troops to arrive, seal off the Bendlerstrasse and protect the conspirators. In the meantime, General Hoepner, Stauffenberg's former superior in the field, assumed Fromm's command. Other conspirators began to appear at the War Office, including Berthold, Stauffenberg's brother, and General Beck, the intended new head of state. When informed that Hitler might indeed have survived, Beck decided the possibility could not be entertained. 'For me,' he said, 'this man is dead.'[12] Such was the premise on which things were to proceed, regardless of the reality.

Shortly after five o'clock, according to eyewitnesses, an SS Oberführer, or colonel, made an ingenuous appearance.

Suddenly thumping footsteps sounded in the corridor. The door flew open and an SS . . . of the typical butcher type appeared in the doorway. A more vivid, more typical SS hangman could scarcely be imagined. This creature clicked his heels with a report like a pistol shot, raised his hand in the 'German' greeting and growled loudly, 'Heil Hitler.'[13]

He had orders, he announced, to question Colonel Count von Stauffenberg. Formal but as genially cordial as ever, Stauffenberg invited the SS man into his office. Here, the SS man was disarmed by Kleist and a colleague, Lieutenant Ludwig von Hammerstein (son of the former German army C-in-C), and placed under guard in the same room as Fromm.

Shortly thereafter, the commander of Berlin's military district appeared, having been summoned by Olbricht. He was horrified to find a coup in progress, refused adamantly to co-operate and yelled repeatedly that 'the Führer is not dead'. In an attempt to escape, he dashed down the corridor towards the exit. Here he, too, was stopped by Kleist and an NCO with drawn pistols, then placed under guard with Fromm and the SS colonel. When he invoked his oath of loyalty to the Führer, Beck replied:

'How dare you talk of oaths? Hitler has broken his oath to the constitution and his vows to the people a hundred times over. How dare you refer to your oath of loyalty to such a perjurer?'[14]

For the next four hours, the War Office was a maelstrom of frenzied activity. Confirmations were received that troops everywhere were ready to move. Instructions for Operation Valkyrie were transmitted beyond the precincts of the Reich, to Austria, Italy, Czechoslovakia and France. The orders previously promulgated within Germany proper were now promulgated in occupied territory as well. Martial law was declared to be in effect. The army was to assume absolute control. All SS, SD, Gestapo and Party personnel were to be arrested or placed under military authority.

It was already too late. The delay during the afternoon had been fatal, and so had at least two other factors. Stauffenberg was urged to deal with Goebbels, who remained safely ensconced at the Ministry of Propaganda in the nearby Prinz Albrechtstrasse. For the first and only time in the course of that crucial day, he hesitated, as did the more senior of his colleagues. Perhaps – although it seems inconceivable – they underestimated Goebbels' importance. Or perhaps they shrank from the prospect of unleashing a reign of terror in Berlin. To assassinate the Führer was one thing. To embark on a wholesale purge was quite another, entailing precisely the same evils they were endeavouring to overthrow. They had no wish to perpetrate their own Night of the Long Knives.

Beck, Olbricht, Hoepner and Stauffenberg all procrastinated when Gisevius tried to impress on them the need to radicalize the coup by summarily executing some top Nazis. The very outrage at the methods of the Nazi régime became an impediment to a coup d'état, which depended, in part, on those same methods.[15]

Such scruples were present even though the conspirators at the War Office had now been joined by the head of the Ecumenical Section of the Evangelical Church, with a pistol as well as a Bible in his pocket. On a day such as this, the clergyman had declared, a day which involved revolt against monsters like the SS and National Socialist Party leaders, shooting must be expected. Excessive probity, he argued, would endanger both the coup and its participants.

Of equally fatal consequences was the conspirators' failure to shut down, effectively and completely, all broadcasting. They had dispatched contingents of troops to occupy the relevant radio stations and transmission centres, but these troops had lacked the technical expertise to do anything more. As a result, broadcasting by Nazi authorities was soon to recommence and continue uninterrupted; and the loyalties of the troops sent to curtail it were soon to be disastrously divided.

By five-forty-two, orders were issuing from the Führer's head-quarters and other bastions of Nazi power, contradicting those from the War Office. In the War Office itself, telephone wires were clogged by confused commanders besieging the conspirators. Kassel and Hannover rang. Nuremberg rang. Vienna rang. Prague rang. Stauffenberg personally answered all requests for clarification. At the same time, he and Hoepner were also ringing out, galvanising their network in Königsberg, in Stettin, in Münster, in Breslau, in Munich and Hamburg.

By this time, it was clear to Stauffenberg that the conspiracy was doomed. He refused, however, to capitulate – or to perform some such facile gesture of martyrdom as, say, shooting himself. He continued to inspire his colleagues and to comport himself as if success were still within easy reach. The eyewitness Otto John has described him at his desk, answering the telephone. John's words may not be accurate in every detail, but they convey a stirring impression of Stauffenberg, single-handedly trying to keep the coup on course:

'Stauffenberg here – yes – yes – they are all C-in-C's orders – yes, that stands – all orders to be carried out at once – you must occupy all radio and signal stations forthwith – any resistance will be broken – you will probably get counter-orders from the Führer's head-quarters – they are unauthorised – no – the Wehrmacht has assumed plenary powers – no one except the C-in-C Replacement Army is authorised to issue orders – do you understand? – yes – the Reich is in danger – as always in time of supreme emergency the soldiers are now in full control – yes, Witzleben has been appointed Commander-in-Chief – it is only a formal nomination – occupy all signal stations – is that clear? – Heil.'[16]

Here and there, this arrogation of authority proved convincing and effective. In Vienna, all SS officers were arrested and the army occupied key installations. In Paris, General Karl Heinrich von Stülpnagel (commander-in-chief of France and a long-standing member of the conspiracy) imposed martial law and imprisoned all SS, SD and Gestapo personnel. Summary courts-martial were scheduled for that night and sandbags were piled up in the barracks for the shooting of those condemned to death. For a few hours at least, and in certain areas, the Third Reich was actually overthrown.

But time was running out. On the radio an increasing number of reports stated that the Führer had survived an attempt on his life. Himmler was on the telephone giving orders to SS units in Berlin. There was even one announcement that Himmler himself was now to be placed in command of the Reserve Army. In Rastenburg, Hitler, propped up by aides and still shaken, was recording a speech. It would not be broadcast until one in the morning, but the gist of it was already on the airwaves:

A small clique of ambitious, irresponsible and at the same time senseless and criminally stupid officers have formed a plot to eliminate me and the German Wehrmacht command. The bomb was placed by Colonel Graf von Stauffenberg ... I myself sustained only some very minor scratches, bruises and burns. I regard this as a confirmation of the task imposed on me by

Providence to continue on the road of my life as I have done hitherto . . .[17]

In Berlin, the commander of the city's standing garrison, Major Otto Ernst Remer, had spent much of the afternoon in a quandary. There had never been any question of him becoming associated with the conspiracy – he was too mindlessly fervent a Nazi for that – but the confused situation had already taxed far more capacious brains than his. At four-thirty, he had received the alert for Operation Valkyrie and driven off to report to the city's commandant, a member of Stauffenberg's circle. The commandant had told him the army was assuming supreme power and ordered him to deploy his battalion in a protective cordon around all government buildings, including the War Office in the Bendlerstrasse. Although he later claimed to have been immediately suspicious, he nevertheless complied, and the cordon was in place by six-thirty. Remer was also instructed, albeit belatedly, to arrest Goebbels at the Ministry of Propaganda; but this, he decided, 'would be asking too much of the troops' because Goebbels was their honorary colonel.

Shortly thereafter, Remer was summoned by Goebbels himself. Remer dithered. In the meantime, Goebbels established contact with Rastenburg, spoke to Hitler personally and learned precisely what had happened. Not knowing how far the coup in Berlin had proceeded, he was badly frightened. He alerted a local SS detachment but simply ordered the men to stand by, unsure whether or not to trust them. As a precaution against capture by the conspirators, he slipped a number of cyanide capsules into his pocket. Then, at last, around seven o'clock, Remer appeared, having finally decided at least to find out what was happening. Goebbels must have been profoundly relieved. Remer's would have been the first even potentially friendly face he had seen all day from outside the Ministry of Propaganda, and it was not difficult to ensure the allegiance of so embryonic a mind. He rang Rastenburg again and let Remer speak to the Führer in person. Hitler promoted Remer to colonel on the spot and entrusted him with control of all security measures in Berlin. Remer briefed his subordinates and re-deployed his troops. They were ordered to surround the Bendlerstrasse and, if necessary, storm the War Office.

In the War Office itself, the minions of the Reich had also begun to regroup. Overlooked by the conspirators, a handful of officers loyal to General Fromm had contrived to arm themselves. Around ten-thirty, gunfire suddenly erupted inside the building. As Stauffenberg hurried down a corridor, a shot cracked behind him and a bullet tore into his shoulder. Staggering, he turned and managed to draw his own pistol. According to most accounts, he returned fire, though one eyewitness reports he did not.[18] Alerted by the noise, other conspirators rushed to the scene and more shots were exchanged. It was clear, however, that the situation was hopeless. Stauffenberg, partially supported by colleagues, was bleeding profusely. Morale among the other conspirators was haemorrhaging away. Outside, Remer's battalion of troops was preparing for a full-scale assault.

Stauffenberg and his immediate attendants did not surrender their weapons, but allowed themselves to be conducted to Fromm's office. A few moments later, Fromm himself entered, released from the adjacent room in which he had been confined. Haeften drew his pistol and levelled it at the general. Fromm cringed. Despite his wound, Stauffenberg, his will again asserting itself, held himself erect. He is said to have fixed Fromm with a glare of withering contempt; then, with a glance, he signalled Haeften to lower the pistol trained on his former superior. His personal code of honour precluded petty vindictiveness and revenge; and the death of a single abject general could hardly accomplish anything now. Fromm was doomed anyway. In the days to come, he would equivocate, prevaricate and lie outright in an attempt to exculpate himself, but the scythe of Hitler's vengeance would sweep through the ranks of anyone even remotely connected with the conspiracy, and Fromm would be among the first to fall. The charge against him would not be treason, but cowardice, thus setting the seal on his ignominy.

Now, released from his confinement, Fromm surveyed the men before him, the nucleus of the coup that had come so near to success. These men, he realised, were not only an embarrassment. They were also a dangerous liability, for they could testify to his own involvement in the conspiracy, tepid though it had been. To leave them alive for interrogation would be too risky. They would have to be dispatched at once. Fromm pronounced them officially under arrest and declared that he had just convened a summary court martial. Provoked further by their comportment of continued defiance, he sentenced four of them to immediate execution. 'Colonel Merz, General Olbricht, this colonel whose name I will not mention and Lieutenant von Haeften are condemned to death.'[19]

At this point, Stauffenberg spoke for the first time. 'In a few short clipped sentences, he assumed responsibility for everything.'[20] His colleagues, he said, had simply conducted themselves as soldiers and as his subordinates. They had been guilty of nothing save carrying out his orders.

It is likely that Beck would also have been sentenced to summary execution. The old and beloved general requested to keep his pistol, however, 'for private use'. Fromm consented, ordering him 'to hurry up'. Under armed guard, Stauffenberg, Olbricht, Haeften and Merz von Quirnheim were escorted down the stairs to a courtyard below. Stauffenberg was still bleeding copiously from his shoulder, and Haeften again supported him. All four men walked calmly, 'showing no emotion'. In the room to which he had retired, Beck shot himself twice. When he was found to be still alive, Fromm ordered an officer to administer the *coup de grâce*. The officer could not bring himself to do so, and entrusted the task to a sergeant.

\*

For the Nazis, one of the greatest (and most improbable) 'heroes of the hour' was the toadying and robotlike young Major Remer. By the end of the war, he had risen to the rank of major-general. Age was to bring no very marked wisdom in its wake. After the cessation of hostilities, Remer remained a dedicated Nazi, eager to disseminate his warped *Weltanschauung*. In 1950, he joined the neo-Nazi Socialist Reich Party (SRP) and became its second chairman. With bizarre sanctimoniousness and sententiousness, he fulminated against Stauffenberg and other members of the conspiracy, branding them 'traitors to their country' and a 'stain on the shield of honour of the German officers' corps'. They had, he blustered (in an all-too-familiar clichéd phrase) 'stabbed the German army in the back'. 'The time will come,' he frothed in 1951, 'when men will be ashamed to admit that they were part of the 20 July Putsch . . .'[21]

In the same year, a statement was issued by an ex-officer, one of Remer's wartime colleagues:

> We, his former comrades, have deeply regretted that destiny confronted this young officer in July, 1944, with a situation with consequences the bearing of which I should assume are beyond the powers of a human being. No judgement will be made here as to whether his decision on July 20 was right or wrong. But the consequences of his decision were so terrible, and have cost so much of the best German blood, that we old soldiers had expected that a man to whom destiny gave such a burden to carry until the end of his life would recognise this, and would thereafter live quietly and in seclusion. We, his former comrades, lack any sympathy for the fact that Herr Remer fails to summon up this attitude of self-effacement.[22]

In the spring of 1952, Remer was sentenced to three months in prison for the 'collective libel of the Resistance circle'. He promptly fled Germany, re-surfacing in Egypt. But stupidity, as Schiller observed, is something with which the gods themselves must contend. Forty years later, in October 1992, Remer was again arrested in Germany and sentenced to twenty-two months in prison for publishing neo-Nazi propaganda and denying the occurrence of the Holocaust.[23] One can perhaps be forgiven a certain outrage at the fact that this creature is still alive, continuing to pollute the cosmos with his existence.

While Remer survived to preen himself on his comportment in Berlin, the aftermath at Rastenburg was less conducive to such vanity. Mussolini had been scheduled to arrive for a meeting at four o'clock. When he did so, the Führer was still dazed and over-wrought, and even more prone to hysteria than usual. This hysteria was contagious, transmitting itself to the other Nazi leaders present. The arranged 'talks' quickly degenerated into a sequence of manic and unseemly rows. Goering at one point challenged Ribbentrop's right to parade a 'von' before his surname. Ribbentrop retorted by calling Goering a 'champagne salesman'. Apoplectic with rage, the Reichsmarshal threatened to batter the foreign minister with his bejewelled baton. His nerves further abraded by this dissension among his associates, Hitler lost all vestiges of control and launched into a tantrum. He would be ruthless, he screamed: he would annihilate everyone associated with the conspiracy, would exterminate them all, would show no mercy, would exact revenge even from women and children. In the past, Mussolini had been awed and cowed by what he saw as the forbidding majesty of the Reich's hierarchy. When he left Rastenburg, he was shaken and bewildered, feeling, as he reported afterwards, that he had been in a madhouse.

Command of the Reserve Army was now entrusted to Himmler, which rendered it subordinate to, and eventually all but subsumed by, the SS. In hunting down conspirators, Hitler urged his deputy to be ruthless. 'My Führer,' Himmler replied with a smile, 'you can rely on me.' On 3 August, a fortnight after the attempted coup, he formally introduced the doctrine of *Sippenhaft*: 'blood guilt' or 'blood liability'. According to this doctrine, allegedly rooted in ancient Germanic tradition, treachery was a manifestation of diseased blood, not only in the culprit himself, but in all members of his family. In consequence, Himmler concluded, 'all were exterminated, to the last member of the clan'. The doctrine of *Sippenhaft* was now to be invoked anew. 'The family of Graf Stauffenberg will be extinguished to the last member.'[24]

In the end, Himmler was balked by his own doting reverence for aristocracy and antique lineage. The blood of such families as the Stauffenbergs, he concluded, was too precious to be indiscriminately squandered. In this blood resided the *puissance*, the *vertu*, of Germany's future leadership. As a result, most members of the Stauffenberg family escaped extermination. Many of them were consigned to internment camps. Relatives were wrenched apart, children separated from their parents and entrusted to the care of the State. Claus and Berthold von Stauffenberg's wives and children survived. So, too, did their brother, Alexander, who had not been implicated in the conspiracy.

There were other conspirators, at least eight of them, who, like Beck, eluded the Führer's vengeance by committing suicide. One such was the gallant Henning von Tresckow on the Russian front. According to some accounts, Tresckow walked from his headquarters to the front line and there shot himself. According to others, he simply strode out, amid an artillery barrage, into the no-man's-land between German and Russian lines.

Tresckow was very much in the minority. Most of the conspirators not only chose to stay alive, but even, with surprising docility, allowed themselves to be arrested. It has been suggested that they may not have expected as severe a punishment as they were subsequently to receive, but this seems unlikely. They cannot have had many illusions about what was in store for them. In fact, most of them welcomed the opportunity to speak out to their interrogators and, more publicly still, in court, where they hoped to be heard by the German people. They were eager to turn the indictments brought against themselves into indictments against the régime. In more than a few instances, they made a genuinely profound impression on their persecutors. Some were even seduced into sympathy.

Dr Georg Kiesel offers one such example. In the aftermath of 20 July, Hitler had demanded from Ernst Kaltenbrunner, head of the SD, a comprehensive enquiry into the conspiracy and a detailed report. Kaltenbrunner issued personal instructions that the Führer 'must be given an uncompromising account of the motives for the assassination attempt. So many men of distinguished character and office were involved in the conspiracy that Hitler would, it was hoped, receive the shock he needed to make the necessary changes.'[25]

Kiesel, an SS interrogator and investigator, was assigned by Kaltenbrunner to compile much of the required documentation. To what must have been Hitler's profound consternation, Kiesel described Stauffenberg as 'a truly universal man' and 'a spirit of fire, fascinating and inspiring all who came in touch with him'.[26] He actually went so far as to depict the Führer's would-be assassin as 'a revolutionary aristocrat, careless of himself, without a trace of vanity or ambition', a eulogy that even Stauffenberg's staunchest supporters might find slightly extravagant. Kiesel was equally impressed by his interrogation of Stauffenberg's brother, Berthold:

> His short evidence was the clearest and most important document indicting Hitler that may ever have been written and shown to him. It manifested a type of German manhood with deep religious, political and artistic principles, utterly divorced from Hitler and National Socialism.[27]

Kiesel was not alone. Reports by other interrogators spoke with consistent respect of Stauffenberg, citing his 'vision and struggles' and his desire 'to combine ethical socialism with his aristocratic traditions'.[28] For many of the interrogators, their work was not without some considerable discomfort. They may have been vicious and sadistic bullies, but they were not fools, and had been inculcated since childhood with respect for those they regarded as their 'betters'. Their victims were precisely such betters, men whom, for various reasons – caste or lineage, social standing and prestige, military or other accomplishments, intelligence and articulateness – they had revered. It must have been disconcerting to hear the well-reasoned and eloquently enunciated arguments of such men – arguments whose validity the interrogators themselves would have had difficulty ignoring. No one, after all, could be oblivious to the disaster which, by 1944, Hitler and the National Socialist hierarchy had brought down upon Germany. No one could be oblivious to the deteriorating military situation: the Western Allies driving eastwards from Normandy, the Red Army advancing westwards, British and American heavy bombers raining death down on German cities by day and night. And no one could be oblivious to the atrocities of the régime, the wholesale murder of Jews, Slavs and others, which the conspirators again and again cited as one of their primary reasons for action.

Under brutal torture – what the Gestapo, with typical bureaucratic euphemism, called 'sharpened interrogation' – the conspirators displayed extraordinary bravery and tenacity. Fellgiebel suffered for three weeks before divulging any names. When he finally did speak, he involved only those he knew already to be dead. By virtue of such courage, a number of imprisoned individuals were released, and others were never arrested at all. Thus did men such as Axel von dem Bussche, Ludwig von Hammerstein and Ewald von Kleist escape and survive.[29]

All officers implicated in the conspiracy were expelled from the army by a spurious 'court of honour' – a total of fifty-five men, including ten generals and a field marshal (Witzleben). This semblance of legality allowed them to be tried, along with their non-military colleagues, as civilians. There followed a series of grotesque 'show trials' in the notorious 'People's Court', under the auspices of its so-called President, Roland Freisler, one of the most loathsome figures in the entire macabre history of National Socialism. No pretence was made to anything even approximating judicial procedure. Freisler interrupted the defendants, shouted them down, insulted them, swore at them, endeavoured to humiliate them by every means possible.

It is not known how many Germans altogether died in reprisal for the abortive coup, but the total number has been estimated as high as two or three thousand. In the 'People's Court' alone, some two hundred were sentenced to death before Freisler, on 21 December 1944, was fatally injured in an Allied air raid. He was holding, at the time, the papers pertaining to the case of Fabian von Schlabrendorff, Tresckow's subordinate, who consequently escaped.

Those condemned by Freisler's court were hanged in Berlin's Ploetzensee prison. The method employed did not, as in conventional hangings, break the neck. It was a slow and painful death by strangulation, which sometimes lasted as long as twenty-five minutes. On Hitler's express orders, the executions were filmed. Even Kaltenbrunner objected to this obscenity, but the Führer remained adamant. Nine camera-men were employed by turns, but filming, after the first day, was curtailed. According to their director: 'I declared that I could not expect my camera-men to film any more of such cruelties. All the camera-men were with me on that.'[30]

In the company of close friends, Party officials and selected guests, Hitler would spend whole evenings watching such footage as had been filmed. He also had stills made, which Albert Speer reports seeing on his desk. Speer himself was invited to a showing, but declined in revulsion. The audience, he observed, consisted primarily of civilians and junior SS personnel. 'Not a single officer of the Wehrmacht attended.'[31]

Despite the grisly fate awaiting them, the conspirators remained defiant, even parrying Freisler's abuse in the 'People's Court' and making themselves heard above his hysterical tirades. When sentenced to hang, Fellgiebel replied, 'Then hurry with the hanging, Mr President; otherwise you will hang earlier than we.'[32]

'Soon you will be in hell,' Freisler sneered at the lawyer Dr Josef Wirmer, one of the civilian conspirators.

'It will be my pleasure when you follow shortly, Mr President,' Wirmer retorted.[33]

Field Marshal von Witzleben issued a similar prophecy: 'You can hand us over to the hangman. In three months, the enraged and tormented people will call you to account, and will drag you alive through the muck in the street.'[34]

Hans Bernt von Haeften, brother of Stauffenberg's aide, was asked how he could possibly have broken faith with the Führer.

'Because,' Haeften answered, 'I consider the Führer the executor of the evil in history.'[35]

On 21 July, the day after the abortive coup and just before his own suicide, Tresckow stated:

> Now they will all fall upon us and cover us with abuse. But I am convinced, now more than ever, that we have done the right thing. I believe Hitler to be the arch enemy not only of Germany, but indeed of the entire world . . . No one among us can complain about his death, for whoever joined our ranks put on the poisoned shirt of Nessus. A man's moral worth is established only at the point where he is prepared to give his life for his convictions.[36]

He went on to say:

> In a few hours' time, I shall stand before God and answer for both my actions and the things I neglected to do. I think I can with a clear conscience stand by all I have done in the battle against Hitler. Just as God once promised Abraham that he would spare Sodom if only ten just men could be found in the city, I also have reason to hope that, for our sake, he will not destroy Germany.[37]

Tresckow's unwavering certainty was echoed in the last words of other conspirators. Immediately before his execution, Julius Leber sent a statement to his associates:

> One's own life is a proper stake for so good and just a cause. We have done what lay in our power. It is not our fault that we all turned out like this, and not otherwise.[38]

In a farewell letter to his mother, one of Stauffenberg's cousins, Peter Yorck von Wartenburg, wrote:

Perhaps there will yet come a time that will judge us not as scoundrels but as prophets and patriots.[39]

The night before his death, Yorck wrote to his wife:

> I, too, am dying for my country, and even if it seems to all appearances a very inglorious and disgraceful death, I shall hold up my head and I only hope that you will not believe this to be from pride or delusion. We wished to light the torch of life and now we stand in a sea of flames.[40]

One of Stauffenberg's closest friends and associates was Count Fritz-Dietlof von der Schulenburg. Schulenburg's was among the oldest and wealthiest of Prussian 'Junker' families. Like Stauffenberg and Tresckow, Schulenburg himself was a passionate devotee of Stefan George's poetry. His wife's birthday was on 20 July. On the evening of the 18th, he had returned home to visit her, saying he wished to celebrate in advance.

> The children were to be got out of bed again . . . When he drove away again in the early morning and sat on the driver's seat he . . . waved his cap like a civilian, bowed low and gravely and went off, to the laughter of the gesticulating children.[41]

No sooner had he reached Berlin than he learned that his brother had been killed in Normandy.

In his trial before the 'People's Court', Schulenburg stated:

> We have accepted the necessity to do our deed in order to save Germany from untold misery. I expect to be hanged for this, but I do not regret my action and I hope that someone else in luckier circumstances will succeed.[42]

Just before his execution, he wrote to his beloved wife: 'What we did was inadequate, but in the end history will judge and acquit us.'[43]

Berlin's Ploetzensee Prison is still in use today, but the room in which the conspirators died is not. It is a cold room. At the end of it opposite the entrance, five bleak meat hooks swing from a metal beam. In front of these hooks, there are usually banks of flowers.

Despite its grimly stark appearance, the atmosphere of the place suggests something of a shrine. People approach it deferentially, in small groups or singly. Their talk ceases. They stand in contemplative silence for a few moments, then walk slowly on.

The nine months between 20 July 1944 and the end of the war in Europe were to witness an appalling loss of life. There was the prolonged Allied thrust from the Atlantic wall into Germany, with such major engagements as Arnhem and the so-called Battle of the Bulge; and the even more costly Russian advance from the east, into the shattered ruins of Berlin. There was also the Allied air offensive, with its sickening toll of both air crew and German civilians, which culminated in the devastation of Dresden. Lives continued to be lost at sea, as well as in occupied countries such as Greece and Yugoslavia. Thousands died in London from V-1 'buzz-bombs' and V-2 rockets. Most appalling of all, millions were exterminated in the death camps. Altogether, the last nine months of the war in Europe took more lives than the previous four years and eleven months of conflict. This statistic offers some gauge of the stakes involved in Stauffenberg's conspiracy. Had Hitler died on 20 July 1944, the total casualties of the Second World War could have been halved.

\*

Stauffenberg himself eluded Hitler's vindictive sadism and the gruesome fate that befell so many of his co-conspirators. Shortly after midnight on the morning of 21 July, he, Olbricht, Haeften and Merz von Quirnheim were lined up before a pile of sand in an inner courtyard of the War Office. They were supposed to be shot in order of rank: Olbricht first, then Stauffenberg, then Merz, then Haeften. One of the latter two – Haeften according to some accounts, Merz according to others – is reported to have lunged in front of Stauffenberg and received the bullets intended for him. The firing squad was compelled to take aim again. An instant before the fatal shots cut him down, he shouted something defiant into the faces of his executioners. Amid the reverberating echoes from the surrounding walls, the words were indistinct. According to some accounts, he shouted: '*Es lebe unser heiliges Deutschland!*' ('Long live our sacred Germany!') According to other accounts (and these would appear to be more accurate), Stauffenberg's last words invoked his master, the poet Stefan George, and the title of George's poem he had conferred on the German resistance: '*Es lebe unser geheimes Deutschland!*' ('Long live our secret Germany!').[44]

# Part Two

———

## THE RISE OF PRUSSIA

# 4
# Blood and Iron

By the dawn of the twentieth century, if not before, the name of Prussia had become synonymous in the English-speaking world with everything most quintessentially German. Among other things, it connoted militarism, aggression, obedience, rigorous discipline and assiduous service to the state. It often conjured up an unthinking robotlike efficiency, and it was associated with what outsiders believed to be the nucleus of the German aristocracy – the old, so-called 'Junker' class, the very name of which implied something pejorative. In 1900, the terms 'Prussian' and 'German' were habitually used by non-Germans more or less interchangeably. Even today, something of this association lingers. In 1947, according to Law Number 46 of the Allied Control Council, Prussia was formally and officially 'abolished': 'The Prussian State which from early days has been a bearer of militarism and reaction in Germany has *de facto* ceased to exist.' Prussia exists today only as a nebulous geographical entity, a generalised and vaguely defined region. It no longer appears on any map, no longer has any precise delineation or frontiers, has no political or administrative status of any kind. Yet even today, in the English-speaking world, the word 'Prussian' evokes something more uniquely, more distinctively and more undilutedly German than, say, 'Saxon' or 'Bavarian'.

Yet Prussia was a relatively late development, not just on the stage of world history, but on that of German history. It was one of the most recent powers to appear in the context of European politics. During the thirteenth century, when England and France were already developing specific national identities, 'Germany' had nothing whatever to do with Prussia. To Western Europe, Prussia was pretty much what the American West was to denizens of Boston and New York at the beginning of the nineteenth century – before the California Gold Rush, before the Civil War, before the pioneers in their wagon trains had pushed the nation's 'manifest destiny' even to the Mississippi, still less as far as the Pacific. Prussia was an unmapped wilderness, a forbidding hinterland peopled only by 'heathenish' tribes as divorced from Western 'civilisation' as were the American Indians.

Between the thirteenth and early sixteenth centuries, Prussia was part of the territory known as the Ordenstaadt, or Ordensland. This was the unique domain of a military-chivalric institution, the Teutonic Order or Teutonic Knights, an offshoot of the medieval Knights Templar. It was they who colonised the region known as Prussia, as well as the Baltic coast as far as the Gulf of Finland, an area consisting of large parts of Poland, Lithuania, Estonia, Latvia and north-western Russia. The process had much in common with the colonisation of the American West. Indigenous tribes, including the Balts and native Prussians, were exterminated wholesale, and the land was parcelled out to agricultural settlers from Christian Europe.

Like the other military-chivalric orders – the Templars, the Knights Hospitaller, and their equivalents in Spain and Portugal – the Teutonic Knights functioned as the vanguard of Christendom, carrying the banner of the Church into pagan territory. The colonisation and settlement of Prussia and the Baltic was officially described as a 'crusade' – as much so as the 'crusades' that temporarily annexed the Holy Land, that exterminated the Cathar heretics of the Languedoc, that drove Islam from the Iberian peninsula. And like the other military-chivalric orders, the Teutonic Knights served as a kind of repository for Western nobles seeking to gain experience of the battlefield, and obtain military initiation and expertise. Campaigning in Prussia and the Baltic became a kind of blood sport. The Teutonic Knights played host to aristocrats from all over Europe in quest of the excitement of combat – and Papal dispensation. Among them were a number of Scots, such as Henry Sinclair of Roslin. Henry, Earl of Bolingbroke, the future Henry IV of England, on being exiled by Richard II, also campaigned with the Teutonic Knights. From them, he learned many of the martial and political skills that would enable him eventually to return to England, depose Richard and establish his own dynasty.

At the end of the fourteenth century (the time when Bolingbroke was serving with them), the Teutonic Knights were at the peak of their power. The Ordenstaadt over which they presided encompassed the whole of Christianised north-eastern Europe, a fiefdom the size of England, Scotland and Wales combined. It was effectively remote from all other authority, spiritual or temporal. Operating well beyond the reach of the Pope and all secular Western potentates, the Teutonic Knights were a law unto themselves, and the Ordenstaadt was regarded as a nation-state in its own right. It had its own capital at Marianburg (now Malbork, in Poland), and its own political and administrative machinery. It sent and received its own embassies to and from Western courts, to and from Rome. The governing hierarchy, headed by the Grand Master, was accorded the same respect, status and honours as that of any Western European principality.

Then, in 1410, at the Battle of Tannenburg – some sixty miles from where Hitler was subsequently to build his 'Wolf's Lair' at Rastenburg – the Teutonic Knights suffered a decisive defeat at the hands of a combined Polish and Lithuanian army. From that point on, their domain began to shrink, their power to decline, although the Ordenstaadt survived for another century.

At last, in 1525, Albrecht von Hohenzollern, Grand Master of the Teutonic Knights, came under the influence of Martin Luther and converted to Protestantism. He was followed by others, and the Order itself was secularised. Later that year Albrecht was made Duke of Prussia, owing allegiance to the Polish throne, and Prussia became a defined political and administrative entity. In the domains of the newly created duchy, brethren of the Teutonic Knights – the younger sons of a much older German aristocracy – began to marry, bring up families and establish their own land holdings. It was these men, and, even more, those they had ushered into the region as settlers and colonists, who comprised the so-called 'Junker' class.

In 1618, the duchy of Prussia passed into the hands of another branch of the Hohenzollern family, who ruled the territory known as Brandenburg. Brandenburg and Prussia were thus amalgamated. Then, in 1701, Albrecht von Hohenzollern's descendant assumed the title of Friedrich I and proclaimed himself 'King *in* Prussia', being anointed by two Protestant bishops but placing the crown on his head himself.

When Prussia emerged as a kingdom, Queen Anne's reign in England was about to begin, while that of Louis XIV in France was nearing its end. French military supremacy on the continent was soon to be challenged by the Duke of Marlborough and his Austrian colleague, Prince Eugène of Savoy. Yet within half a century, Prussia was abruptly to assume the rôle of Europe's predominant martial power. She was to do so under only the third of her kings, Friedrich II, better known as Frederick the Great, the single most brilliant and resourceful commander of the eighteenth century. Under Friedrich, Prussia – a mere minor duchy only a few years before – became one of the most important components in the shifting kaleidoscope known as the European 'balance of power'. Her army was regarded as a model, and duly emulated by those of Britain, France, Austria and Russia. And the Junker class, the country's military and administrative élite, consolidated their ascendancy.

Not even by this time was Prussia synonymous with Germany. So far as Germany was concerned, Prussia was still largely alien territory. Germany, in the world's eyes, lay elsewhere, and the Germans resided elsewhere. Even England – with her Saxon heritage, seventeenth-century dynastic links with the Palatinate of the Rhine and eighteenth-century Hannoverian monarchs – was considered more 'German' then Prussia, much of whose population consisted of Balts, Poles, Lithuanians, Latvians, Estonians, Russians and Scandinavians. And the Hohenzollerns, as well as the Junker class, were regarded, especially by the older aristocracy of southern Germany, as mere parvenu upstarts, backwoods yokels or semi-barbarians, only partially civilised and descruffed, still damp with vestiges of hyperborean mist.

Despite more recent assumptions, then, the real heartland of old

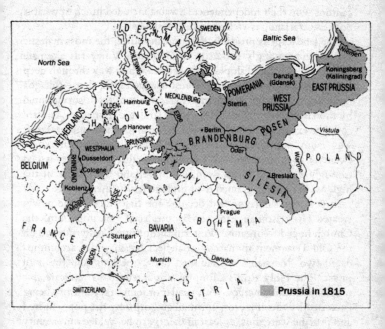

After the Napoleonic Wars the 1,789 domains comprising Germany were reduced in number to 39. Of these Prussia benefited most and, with its consolidated domains, was now in a position to challenge Austrian influence over such principalities as Bavaria, which included the Stauffenbergs' native home near Stuttgart in the ancient region of Swabia.

Germany had nothing whatever to do with Prussia; and the original German aristocracy – the aristocracy from which the Stauffenberg family issued – long pre-dated that of the 'uncouth' east. Old Germany's heartland consisted of the Rhine and its environs, particularly the region known as Schwaben or, in its anglicised version, Swabia. Swabia lies in the northern foothills of the Alps. On the west, it is bounded by the Rhine, on the east by the river Lech, beyond which lies Bavaria. Its principal cities are Ulm, Augsburg and Stuttgart. Prior to the fourteenth century, when the cantons won their independence, Swabia included much of what is now Switzerland, as well as Lake Constance.

The landscape is probably the most beautiful, the most majestic and most hauntingly evocative in Germany. Vineyards alternate with thickly wooded slopes. Rivers thread their way through deep valleys nestled between steep forest-shagged hills, dense-foliaged mountains and stark projecting crags, many of them surmounted by monasteries or castles. From these strategic eminences, control could be exercised over fords, bridges, road junctions and passes. It was from one such eminence – Castle Hohenstauffen, some twenty-five miles to the east of Stuttgart – that the dynasty issued through which the Holy Roman Empire, and the culture of the high Middle Ages, attained their highest achievements.

In 800, Charlemagne had become the first ruler of the newly created Holy Roman Empire. By means of this imperium, the Church hoped to organise Western Europe into a pattern based on the Old Testament monarchy of ancient Israel, which accommodated two 'Messiahs' or 'anointed ones', the king and the high priest. The Holy Roman Empire was intended to replicate this religio-political structure, with secular or temporal authority being exercised by the emperor, spiritual authority by the pope. Sacred and profane were thus, at least in theory, to be welded into a unity that facilitated the process of administration and government – and firmly subordinated, again in theory, secular affairs to those of the Church.

On Charlemagne's death, the secular empire he had yoked inseparably to the Papacy ws sub-divided among his sons. The temporal sphere of the intended pan-European theocracy became increasingly more fragmented, increasingly a law – or multitude of laws – unto itself. By the Middle Ages, France, England, Italy, Spain and other nations had begun to evolve national, cultural and, in some cases, political identities of their own, often with their own autonomous rulers and administrative apparatus; and the Holy Roman Empire, though it continued to exist under that name, had become, to all intents and purposes, the German Empire, the first Reich. In the language of the time, it was accepted as commonplace to speak of the Holy Roman Emperor as the German Emperor, and of the empire itself as simply Germany.

Swabia was created as a duchy in 917. By the end of the eleventh century, the duchy had passed into the hands of the Hohenstauffen ('High Stauffen') dynasty. In 1155, the Duke of Swabia, Friedrich III von Hohenstauffen, became the Holy Roman Emperor Friedrich I, also known as Friedrich Barbarossa ('Red Beard'). When he ascended the imperial throne, he was already a veteran of the ill-fated Second Crusade of 1147 and, in 1154, had embarked on a project that was to occupy him for much of his life, the subjugation and annexation of Italy. This was to bring him into conflict with the pope, who, in 1160, excommunicated him – thus, rather embarrassingly, leaving the Holy Roman Empire neither holy nor Roman. Friedrich responded by storming Rome itself and, in 1166, installing his own puppet pontiff, Paschal III, a personage still unrecognised in the Vatican's official history. For the next six years, and with the blessing of his pet anti-pope, Friedrich busied himself extending his domains to include Bohemia, Hungary and Poland. Then, in 1174, he made peace with the newly elected 'official' pope, Alexander III. He had to abase himself, kneel and kiss the pontiff's feet, in exchange for which his excommunication was lifted. In the following year, Friedrich contrived to get himself crowned King of Burgundy, which at that time stretched from Marseilles to Basle. By 1184, however, his renewed designs on Italy had brought him into conflict with the Papacy again; and when Urban III ascended the throne of St Peter, open warfare erupted between pope and emperor.

In 1189, Friedrich embarked from Germany with an immense army, intending to join King Richard I of England (Richard Coeur de Lion) on the Third Crusade, but on the way to the Holy Land, while crossing the river Göksu in Turkey, he drowned. His burial site remains a mystery. According to later legends, he lies sleeping in a cave deep within Mount Kyffhäuser, south of the Harz Mountains, awaiting the call to awake and rescue his country in the hour of need.

Friedrich Barbarossa was a vivid and archetypally evocative figure, but his grandson, Friedrich II, was an even more flamboyant personality, who, seven centuries later, was to exert a profound influence on the thinking of the poet Stefan George and of the young Claus von Stauffenberg. Under Friedrich II, the Hohenstauffen dynasty and the Holy Roman Empire attained their zenith. He was born in Italy in 1194 and in 1220, at the age of twenty-six, ascended the imperial throne. By that time, most of the Holy Land had already been lost to Islam, but instead of waging war against the 'infidels', Friedrich chose to treat with them, and obtained by negotiation what the crusaders could not by conflict. In 1229, he was crowned King of Jerusalem, entered the Holy City in triumph and obtained Bethlehem, Nazareth and the surrounding countryside as well.

At their maximum extent, Friedrich's European domains were to include the whole of what is now Italy, as far south as Sicily. They were to include Burgundy, from Provence across the Rhine to Lorraine. They were to include Austria, Swabia, Bavaria, Franconia, Saxony, Brandenburg, Brabant and other duchies, counties and marches in what was then German territory. They were to include Silesia, Pomerania and as much of Prussia as had been conquered and colonised. They were to include Bohemia, Hungary and Poland. In effect, the Hohenstauffen empire encompassed virtually the whole of Europe except for Scandinavia, France, the Iberian peninsula and the Balkans. Friedrich's temporal power, like that of his grandfather, inevitably brought him into conflict with the Papacy and, like his grandfather, he was excommunicated. Unlike his grandfather, however, he did not care, making no attempt to come to an accommodation with Rome.

Whatever Friedrich's accomplishments in politics and diplomacy, they were to be eclipsed, at least for posterity, by his activities in other spheres. He was a kind of pre-Renaissance 'Renaissance Man', and his mind was one of the most brilliant, most energetic, most insatiably voracious and audacious of the entire Middle Ages. He was to play a crucial rôle in the coalescence of modern Western culture. He spoke six languages, wrote poetry, was impressively versed in falconry, music, philosophy, mathematics and the spectrum of esoteric teachings available to his time. His opulent, cosmopolitan and ultra-sophisticated court in Sicily was a centre and a haven for Judaic and Islamic scholars; and it was through this court that much of their knowledge – algebra, for example, and Arabic numerals – was transmitted to the West. To propagate and disseminate such knowledge, Friedrich founded the University of

Naples. Not surprisingly, his encyclopedic and heterodox thinking provoked as much antipathy in the Papacy as did his territorial expansion. He was repeatedly accused of heresy and, even worse, apostasy; and he seems, indeed, seriously to have considered converting to Islam. Although he remained nominally Christian, his attitudes towards most things had little in common with the orthodoxy of the era. This included his attitude towards wedlock. His first marriage, at the age of fourteen, was to the daughter of the King of Aragon and the widow of the King of Hungary. His second was to Isabella, daughter of King John of England. Neither of these dynastic alliances prevented him from maintaining a harem in the Arab style.

From the milieu of the Hohenstauffen emperors, and particularly from that of Friedrich II, there sprang such phenomena as the poetic mystique of the Rhine, as expressed in the early thirteenth-century epic *The Nibelungenlied*, which provided, of course, the basis for Wagner's *Ring*. From the same milieu there also sprang perhaps the supreme flowering of medieval high culture. One especially important and durable manifestation of this was the work composed by Hartmann von Aue, Gottfried von Strassburg, Wolfram von Eschenbach, Walther von der Vogelweide, as well as the *Minnesänger* and *Meistersänger* who midwifed the epoch's great corpus of lyric, dramatic and narrative poetry. At the court of the Hohenstauffen, poetry contests and festivals were a regular occurrence, and bards competed with each other as they did in Ireland and Wales centuries before. The ritual of the poetry festival spread as far east as Marianburg, where it became a feature at the court of the Grand Master of those supposedly ascetic and austere warrior-monks, the Teutonic Knights.

It was also from the milieu of the Hohenstauffen empire and its high culture that the Stauffenberg family first issued. The family name, Schenk, now usually means 'publican', but it can also signify 'cup-bearer', and this was the sense attached to it in Hohenstauffen times. 'Cup-bearer' was an officially recognised court title and position (rather like 'Steward' in Scotland, which evolved into a family surname and then, as 'Stuart', into the name of a royal dynasty). The ancestors of the modern Stauffenberg family first appear on the stage of history as *Schenken*, or 'cup-bearers', to the powerful Swabian Counts of Zollern, who, from the mid-fourteenth century on, were known as the 'High Zollern', or Hohenzollern. Ruins of the original Stauffenberg castle can still be seen at the tiny Swabian hamlet of Stauffenberger Hof.

It is not known precisely how far back in time the family extends. The first name to appear officially in the record is Werner, Schenk von Zollern, in 1257. The family's full name first appears on a deed dating from 1317 which bears the signatures of three brothers: Burkhard Schenk von Stauffenberg, Berthold Schenk von Stauffenberg and Werner Schenk von Andeck. It is from the last of these, through his son, Hannes Schenk von Stauffenberg, that the modern Stauffenberg family descends.[1]

The family produced a predictable number of military figures. At least three Stauffenbergs served with the Teutonic Knights and at least two others with the Knights of St John, one of them becoming a high functionary of that order. Another served in the army of Charles, Connétable (Constable) de Bourbon, who rebelled against François I, joined the Habsburg Emperor Charles V to defeat and capture the French king at the Battle of Pavia in 1519, then went on to besiege Rome. There were also many ecclesiastics in the family, and a significant number of scholars. As early as 1310, two of Hannes Schenk von Stauffenberg's brothers were enrolled at the University of Bologna, and a tradition of learning was to persist in the line from then on. So, too, did a tradition of piety. In 1468, two Stauffenbergs, with an entourage of forty men, embarked on a pilgrimage to the Holy Land, visiting Bethlehem and the Jordan.[2]

Within Germany proper, the Stauffenbergs enjoyed the status of Free Knights of the Empire. This was denoted by the title 'Freiherr' and, like that of an English baronetcy, was hereditary. Indeed, 'Freiherr' is often translated as 'baron' to differentiate it from 'Ritter', which denotes an 'ordinary' knight. The Free Knights of the Empire were a uniquely German institution. Some were immensely wealthy, others poverty-stricken; some owned vast estates, others no more than a single castle or, even less, a manor house or fortified farm. But a Free Knight was, as the designation implies, accountable to no one save the emperor – who was usually too far away, or too apathetic, to exercise any control over him. A

Free Knight's holdings might lie in the domains of a count, duke or even king, but none of them could wield authority over a Free Knight, who was deemed, technically, to be a nobleman of equal rank. A Free Knight was exempt from all taxes save those due the emperor, and he could flout with impunity all laws the emperor had not personally decreed.

The Free Knights were symbolic embodiments in Germany of autonomy, self-sufficiency and independence. They were fiercely proud of their independence and defended it tenaciously. In many respects, they were the stuff of legend: romantic, dashing and often buccaneering figures who exemplified a spirit envied by much more powerful, yet also responsible, potentates. Thus do they appear in the late eighteenth-century play *Götz von Berlichingen*, the work with which a then unknown young writer named Johann Wolfgang von Goethe made his literary début.

It was, of course, inevitable that a warrior caste like the Free Knights, enjoying their exemption from constraint and seeking anything from adventure to riches, would often enough turn to crime. By the eve of the Lutheran Reformation, a burgeoning new middle class had begun to swell the wealth of German cities. The Protestant 'work ethic' contributed dramatically to this development, and money once lavishly squandered by feudal nobles and potentates was finding its way into the coffers of such influential banking dynasties as the Fuggers of Augsburg, or those of the Thurn-und-Taxis family, who had established Europe's first commercial postal and courier service. For the Free Knights, the newly prosperous class of merchants, entrepreneurs, bankers and financiers offered enticing opportunities for plunder. Caravans of bullion and commodities plying between such cities as Nuremberg, Augsburg and Frankfurt became fair game for bands of freebooting Free Knights, who would swoop on them like corsairs, or like the later outlaws of the American West. These depredations, which prompted the first use of the term 'robber baron', generated a state of ever intensifying friction between the Free Knights and the cities. Attempts to neutralise them by curbing or curtailing their hereditary rights and privileges were a primary cause of the curious aristocratic insurrection of 1522 known as the Knights' Revolt.

The acknowledged leader and guiding hand of the revolt was the

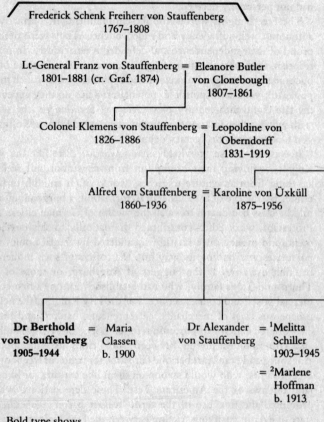

Frederick Schenk Freiherr von Stauffenberg
1767–1808

Lt-General Franz von Stauffenberg = Eleanore Butler
1801–1881 (cr. Graf. 1874)        von Clonebough
                                   1807–1861

Colonel Klemens von Stauffenberg = Leopoldine von
1826–1886                          Oberndorff
                                   1831–1919

Alfred von Stauffenberg = Karoline von Üxküll
1860–1936                 1875–1956

**Dr Berthold**   = Maria        Dr Alexander    = [1]Melitta
**von Stauffenberg**  Classen     von Stauffenberg    Schiller
**1905–1944**     b. 1900                             1903–1945

                                                  = [2]Marlene
                                                    Hoffman
                                                    b. 1913

Bold type shows
members of the Bomb Plot
executed in 1944.

1 Claus von Stauffenberg, a captain in the 6th Panzer Division in 1940.

2 Colonel-General
Ludwig Beck: Chief
Staff, German Army
1935-8, one of the le
of the German resist
to Hitler.

3 Colonel-General
Franz Halder. An ea
prominent member
the opposition to H
he succeeded Beck a
army Chief of Staff.

4 Hitler and his generals: left to right: Hitler, Field Marshal Keitel, Colonel-General Halder, Field Marshal Brauchitsch.

5 Lieutenant Werner von Haeften, who accompanied Stauffenberg on the attempt to assassinate Hitler.

6 Major-General Henning von Tresckow (centre), Chief of Staff of Army Group Centre (eastern front) which he built into an active opposition group. All the officers pictured here were involved in attempts to remove Hitler.

7 General Friedrich Olbricht, a member of the opposition to Hitler.

8 Colonel-General Fromm who arrested and ordered the death of Beck, Olbricht, Stauffenberg, Merz von Quirnheim and Haeften.

9 Dietrich Eckart, occult *éminence grise* behind Hitler.

10 Goering, Bormann and others outside the briefing hut at the 'Wolfsschanze' headquarters in East Prussia where Stauffenberg attempted the assassination of Hitler.

11 Goering, Bormann and others viewing the damage in the briefing hut caused by Stauffenberg's bomb, 20 July 1944.

12 Following the blast an official photograph was issued of Hitler's trousers.

13 Hitler visiting Major-General Scherff who was wounded by the bomb.

14 The ghost of a house: remains of Hitler's headquarters, the 'Berghof' above Berchtesgaden, Bavaria.

## Genealogy of the Stauffenberg family

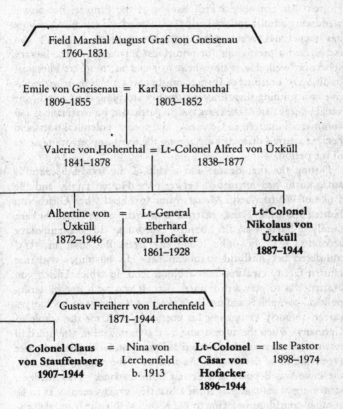

Field Marshal August Graf von Gneisenau
1760–1831

Emile von Gneisenau = Karl von Hohenthal
1809–1855          1803–1852

Valerie von Hohenthal = Lt-Colonel Alfred von Üxküll
1841–1878               1838–1877

Albertine von = Lt-General        **Lt-Colonel**
Üxküll          Eberhard          **Nikolaus von**
1872–1946       von Hofacker      **Üxküll**
                1861–1928         **1887–1944**

Gustav Freiherr von Lerchenfeld
1871–1944

**Colonel Claus** = Nina von      **Lt-Colonel** = Ilse Pastor
**von Stauffenberg** Lerchenfeld   **Cäsar von**    1898–1974
**1907–1944**      b. 1913        **Hofacker**
                                  **1896–1944**

powerful and charismatic Franz von Sickingen. For posterity, however, Sickingen's status has been eclipsed by that of his spokesman and lieutenant, the dynamic and resourceful young Ulrich von Hutten. Descended from a noble Franconian family, Hutten was not only a Free Knight of the Empire, but also a wandering scholar and soldier-poet. Learned and articulate, Hutten has sometimes been called the 'first political German', and established a prestigious (or notorious) reputation in the literary sphere as well. He is now held to stand in the great humanist tradition of Erasmus of Rotterdam, but was much more vituperative and scathing than Erasmus, boldly attacking the Church, the venal bourgeoisie of the cities and, in particular, Italian financial and commercial interests in Germany. His poems, polemical tracts and rasping satirical dialogues are among the most important literature of the period.

During the first decade and a half of the sixteenth century, antagonism had intensified between the Hutten family and the Duke of Württemberg. Matters came to a head when Ulrich von Hutten's cousin, Hans, married a woman of the Stauffenberg family.[3] Such was her beauty, according to contemporary accounts, that the duke found her irresistible and, in 1515, murdered her husband to obtain her. His hostilities with the Hutten family escalated into a blood feud, in which Ulrich von Hutten was to play a prominent part. It was with five blistering political pamphlets against the duke that he launched his literary career, publicly castigating his enemy in print for the whole of Germany. When the duke, stung by this humiliation, attempted to retaliate, Hutten invoked the aid of Franz von Sickingen and other Free Knights of the Empire. As a result of their concerted action, the duke was deposed and driven from his lands. This incident, stemming at least in part from a Stauffenberg woman, was to be another contributing factor to the Knights' Revolt. It imbued the knights with an overestimated sense of their own power and spurred them on to more reckless undertakings. Their success in toppling a powerful secular authority generated fresh alarm and antagonism among the urban bourgeoisie.

As for the Stauffenbergs themselves, Jakob Schenk von Stauffenberg and his wife were early converts to Lutheranism, but other members of the family continued to adhere to their Catholic heritage.[4] In the seventeenth century, one Stauffenberg was a Jesuit, while another served in the Catholic armies of the Empire during the Thirty Years War. The brother of this officer became Prince-Bishop of Bamberg. Another Stauffenberg became Prince-Bishop first of Konstanz, then of Augsburg. His brother rose in the Swabian contingent of the Knights of St John to the rank of 'Generalfeld-marschalleutnant'. The family continued to have connections with some of the most resonant names not only in German, but in European, history. The great poet and playwright Friedrich von Schiller was descended from the fourteenth-century Konrad Schenk von Stauffenberg.[5] Prince Metternich, that *éminence grise* of early nineteenth-century continental politics, was the nephew of a Stauffenberg.[6]

In 1874, the 73-year-old Lieutenant-General Franz Schenk, Freiherr von Stauffenberg was raised to the rank of Graf, or count, by Ludwig II of Bavaria.[7] Trained as a lawyer, the lieutenant-general had also had a distinguished career in politics dating from 1837. Between 1877 and his death in 1881, he played a salient rôle in the parliamentary opposition to Bismarck. His grandson, Alfred, married Karoline von Üxküll in 1904. From this union, the three brothers, Alexander, Berthold and Claus von Stauffenberg, were born.

Karoline von Üxküll was of Prussian descent. Her lineage may not have been quite as old as that of the Stauffenbergs, but it included names no less resonant – at least two of which were to figure prominently in the minds of the three brothers. Claus von Stauffenberg was able to claim among his maternal ancestors two of the most distinguished commanders in German military history, two of the most important leaders of the Napoleonic Wars.

One of these was Field Marshal Peter Yorck, Graf von Wartenburg (1759–1830). Yorck began his career as a swash-buckling soldier of fortune. In 1779, at the age of twenty-one, he accused a superior officer of stealing an altar cloth from a church and thereby got himself court-martialled, imprisoned for a year and cashiered from the Prussian army. In 1781, he migrated to Holland, took service with the Dutch East India Company and spent a year at the Cape of Good Hope as well. In 1794, at the beginning of the revolutionary wars with France, he regained his Prussian commission and embarked on a prolonged campaign to update the Prussian army – to modernise the military machine which had rested on its laurels since Frederick the Great's time half a century before and adapt it to the conditions of early nineteenth-century warfare. He was too late to do much at first, but at the Battle of Jena in 1806, where the supposedly invincible Prussians were resoundingly trounced by Napoleon, he managed to bring his regiment through the débâcle intact and with honour. He subsequently commanded a corps (half the force allowed Prussia by treaty) attached to the French army during Napoleon's invasion of Russia. He was to play a crucial rôle in bringing Prussia into the Grand Alliance that eventually toppled the French emperor. He also participated in the mammoth Battle of Leipzig, known as the 'Battle of the Nations', and in the joint Prussian-Russian-Austrian-Swedish-British invasion of France which culminated with Napoleon's capitulation in 1814.

The second of Stauffenberg's illustrious maternal ancestors was Field Marshal August Wilhelm Neithardt, Graf von Gneisenau (1760–1831). A Saxon by birth, Gneisenau served in the Austrian army, then in that of the small German principality of Bayreuth-Anspach. The army of Bayreuth-Anspach was among those recruited as mercenaries by Britain's Hannoverian monarchy for service in the rebellious colonies of North America; and though he arrived too late to see much action, Gneisenau was present during the final phases of the American War for Independence.

Much later, in Prussia, Gneisenau was at the forefront of attempts to introduce social and constitutional reform, but it was as a military reformer that he achieved his most significant and durable success. After the defeat at Jena and the French occupation of Prussia, Gneisenau – together with Yorck von Wartenburg, Gerhard von Scharnhorst and their younger disciple, Karl Maria von Clausewitz – embarked on a dramatic and radical renovation of the entire Prussian military system. This renovation, executed secretly under the very noses of the occupying French, was to transmute the cumbersome old Prussian war machine into one of the most efficient, modern and sophisticated on the continent. Among other things, Gneisenau and Scharnhorst democratised the Prussian officer corps, made men of non-aristocratic status eligible for commissions and introduced universal conscription. They were also instrumental in the creation of the Prussian (subsequently German) General Staff, the first such institution in the world, and in the creation of the General Staff College, prototype for Sandhurst, St Cyr, West Point and other such academies. Like Yorck von Wartenburg, Gneisenau played a prominent part in the Grand Alliance against Napoleon, functioning as the Prussian army's Chief of Staff. In this capacity, he attended – and did the thinking for – the more famous and flamboyantly eccentric Marshal Gebhard von Blücher. When Blücher's army was defeated by Napoleon at Ligny in June 1815, it was Gneisenau who assumed command. He prevented the retreat from disintegrating into a rout, regrouped the scattered Prussian formations and enabled them, in the nick of time, to come to Wellington's aid at Waterloo.

*

With illustrious ancestors constantly in mind, Claus von Stauffenberg and his two brothers grew up and came to maturity. But the Germany they inhabited was a very different Germany from that of Gneisenau's and Yorck von Wartenburg's time. In a span of some fifty-five years, the country had undergone a revolution as dramatic, and traumatic, as that of France in 1789 or Russia in 1917, but the revolution was of a very different kind.

In 1789, on the eve of the French Revolution, Germany was divided into no less than 1,789 separate domains. There were 51 Free Cities of the Empire, including Hamburg, Bremen, Nuremberg, Augsburg, Ulm and Frankfurt. There were 63 ecclesiastical principalities presided over by clerics. There were 200 other principalities, ranging from the demesnes of counts, through duchies, up to kingdoms like Saxony, Bavaria and Prussia, and there were 1,475 tracts of independent territory held by Free Knights of the Empire.

In the aftermath of the Napoleonic Wars, the Congress of Vienna reassembled this bewildering jigsaw into something more manageable: four Free Cities and thirty-five other principalities. Of these, Prussia was the most powerful militarily, but the 'heart and soul' of Germany were still deemed to lie elsewhere – in Saxony, in Bavaria and, especially, in such regions along the Rhine as the Palatinate,

Hesse, Nassau, Baden and Westphalia, as well as the Stauffenbergs' native Swabia. These regions were to constitute the arena for a new struggle between 1815 and 1866, a social, cultural and political struggle for Germany's 'heart and soul'. The two protagonists in the struggle were to be Prussia under the Hohenzollern dynasty and Austria (after 1848 the dual monarchy of Austria-Hungary) under the Habsburgs.

Although held only tenuously together, and grievously debilitated by the struggle with Napoleon, the Habsburg imperium still remained a major European power, ruled by the oldest reigning dynasty on the continent. It had on its side the weight of tradition, of legitimacy, of nearly a thousand years of high culture, sophistication, cosmopolitan urbanity, diplomatic experience – and the support of the Papacy, which carried much currency in such Catholic regions as Bavaria. Prussia could not compete in these respects, but she had the energy of a newly discovered nationalism, a vital industrial base, an increasingly efficient military machine and the support of the Lutheran Church, which has been described as pretty much an adjunct of the War Office. The rôle of the Lutheran Church should not be overlooked or underemphasised, for it was responsible for promoting the Protestant 'work ethic'. Encouraging progress, commerce, industrialisation and material success, the dynamism of this ethic had, two centuries before, transformed England and Holland, catapulting both to the forefront of European affairs. Now, that dynamism was to find a new sphere of activity in Germany.

Thus the polarity of the mid-nineteenth century took shape. For many Germans at the time, Austria embodied culture and civilisation, but she also appeared decadent, inert and mired in the past. Prussia, though brash, vulgar and tactlessly self-assertive, embodied the qualities associated with youth – energy and idealism. Compared to Austria, she could appear alluringly dynamic. If Austria was old, Prussia appeared young and seemingly bursting with exuberance – even though her governing régime was among the most stodgy and reactionary in Europe.

Until 1866, the struggle between Austria and Prussia for the 'heart and soul' of Germany remained confined to social, cultural and diplomatic spheres. But Prussia was readying herself for more dramatic activity. Quietly, discreetly, virtually unnoticed by the rest of Europe, she had embarked on a process of radical modernisation. This took place under the auspices of the monarch, Wilhelm I, but its real instigator and guiding spirit was the king's so-called 'Iron Chancellor', Prince Otto von Bismarck. And Bismarck, relying heavily on the institutions Gneisenau had helped to devise half a century before – the General Staff and the General Staff College – proceeded to forge, out of 'blood and iron', the most efficient military machine since Napoleon's time. This machine was to be deployed with a single focused objective in mind: the neutralisation of Austria and the unification of Germany under Prussian leadership. Operations were entrusted to the new Chief of the General Staff, Field Marshal Helmuth von Moltke.

In 1864, while Europe's attention was distracted by the civil war raging in the United States, Bismarck and his Chief of Staff undertook to give their war machine a trial run. The target for this exercise, puny little Denmark, was hardly in a position to offer much serious resistance. The conflict lasted six months, although it took just ten weeks to defeat the Danish forces in the field. When Denmark sued for peace, Prussia annexed (with nominal Austrian collaboration) the prized duchies of Schleswig and Holstein.

Having proved itself against a token adversary, the martial dynamo was ready for a more serious and consequential confrontation. At last, after half a century of subterranean diplomatic tussling, Bismarck was intent on settling, once and for all, the long-standing vendetta with Austria. Most outsiders at the time would not have wagered much on his chances, but the Habsburg imperium was militarily feeble, spending only enough on her army, as the novelist Robert Musil later wrote, 'to ensure her position as the second-weakest great power in Europe'. According to jokes then current, the Prussian army made steel while the Austrian army made music; the Prussian army wore iron helmets with spikes, the Austrian cock hats adorned with feathers. Music and feathers were no match for Krupp steel. When war came in 1866, Austria's showing was no more creditable than Denmark's had been. Her troops offered stiffer resistance, but the war lasted only seven weeks, and when it was over, the struggle for the 'heart and soul' of Germany had at last been decided in Prussia's favour. Among the spoils of war were

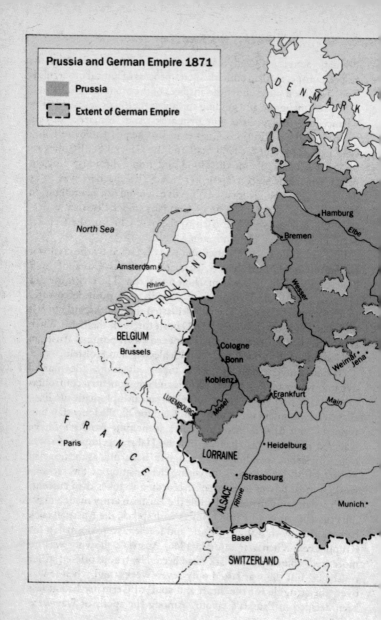

**Prussia and German Empire 1871**

Prussia

Extent of German Empire

DENMARK

North Sea

Hamburg

Bremen

Elbe

Amsterdam

HOLLAND

Rhine

Weser

BELGIUM

Brussels

Cologne

Bonn

Weimar Jena

Koblenz

Frankfurt

Main

LUXEMBOURG

Mosel

F R A N C E

Heidelburg

Paris

LORRAINE

Strasbourg

ALSACE

Rhine

Munich

Basel

SWITZERLAND

Hesse-Cassel, Nassau, Hannover and the Free City of Frankfurt.

Among continental powers, the only serious remaining rival was France and the Second Empire of Napoleon III. By 19 July 1870 (a day after the doctrine of Papal infallibility was proclaimed by the Vatican), Bismarck had skilfully manipulated the French emperor into declaring hostilities. Having thus exonerated himself from any charge of aggression, he responded with the kind of force and speed that would come to be known, seventy years later, as 'lightning war', or 'Blitzkrieg'. The painfully humiliating Siege of Paris was to drag on until the end of January 1871, but effective fighting in the field between French and Prussian armies was over by 2 September 1870, a mere six weeks. When the conflict ended, Napoleon III had capitulated, the Second Empire lay in ruins and France, after careening vertiginously towards full-scale civil war, had pulled herself tenuously together into a chastened and none-too-stable republic. In place of the Kingdom of Prussia and its associated satellite principalities, a new political entity had appeared on the world's maps. On 18 January 1871, while his troops formed a ring of bayonets around Paris and his artillery shelled the helpless city at will, Wilhelm I was proclaimed German Emperor at Versailles. The reborn German Empire, the Second Reich, was an imperium calculated to evoke echoes of the old Hohenstauffen dynasty, but it owed no allegiance whatever to Rome, and its capital was not on the Rhine, but in the Prussian capital of Berlin. Prussia and Germany were now, to all intents and purposes, synonymous, and a military model for the rest of the world even in matters of fashion. Many infantry regiments in the British Army adopted the spiked helmet, and some retain it even today. It also survives in the helmet of the British bobby: essentially a Prussian helmet with an amputated spike.

Nominally at least, the new German Empire was a confederation of kingdoms and principalities, each retaining its own semi-autonomous ruler. Thus, for example, Ludwig II of Bavaria continued to preside over his Wagnerian fairy-tale realm. But the Second Reich was not prepared to brook any insubordination from its constituent components. In 1886, after defying Bismarck, Ludwig was mysteriously and conveniently murdered – at the hands, it is now generally believed, of Prussian agents. It has even been suggested that Prussian policy had something to do with the death of Archduke Rudolf, the Austrian heir apparent, whose body was found, along with that of his mistress, at the hunting lodge of Mayerling in 1889.

The new imperium was a curious, at times hybrid, political entity. Many of the smaller principalities continued to exist as before: enclaves of archaic quaintness and picturesqueness out of the brothers Grimm, with gingerbread castles and a Ruritanian lifestyle unchanged since the Middle Ages. This is how 'Germany' appears in Thomas Mann's early novel *Royal Highness*, published in 1909. But side by side with such kitsch anachronisms (of particular appeal to British tourists), there were burgeoning cosmopolitan cities like Hamburg, Frankfurt and Cologne – and, of course, the massive industrial centre of the Ruhr valley.

In the years immediately preceding the creation of the empire, Prussia had closely monitored the American Civil War. Prussian 'observers' were often to be found hobnobbing with the staffs of both Union and Confederate forces, and much was learned from the North American conflict about the urgent need for industrialisation, about modern weaponry and the advantages of up-to-date artillery, about the possibilities created by railed transport. Bismarck was quick to translate the lessons learned into practice. While he was developing and then flexing his military machine against Denmark and Austria, he was also building railroads. In the scale of this enterprise, Germany rivalled the United States and outstripped Britain, Russia and France; and while the railroads in other countries were designed to link major urban centres, those in Germany were geared specifically to strategic military needs.

During the conflict in the United States, the Confederate General Nathan Bedford Forrest had been asked what constituted the key to martial success. Forrest had replied with a memorably succinct and oft-quoted formulation of the self-evident: 'To git thar fustest with the mostest.' Germany's railway system was structured in precise conformity to this principle – organised to facilitate mobilisation and deploy the maximum number of troops, in the shortest possible time, at the frontiers. On the eve of the Franco-Prussian War in 1870, France mobilised in a traditional leisurely fashion, not significantly changed since the Napoleonic era. In the astonishing span of two days, meanwhile, the German railway network had mustered a quarter of a million soldiers at the border, poised for a concerted thrust into enemy territory. Everyone had imagined that war, when it came, would be fought on German soil. In fact, it was fought entirely on French soil, and culminated with the siege and bombardment of the French capital.

Britain had taken about a century and a half to industrialise. The United States, prompted by the needs of the Civil War, did so in roughly half that time. France, Russia, Austria–Hungary, Italy and other nations proceeded at a much slower pace. Within a quarter of a century, however, Germany's accelerated industrialisation had made her one of the age's 'superpowers', equalling the United States and surpassed only by the British Empire. By 1900, Germany was overtaking even Britain and had the largest iron and steel industry in Europe. By then, too, she was presuming to challenge Britain, France and the United States in the quest for overseas colonies. Attempts were made to establish spheres of influence as widespread as Mexico, what is now Namibia in South-west Africa, Morocco (where a conflict with the States was narrowly averted) and China (where German troops contributed to the suppression of the Boxer Rebellion). By the end of the first decade of the twentieth century, Germany had embarked on what had hitherto seemed the unthinkable. Under her new Secretary of the Navy, Grand Admiral Alfred von Tirpitz, she was engaged in constructing a 'blue water' battle fleet calculated to challenge Britain's sovereignty of the waves. The so-called 'Dreadnought Race' between 1906 and 1914 established a pattern for twentieth-century politics, and presaged the nuclear arms race of the Cold War. Yet German industrialisation, and the power accruing from it, had outstripped the country's social and political maturity. The result was analogous to a precocious and long-bullied adolescent wielding a Magnum or a submachine-gun.

# Part Three

CLAUS VON STAUFFENBERG

# 5

# *The Cult of Stefan George*

It was in the heady, volatile and incipiently belligerent atmosphere pervading a newly fledged 'superpower' that Claus von Stauffenberg was born on 15 November 1907, two years after his twin brothers, Berthold and Alexander. His father was Alfred Schenk, Graf von Stauffenberg and his mother – Gneisenau's great-granddaughter – Karoline, Gräfin von Üxküll. The Stauffenbergs were traditionally, albeit nominally, Roman Catholics, but Gräfin Karoline was Protestant.

Since Hohenstauffen times, the Stauffenbergs had been Free Knights of the Empire, a status cherished more proudly than any conventional title of nobility. In 1874, however Claus's great-grandfather, Franz Ludwig Schenk, Freiherr von Stauffenberg – lieutenant-general and hereditary counsellor to the king of Bavaria – was asked by Ludwig II what form of recognition he desired to commemorate both his seventieth birthday and his twenty-five years of service as president of the Bavarian parliament. 'Anything you like,' the old man replied to the monarch, 'except an additional title.' As a result, he was given one, being created Graf or 'count', the equivalent of a British earl.[1]

Claus's father, Graf Alfred, was a Commander of the Bavarian Order of St George and a major in the cavalry of Württemberg, the kingdom into which, after the Napoleonic Wars, Swabia had been incorporated. Between 1910 and the end of the Great War in 1918, Graf Alfred was also 'General Plenipotentiary' and Senior Marshal to the court of the King of Württemberg, who had retained his throne and nominal independence within the newly created Second Reich. In 1918, however, following the collapse of the Reich and the Kaiser's abdication, the Wittelsbach monarchy of Württemberg – the oldest monarchy in Europe – was abolished, and with it Graf Alfred's official status. Although he had no great affection for the post-war Weimar Republic, he continued to serve his former kingdom as 'General Plenipotentiary' and President of the Chamber of Revenues until his retirement in 1928. He has been described as 'a devout but not political Catholic', a conservative aristocrat and an expert on protocol and court ceremonial, which did not prevent him from being an adept handyman and a keen gardener on his estate. Like many of his class, he winced at sentimentality, invariably responding to it with good-humoured sarcasm.

Claus's mother, Gräfin Karoline, was lady-in-waiting to the Queen of Württemberg. She has been described as romantic, idealistic, dreamy, impractical and highly literate. She was passionately devoted to Shakespeare, as well as to Goethe and other great German poets of the early to mid-nineteenth century: Schiller, Novalis, Hölderlin and Heine. In their work, she sought a refuge from what she deemed the tedium and constricting rituals of court life. In so-called 'practical affairs', she is said to have displayed a naiveté that often yielded comic results.

Until the fall of the Württemberg monarchy in 1918, the Stauffenbergs resided in the 'old castle' of the royal residence in Stuttgart, occupying apartments on the second floor of the massive towered Renaissance building. Subsequently, the family moved to their hereditary manor and estate at Lautlingen, some sixty miles south of Stuttgart and an equal distance north of Lake Constance. The village lies in a valley which forms a pass through the foothills of the Swabian Alps, with a river and a railway following the valley floor. Even today, and despite the noise of traffic, the setting is idyllically pastoral. Cows graze in clover fields between apple orchards. To every side rise hills thickly forested with dark green pines, broken by the occasional birch, beech, larch and mountain ash. On the horizon, the walls and turrets of distant castles can be seen. The road from Lautlingen to Stuttgart is dominated by the silhouette of Burg Hohenzollern, a fairy-tale edifice atop a conical hill. Built in the nineteenth century, this structure housed, until recently, the body of Frederick the Great.

In Lautlingen and the adjacent villages, the houses are of traditional Alpine style, with balconies, wooden shutters and steeply sloped roofs. The Stauffenberg manor – Schloss Stauffenberg – was built in the nineteenth century within the old manor's plastered walls, the fortified towers of which are still visible. The structure, a large plain white-painted mansion, lies in the very centre of the village, its grounds adjoining the churchyard. Today, it is a museum for the history of music, where concerts are regularly held. During Stauffenberg's boyhood and youth, it was surrounded by the cottages of local peasants and artisans. Family and villagers formed a close-knit community, and Gräfin Karoline would customarily visit the neighbourhood's sick and aged – not out of condescending noblesse oblige, but out of a much more deeply rooted sense of service and out of a genuine sympathy and rapport.

It was in this environment that Claus von Stauffenberg, from his eleventh year onwards, spent much of his time. He was officially enrolled at the Eberhard-Ludwigs School in Stuttgart, a famous 250-year-old institution known for its propagation of Swabia's humanist tradition. Homer, Plato, Shakespeare and Goethe were accorded special priority in the curriculum. The headmaster also stressed Schiller's pronouncements on freedom, Hölderlin's Swabian identity and the poetry of Stefan George. Stauffenberg was a sickly and delicate boy, subject to recurring headaches and throat infections, and was often absent from class. During his frequent bouts of illness (and, indeed, during the last two years of his enrollment at the Eberhard-Ludwigs School), he remained at Lautlingen and was privately tutored there. He was thus steeped all the more deeply in the landscape and its history.

Theodor Pfizer first met the Stauffenbergs in the autumn of 1918, when Claus was eleven, and sat in the same class as Berthold and Alexander. He was one of their closest childhood friends and, like them, became a disciple of Stefan George. In 1957, Pfizer published his recollections of the years he shared with the three aristocratic youths. He described how profoundly attached they all were to their native region. 'The Stauffenberg brothers were rooted in this soil, they blossomed in this air . . .'[2] They would speak of Swabia as the true heir to the humanist tradition of the Renaissance, and pride themselves on the fact that Schiller, Hölderlin and the nineteenth-century poet and nouvelle-writer Eduard Mörike 'all had their roots here'. Pfizer also described his many long walks with the brothers in the surrounding hills. Claus, he recalled, was particularly attached to a site known as Torfelsen, the crest of a steep ridge to the south of the family estate, where jagged rocks projected high out over the beech forest below. Here, Pfizer recalled, Claus would retire to meditate, drinking in the panoramic vista of hills and valleys. 'Here we spoke of the future, of the painful development of a new Germany, of the tasks of the state, the possibilities of having an effect on it, of career hopes and desires.'[3]

Along with an indelible attachment to the landscape, Stauffenberg acquired at Lautlingen a pervasive self-awareness of his own patrician caste. He was an aristocrat, and always conscious, even if only subliminally, of being one. For him aristocracy was not merely an exalted social status, something assumed, something put on and worn like an outer garment. It was a basic premise of his existence, something akin to a vocation, a mission and an ongoing obligation to service. It required an ever-present deference to duty, as if a debt had constantly to be repaid to the community in exchange for the privileges that community conferred. In other words, it was an integral part of a reciprocal arrangement. One could not simply benefit from those whom chance or fate had assigned a different social position: one was responsible for them and accountable to them, not just paternally, but fraternally as well; and one had to return to them something of what one had received from them.

For Stauffenberg's caste, possession of land – and especially the old inherited family estate – was not its own self-justification, nor was it sufficient to validate one's own existence: it was a means to an end. It served the utilitarian purpose of ensuring a sufficient standard of living, not just for the individual, but for the family, the line, and its continuity. Land guaranteed that descendants would receive the education and training required to assume responsibility in their turn – the responsibility of a class born and bred to the often onerous obligations of leadership. As a consequence, there were, ultimately, more important duties than merely looking after an estate. The most worthy and estimable of these was service to the community.

In 1934, at the age of twenty-seven, Stauffenberg wrote to one of his wife's cousins: 'The true aristocratic attitude – which is the primary thing for us – demands service to the state, regardless of the specific profession.'[4] A crucial characteristic of this attitude, he stated on another occasion, was 'firmness'. 'Firmness lies in a measured progress in spite of one's own doubts, in the unconditional obedience to the self . . .'[5] At the same time, he deplored men 'of the same level of education' as his own, but without the sense of responsibility and service – men 'whose pride is stupid arrogance and whose camaraderie is wretched egotism'.[6]

In conversation with a co-author of this book, one of Claus's sons, Major-General Berthold von Stauffenberg, gave his view of the obligation of service: 'This was in the family tradition. We are not really a military family. Public service, really. I absolutely feel the sense of public service.' In his opinion, his father 'was very patriotic for Germany. Not necessarily for Prussia. For Germany', and the conspiracy to assassinate Hitler 'was not that much out of line for our family'. Certain families felt 'a pressure to live up to' the example set by the conspirators, but they did not really understand what was involved. The Stauffenbergs were free of such pressure because the conspiracy followed naturally from the logic which had always governed the family's thinking. 'As I understand it,' he concluded, 'this feeling is part of nobility.'[7]

Similar attitudes were expressed by survivors among Claus von Stauffenberg's aristocratic co-conspirators. Before his death in 1992, Axel von dem Bussche described how he saw long lines of Jews being shot by the SS behind the lines on the Eastern Front.

> Some traditional harmony had been destroyed here. We had seen it, but we were not able to put it in words. Something was shattered there. It is my responsibility and guilt that I am still alive.[8]

In an interview Ewald von Kleist was equally forthright about the horror he felt when he first discovered that 'the state had become a murderer'. 'The basis of politics must be morality,' he said. 'We felt terribly ashamed of what happened to Germany. One cannot blame a rank-and-file soldier who knew little of what was going on, but one can blame a person at the top who knew what was going on and yet did nothing.'[9] In speaking of the German aristocracy, Kleist again laid stress upon service:

> The German aristocracy were very different from the English. They were generally not as rich and were educated, furthermore, in serving . . . They liked to serve. The intention was not to become rich by serving, unlike the English, who would use the colonial service as an opportunity to make their family rich for generations. A German was not expected to come home a rich man.[10]

For Kleist, the ideal of aristocratic service was embodied by the monarchical system and incarnate in the king, the people's supreme servant. He emphasised, however, that he was speaking of the king, not the emperor or Kaiser. 'The fact that the Kaiser was a king was more important than him being a Kaiser.'[11] The First World War was a disaster for Germany not because of the dissolution of the German Empire or the abdication of the Kaiser, but because of the collapse of the monarchical system within the various German states.

> Morality is important. The concept of dishonesty violated an unwritten code which was part of a hierarchy with the king at the summit. It wasn't always so intelligent, this code. It was often narrow-minded, but it made life easier because everything existed within a framework. The difficulties began when the monarchy had gone. This code became a part of the *Widerstand*, but just one part.[12]

For almost everyone who knew him, Stauffenberg embodied the ideal of aristocratic service and the code of which it was part; this underpinned his capacity for leadership. General Franz Halder, architect of the abortive coup of 1938 and Chief of the General Staff until 1942, explained:

> I recognised in Claus von Stauffenberg a born leader, one whose whole outlook on life was rooted in his sense of responsibility towards God, who was not prepared to be satisfied with theoretical explanations and discussions, but who was burning to

act . . . My concept of a born leader is a man who, unlike most people, does not allow his thoughts and actions to be dictated by external influences; by 'born leader' I mean a man who has both the courage and the will power to deal with the problems of life on his own responsibility. There is no incompatibility between 'leadership' and 'service' when a natural leader of his own free will decides to serve . . . his country or an ideal.[13]

In addition to the imperatives of service and responsibility, Stauffenberg's sense of his own aristocracy involved a distinctive awareness of his relationship to the past. This can best be understood through an essay, published in 1936, by Thomas Mann, who described what he called 'mythic consciousness', a particular kind of mentality whereby certain individuals defined themselves.

The ego of antiquity and its consciousness of itself were different from our own, less exclusive, less sharply defined. It was, as it were, open behind; it received much from the past and by repeating it gave it presentness again.[14]

When confronted by a crisis, the leader of antiquity 'searched the past for a pattern into which he might slip'. Once mantled with such a precedent, tested and validated by history, tradition and his own ancestry, he might confront the present situation, not nakedly, so to speak, or alone, but from within a time-hallowed context. 'Thus his life was in a sense a reanimation, an archaizing attitude. But it is just this life as reanimation that is the life as myth.'[15] Alexander, Mann explains, saw himself as walking, quite consciously, 'in the footsteps of Miltiades', the Greek commander against the Persians at the Battle of Marathon. Caesar identified himself similarly with Alexander. 'But such "imitation" meant far more than we mean by that word today. It was a mythical identification . . .' And while it was characteristic of antiquity, '. . . it is operative far into modern times, and at all times psychically possible.'[16] Mann cites Napoleon, whose charismatic leadership again stemmed in large part from his conscious identification with the great commanders of the past.

How often have we not been told that the figure of Napoleon was cast in the antique mould! He regretted that the mentality of the time forbade him to give himself out as the son of Jupiter Ammon, in imitation of Alexander. But we need not doubt that – at least at the period of his Eastern exploits – he mythically confounded himself with Alexander; while after he turned his face westwards he is said to have declared: 'I am Charlemagne.' Note that: not 'I am like Charlemagne' or 'My situation is like Charlemagne's,' but quite simply: 'I am he.'[17]

Mann concludes:

Life then – at any rate, significant life – was in ancient times the reconstitution of the myth in flesh and blood; it referred to and appealed to the myth; only through it, through reference to the past, could it approve itself as genuine and significant. The myth is the legitimization of life; only through and in it does life find self-awareness, sanction, consecration.[18]

One of the key words in this passage is 'legitimization'. By invoking and identifying with illustrious precedents or antecedents, an aura of 'legitimacy' was acquired for oneself and one's actions. Thus, for example, did Jesus in the New Testament acquire 'legitimacy' by modelling his behaviour on Old Testament prophecies. Thus, in a rather more sinister fashion, did Hitler augment his personal charisma by encouraging the German people to see him as everything from a biblical Messiah to a modern avatar of the old Hohenstauffen emperors; and thus was his régime called the *Third* Reich. Thus, in our own era, did Margaret Thatcher profit from mythic identifications with Churchill, with Elizabeth I and with Boadicea. And thus does Bill Clinton in the United States today attempt to foster a mythic identification with John F. Kennedy. Such identifications exercise authority because, whether validly or not, they seem to have a 'legitimacy' behind them – the 'legitimacy' of the past, of history and tradition through which, as Mann says, life finds 'self-awareness, sanction, consecration'. The leader who fosters no mythic identification – John Major, for example, or George Bush, or Jimmy Carter – seems to lack authority precisely because he lacks the semblance of 'legitimacy'.

For a figure like Claus von Stauffenberg, 'mythic consciousness' as defined by Mann involves something even more: a pervasive awareness of oneself not only as an individual, but also as the temporary manifestation, or embodiment, of an age-old and ongoing *continuity*. Individual life is part of a greater continuum: the transient incarnation of a sequence of ghostlike selves, antecedents and descendants, extending back into the past and forward into the future. One is part of a process, or procession; and it is to this, not to its particular ephemeral form at any given moment, that one's obligation lies. And from such a perspective, death is almost incidental. Indeed, death – and especially death through noble self-sacrifice – is less an end than an integral phase of the process.

From his subsequent letters and statements, from his behaviour, his attitudes and actions, it is clear that Stauffenberg regarded himself with precisely the kind of 'mythic consciousness' Mann describes. Thus, too, did he regard his relationship to his family and to German history. As Napoleon, in Mann's example, saw himself as the nineteenth-century avatar of Charlemagne, so Stauffenberg in boyhood saw himself as a twentieth-century avatar of Gneisenau, of Yorck von Wartenburg, ultimately of the Schenk von Stauffenberg knights who served the Hohenstauffen emperors of the high Middle Ages. In adulthood, this attitude would become less simplistic, more tempered and sophisticated, but it would continue – encouraged by Stefan George – to operate as a determining principle throughout his life. The impulse to see oneself, either in the present or potentially, as ' a man of importance' can, of course, readily be ascribed to 'delusions of grandeur', but the final word on the matter is perhaps best left to the great Austrian novelist Robert Musil:

> It is true that such an urge may be a sign of vanity and stupidity; it is no less true, however, that it is a very fine and proper desire, without which there would probably not be many men of importance.[19]

\*

During his boyhood, Stauffenberg was imbued with an ideal of aristocratic service and responsibility that motivated him throughout his career – through his service in the Reichswehr and the Wehrmacht, through his activities during the war and his leadership of the German resistance. It was during his boyhood, too, that he began to cultivate another characteristic that would be manifested dramatically throughout his life. Even before he was able to read philosophical theories about such matters, much less formulate his own, he instinctively developed a sense of determination and resolve, verging on a kind of 'cult of willpower'. He refused to be immobilised by his recurring illnesses and constant throat infections. With a fierce single-mindedness, he seems in fact to have *willed* himself into health. The once-feeble boy contrived to turn himself into an impressive athlete, noted for stamina and resilience. At Lautlingen, he would revel in helping the local peasants with the harvest, taking particular pride in being able to scythe hay – uphill, as well as on level ground – no less energetically than the village boys. This may in part have been dictated by a simple adolescent desire for acceptance, but it also reflects a remarkable capacity to surmount physical disability, to assert the supremacy of spirit, mind and will. The same qualities would later turn him into a candidate for Germany's Olympic equestrian team. They would enable him to display an indefatigable energy and aptitude for physical exertion that would strike his colleagues as one of his most extraordinary traits, and impel him, during his convalescence from the wounds incurred in North Africa, to refuse all pain-killing drugs. In his tenacious unwillingness to be handicapped, Stauffenberg is reminiscent of Nelson.

The life of action and physical exertion for which Stauffenberg took pains and pride in qualifying was not his sole, or even his primary, sphere of activity. Swabia's humanist tradition dictated that Germany's – and the West's – cultural heritage be an integral part of a young aristocrat's training, and Gräfin Karoline von Stauffenberg's passionate devotion to the arts made them more vital and immediate to her sons than any mere academic chore. She herself was one of the numerous patrician ladies who comprised Rainer Maria Rilke's doting fan club, and, like others, took pride in her acquaintance and correspondence with the great poet. It is therefore not surprising that the three Stauffenberg brothers were steeped in aesthetic matters.

All three immersed themselves enthusiastically in poetry, philosophy, history, painting and music. Musical evenings were a regular feature of the Stauffenberg household, with Claus playing the cello, Berthold the piano and Alexander the violin. While still at school, Claus expressed a desire to become a professional musician, possibly a composer. He also began to develop an interest in architecture, and, until the age of eighteen or so, dreamed of becoming an architect. After the Great War, Graf Alfred, the brothers' father, refused to attend the former Royal Theatre because it was in republican hands, but the brothers remained devoted theatre-goers. They also threw themselves into school theatricals. In a production of *Julius Caesar*, Claus played the part of Lucius, while Alexander played Brutus and Berthold Caesar's ghost. Claus also took the part of the revolutionary anti-establishment Stauffacher in a production of Schiller's inflammatory *Wilhelm Tell*, as if rehearsing the rôle he would later play in reality and history.

> Yes! There's a limit to the tyrants' power!
> When man, oppressed, has cried in vain for justice
> And knows his burden is too great to bear,
> With bold resolve he reaches up to heaven
> To seize those rights which are forever his[20]

One of the most influential trends among German youth during the 1920s was the *Wandervögel* movement (to be translated literally as 'Wandering Birds' or, more lyrically, 'Birds of Passage').[21] The movement owed something to the Boy Scouts created some years before by Robert Baden-Powell, but, unlike the scouts, the *Wandervögel* philosophy had less to do with the conventional social virtues than with something more metaphysical, a form of simplistic pantheism. Although later stigmatised because of the ease with which it was taken over and shaped to sinister ends by the fledgling National Socialist Party, during the first two and a half decades of the twentieth century the movement was innocent enough.

Despite their father's disapprobation, Claus and Berthold joined a youth group of *Wandervögel* 'pioneers', the so-called 'New Pathfinders'.[22] In this capacity, they embarked on camping trips, practised spear-throwing, sang folk songs around campfires and recited from Stefan George's poetry. At the time, George's reputation in Germany eclipsed even Rilke's. And while Rilke was of Bohemian-Austrian background, George was German, a native of the lands along the Rhine. It was natural enough that his symbol-laden mythic verse, his archetypal orientation and mystically pantheistic vision should endear him to the young.

Another contemporary author of significance to the Stauffenbergs was Hermann Hesse, also a Swabian and thus a 'kindred soul'. Hesse's early novel *Peter Camenzind* (1904) offers perhaps the supreme prose evocation of the Swabian landscape the Stauffenbergs so loved. *Demian*, published in 1919, became a bible for German youth of the Stauffenbergs' generation. Among more traditionally established figures, the most esteemed by the Stauffenbergs were Goethe and Friedrich Hölderlin. Hölderlin, whom many would rank above Novalis, Heine and perhaps even Goethe in the pantheon of nineteenth-century German poets, was a major influence on Stefan George. Like Hesse, he was a Swabian, and his fusion of uniquely Germanic material with the most lofty elements of classical Greek myth and tradition endowed him with a special significance for the Stauffenbergs. At Christmas 1922, Claus decorated his schoolroom and, by the light of the tree, recited from Hölderlin – and, in an unintentionally heretical juxtaposition, St Paul's Epistle to the Corinthians.

Accounts of Claus von Stauffenberg during his late teens and early twenties portray him as more than a little bohemian. He already displayed the cavalier insouciance about protocol and etiquette that would characterise his later career. He was lazy about shaving. He paid scant attention to the cut of his hair or the correct fit of his school uniform. And he was equally indifferent to such matters in other people. Photographs of the time show a youth with a face that appears narrow in profile but wider when viewed head-on, with symmetrical features, broad cheekbones, a strong and slightly cleft chin. His hair was dark, slightly wavy and, when he bothered to have it cut, fairly close-cropped. His eyes, of a dark metallic blue, were described as among his most striking physical traits. By his late teens, he was already, as General Halder was later to say of him, 'accustomed to making up his own mind and having his views accepted – to taking the lead or feeling an obligation to do so, which in his eyes amounted to the same thing.'[23]

His attitude towards others was dictated largely by his assessment of their inherent qualities rather than by anything stemming from convention. He would keep coldly aloof from certain flamboyant 'personalities', despite their overtures to him. He often displayed indulgence towards people's weaknesses, but could be uncompromising – to the point of harshness, even brutality – when confronted with subterfuge, deviousness or underhand behaviour. According to Ludwig Thormaehlen, a member of Stefan George's circle who met him in 1924, he was temperamentally very different from his twin brothers and 'gave, by his open ready cheerfulness, the image and impression of a steadfast dependability'.[24] Thormaehlen continues, in the somewhat florid style of the time and with more than a little effusiveness:

> Young though he was, his radiant energy, which he was ready to turn to everything around him, produced an impression of absolute reliability . . . Quickness of intellect, rapidity of action, determination to do fully and at once whatever his emotions, his brain or the circumstances indicated should be done – all this Claus had in full measure. With him there was neither differentiation nor interval of time between thinking and doing, between realisation and action. He did not perhaps possess the enigmatic depths of Berthold, the versatility and fullness of Alexander, but he was moulded without inhibitions and he was pure and strong . . . endowed with a complete and totally balanced unity of being, the embodiment of a courageous, awake, living manliness . . . One did not just like or admire Claus – he awoke enthusiasm and delight immediately and everywhere he went. His joie de vivre, his affirmation of himself and of every worthwhile value whenever he came across it were so infectious that they swept everybody along . . .[25]

\*

On 5 March 1926, Claus von Stauffenberg passed his *Abitur*, a public examination administered by the state to determine eligibility for higher education. By this time, he had relinquished ideas of becoming a musician or an architect and decided on a career in the military. The decision was made so abruptly as to startle his family and friends. It also provoked objections from his father, Graf Alfred. Ordinarily, of course, the old man might have approved, a military career being appropriate enough to the dignity of the family name, but he despised the politicians of Weimar as 'lumpenproletariats who could not serve a decent human being'. For a son to serve in the army of any republic – and especially a republic governed by such people – was an alarming prospect.[26]

Claus remained firm, however, and displayed a characteristic self-confidence verging on arrogance. By the Treaty of Versailles which ended the First World War, the Reichswehr – the army of the Weimar Republic – had been denied all aircraft and tanks and was limited to 100,000 men, a diminutive force compared to that of other European powers. (Even the British Army, always small, was appreciably larger. The French Army numbered some 600,000 men.) The Reichswehr's restricted size inevitably meant there were far fewer officers' commissions available than there were candidates (more than seven applicants for each vacancy). Nevertheless, and despite the chronic illnesses of his youth, Stauffenberg seems to have had no doubts about his own qualifications – or about his ability to obtain one of the limited number of places. When asked why he had abandoned his commitment to architecture, he replied that it now seemed to him too much focused on 'things' and too little on people. The army, he explained, would provide him with opportunities for planning, for the management of men, for assuming responsibility and for service to the community.

At least some part in Stauffenberg's change of career had been played by the poet Stefan George, whom he and his two brothers had met in 1923, when he was sixteen. This meeting, and the relationship that developed, were to be among the most influential experiences of his youth, and – occurring at a formative age – were to shape his development, his attitudes, his values, his entire *Weltanschauung* from then on. According to Ludwig Thormaehlen, 'For Claus von Stauffenberg, George's environment and his relationship with the poet remained the decisive factor in his life.'[27]

George's reputation at the time was ambiguous. While regarded as the greatest German-language poet of the age – a figure who, in his lifetime, enjoyed a literary prestige comparable to, say, Yeats or T. S. Eliot – he was also revered as a prophet and magus, a magisterial 'guru' and oracle presiding over an élite hand-picked cadre of intellectual and cultural intiates who 'stood in awe of him' as one might of a high priest. In Berlin, Munich and especially Heidelberg, he held court to a small circle of the brightest, most imaginative and dynamic young men in Germany – the hope, as he saw them, of the country's future. From this cenacle, he issued his often arcane and enigmatic pronouncements, as well as publishing the cryptic verse that became a cultural beacon to a generation.

At the same time, his exalted sense of his own rôle and mission – 'For George, the poet was the appointed keeper of the nation's inner strength'[28] – inevitably provoked hostility, and rumours about him were rife. In his book on George, Professor E. K. Bennet stated that: 'George's fundamental obsession with power, expressed even in his ideal of a highly disciplined personal life, stands openly revealed.'[29] His lofty patrician aloofness, and his insistence on a 'spiritual aristocracy' or 'aristocracy of the spirit', were hardly calculated to endear him to the left-wing intelligentsia of the period – adherents of socialism such as Ernst Toller, Alfred Döblin, Heinrich Mann and the young Berthold Brecht. Among devotees of more popular, more accessible and more traditional literature, he was considered too rarefied, too exclusive, too impenetrable. For adherents of the 'egalitarian esotericism' exemplified by Rudolf Steiner, George was too overpowering: 'the creator of his own intellectual empire'. They respected him, but kept their distance. According to a member of the Steiner organisation in London, George and Steiner met on a number of occasions. Steiner is said to have sympathised with much of the poet's thinking, but to have found him personally too arrogantly Olympian. This is hardly surprising. Steiner, by then, had begun to practise a disarming candour and meekness, a gentleness that found an artistic echo of sorts in Rilke. George would unquestionably have seemed too assertive, too aggressive, too forbidding. These qualities are apparent, almost to the point of self-parody, in photographs of George. Among the great artist-magi of the last two centuries, it would be difficult to find one who so impressively looked the part.

Even more detrimental to George's personal reputation were allegations of homosexuality. He was generally assumed to be a practising homosexual, and this belief persists even today. Certainly the few women admitted to his circle were relegated to subordinate rôles. There were what seemed to be flagrantly homosexual references in his poetry, and rumours abounded about homosexual orgies, often linked with lurid secret ceremonies involving rituals, incense, incantations, elaborate robes and regalia. The popular image was that of something resembling a specifically homosexual version of the Order of the Golden Dawn in England (the coven of would-be magi which included such figures as Yeats, Conan Doyle, Arthur Machen and, at the beginning of his garish career, the young Aleister Crowley).

George himself made no attempt to dispel or correct this image. If anything, he actively encouraged certain aspects of it. He ran his circle as a cult, demanding a binding oath of allegiance from his disciples, who regarded him as their autocratic 'Master'. He sometimes interfered in their personal lives, pronounced peremptory judgement on their private affairs and presumed to make decisions for them. He swore his entourage to secrecy about his teachings. He turned the reading and writing of poetry into an almost religious ritual, a solemn hieratical ceremony accompanied by the burning of incense. George would sit 'at the head of a long table, at the sides of which sat a number of young males who in succession arose and read one or another of his poems in a sonorous but expressionless voice.'[30]

Postulants for admission to his circle were subjected to initiation rituals and rites which involved such arduous undertakings as writing worthy poems. Members of the circle were all given new cultic names that reflected their individual qualities – except, significantly, for Claus von Stauffenberg, who kept his own. George also invented his own private language, in which he composed a number of evocative poems and expected his disciples to be versed. Lines in this language, which owes much to Spanish and Portuguese, were often woven into his German poems as well:

CO BESOSO PASOJE PTOROS
CO ES ON HAMA PASOJE BOAÑ. [31]

It is now clear that much of the bizarre and exotic extravagance attributed to George was, at least to some extent, misplaced. In a lecture after the war, Alexander von Stauffenberg stated:

Previously there was talk of a kind of 'ritual' – of gorgeous robes, incense and secret ceremonies. Whatever substance there may have been in these rumours at the time (and they were undoubtedly exaggerated), we never detected a trace of anything of the sort. Life went on very normally – meals, walks in the country, discussions in the evening – all completely simple . . . Only for the major poetry readings was there a special atmosphere of solemnity, and that was quite understandable . . .[32]

To the mother of the three Stauffenberg youths, the rumours were nevertheless disquieting. Given her devotion to poetry, Gräfin Karoline was, of course, already familiar with George's work, but the prospect of her three sons being apprenticed to him was altogether a different matter. The countess undertook her own investigations. According to some accounts, she even employed a private detective. She herself drove to Heidelberg to meet the 'Master' and assure herself that he was unlikely to corrupt her children. George emerged from the countess's enquiries unscathed.[33] In her meeting with him, Karoline was not only appeased, but also impressed and converted. Her sons, she concluded, could not have a better mentor. Stauffenberg's most recent German biographer, Peter Hoffmann, also acquits George:

The suspicion of homo-eroticism surfaced, but it was also misplaced, although it was understandable because the circle consisted only of men . . . . The study of Greek culture, particularly Plato, undoubtedly provided grounds for assuming sundry things. There are also poems from the circle of friends which seem to hint at homo-erotic relationships. But for the Stauffenberg brothers, it was all a matter of the mind; and Claus later defended to his officer friends the Greek Eros praised by Plato . . . so energetically and clearly that they were convinced. One is wrong to assume that George ever did anything untoward along the hinted lines . . .[34]

The evidence seems effectively to counter the allegations against George. The milieu, after all, was not the cabaret society of decadent Berlin, but the provincial world of conservative Württemberg.

Homosexuality was not only more of a stigma than it is now. It was also a criminal offence. And the Stauffenbergs were not just punctilious in their respect for the law, but also acutely sensitive about any potential stain on the family name and honour. Were there even the slightest grounds for crediting the rumours about George's circle, it is inconceivable that Gräfin Karoline would have allowed her sons to become members.

Berthold and Alexander joined the circle in the summer of 1923, Claus at the end of 1924, when he was seventeen. Their reception into the exclusive group was a source of mutual enthusiasm. The Stauffenbergs had long been devotees of George's work, and all of them knew many of the 'Master's' poems by heart. Other disciples 'seemed to see something regal in the Stauffenbergs', regarding them as avatars of heroic figures of the past, the knights who had served the Hohenstauffen emperors. George himself, as well as other members of the circle, wrote poems specifically dedicated to Berthold. As for Claus, Ludwig Thormaehlen reported panegyrically:

> The future seemed to be tangible in him. One can imagine the enthusiasm that George felt at the advent of this youth . . . George was a passionate guardian of youthful potential . . . Claus flourished in this milieu of humanitarian education and was nurtured in the poetic. The intellectual and creative came naturally to him. The poetic was necessary to him. His love and admiration for George were unquestionable, direct yet without any unhealthy deference . . . His rare presences delighted the poet, brightened the poet's spirits. In his direct and fresh fashion – a fashion appropriate to his age – he participated in every conversation with equal degrees of reserve and intelligent intervention. Like Berthold, he was, in his own way, a master of the free and lofty. He recognised nothing to be above him, nothing to be beneath him . . . His exchanges with George were warm and straightforward. The oath of allegiance was made immediately and candidly, as though between loved and honoured members of an extended family.[35]

The oath of allegiance to George was of profound significance to all three of the Stauffenberg brothers, but seems to have exercised a particularly strong hold over Berthold. Lacking Claus's fierce independence, he sought the 'Master's' approval for a number of his decisions. When he was in Paris, during 1927–8, he made a point of obtaining George's permission before embarking on a holiday to the south of France. In 1931, he became engaged to a woman of whom George disapproved. The following spring, George (then in exile in Switzerland) summoned Berthold for a weighty consultation. On what appears to have been the 'Master's' decree, Berthold withdrew from the marriage – though he did finally marry the woman after George's death.[36] Years later, when George was long dead, Berthold continued to maintain that his allegiance to the 'Master' took priority even over his obligations to the State.

> The Stauffenbergs had signed a secret pact, whose tenets were above those of personal relationships. They demanded the energy and commitment of the whole person. Ultimately, it was about an idea. George's circle fostered, especially for the youths, the spirit (later) to be engendered by the conspiracy: Secret Germany.[37]

As members of George's circle, the Stauffenberg brothers read and discussed literature, philosophy, aesthetic theory and a corpus of what today would be called 'esoteric' teachings. They also read and wrote poetry, which Berthold and Alexander continued to do into adulthood and maturity. Claus, as far as is known, abandoned his efforts after the age of eighteen or so, but there were many other activities in George's circle to keep him stimulated. There were constant discussions, conversations and debates traversing the vast spectrum of George's interests. There were the 'divagations' (to use the word of one of George's own mentors, the French symbolist poet Stéphane Mallarmé) of the 'Master' himself, an unfailing source of inspiration to his disciples. There were communal meals and walks in Heidelberg and the surrounding countryside, especially to scenic or historically resonant sites along the Rhine, where the Stauffenbergs' own sense of legend, tradition and the sacred nature of the river were echoed by the 'Master's' orphic pronouncements. Intimidating though George could be, Claus was not cowed. He adapted eagerly and comfortably to the prevailing ambience, and made himself an integral member of the group:

He would intervene in a manner which showed his intelligence – frank and honest in opposition, good humoured in criticism, but equally vigorous in agreement or in support of any justified demands by others.[38]

George was not just a self-proclaimed magus advocating a pure aestheticism based on 'l'art pour l'art', not just a mystic advocating personal self-perfection and self-refinement. He was fervently committed to the necessity for action, and though he despised politics as such, he was profoundly concerned about the cultural future of the West as a whole and Germany in particular. When asked what he considered his most important work, he replied: 'My friends.'[39] He might equally have said, 'My protégés.' Ultimately, George saw himself as a kind of Chiron or Pythagoras, grooming a select cadre of 'spiritual aristocrats' for the weighty task of leadership. This, he felt, was his real legacy. And his insistence on service and responsibility to the community, on an enlightened few to function as beacons, would have meshed perfectly with the values and attitudes the Stauffenbergs had acquired through their family. Indeed, George's mentorship would have reinforced those values and attitudes, and imparted a new, more focused direction to them. His insistence on action, as well as on human interaction, contributed significantly to Claus von Stauffenberg's renunciation of architecture in favour of the army.

In October 1924, shortly before deciding to embark on a military career, Claus wrote to George, citing the 'Master's' own work (and emulating something of the 'Master's' own unorthodox syntax):

> and in this book I learned the sense of wakeful nights: of the rhythms of praying life and the sound of loud supplications. And the clearer Aliveness stands before me: the loftier Humanity reveals itself and the more piercingly the deed shows itself: so much darker does one's own blood become: so much fainter grows the sound of one's own words and so much rarer the sense of one's own life: indeed, until the hour which, in the harshness of its impact and the greatness of its advent, gives the sign. Master, I have learned too much from this poem:
>
> YOU ARE THE CORNERSTONE AND I ACCLAIM YOU.[40]

The line quoted is from a poem published in 1913, but it is the first line of a stanza which could have been addressed to the Stauffenbergs personally. It is not difficult to imagine how George's words could sink like fishhooks into the mind of a seventeen-year-old high-born youth:

> You are the cornerstone, and I acclaim you
> For how you face yourselves, and me, and others,
> Fulfil your tasks and urge to faithful hearts.
> You are the vassals, bearers of the realm . . . what works
> Within it soon will work the whole, and what
> You do not grasp today can never be.[41]

Two months before Claus's letter to George, in August 1924, Alexander von Stauffenberg had composed a poem entitled 'The Warrior'. In it he depicts his younger brother agonising over the question of whether to embark on a military career:

> The yearnings of the soul you barely hide
> Sorrow stirs your young brow: too far away to you
> What moves your fresh youth
> Now you walk at my side silent and serious
>
> Before you were all turmoil and interrupted
> By wild stirrings to us alone appeared your sorrow
> I saw your breast pounding in silent tolerance
> Because fate took away from you the sweet pleasures.
>
> Still it is true that each pain only proves our worth
> And a scout finds a willing guard
> I never saw glow with such tenderness
> And never by such glowing dreams considered.
>
> The stern brow, the pensive spectator
> Towered up cities in the midday country –
> You stand still in the shade by the wall
> Of the cathedral and questioningly raise your hand.

> O self reply, silent companion
> Your picture as before is turmoil and embers and it burns
> And pours in one with the crowned rider
> That our faraway hopes call king.
>
> It shares the fate of the creation of pain
> The noble song, the unstill passion
> After a deed so far away . . . till you in your heart
> The brother find even in decline.[42]

The 'crowned rider' in this poem – the figure standing 'still in the shade by the wall of the cathedral' with questioningly raised hand – is in fact a statue. It is known as 'der Bamberger Reiter' ('the Knight of Bamberg') and stands inside Bamberg's thirteenth-century cathedral, on the left-hand pier of the choir – the eastern end of the edifice just beyond where the transepts join. The statue is believed to date from around 1240, and generally regarded as a masterpiece of medieval German sculpture. The identity of the figure has never been definitively established, though some hold it to be a representation of Saint Stephen, King of Hungary and brother-in-law of the German Emperor Heinrich II.

When Alexander von Stauffenberg invoked 'der Bamberger Reiter', he was again following in the 'Master's' footsteps. Shortly before the First World War, Stefan George had also invoked the statue, in a short poem entitled 'Bamberg':

> You, the most alien, sprang – when there was need –
> A lawful scion from your people's flank.
> Does not this shrine portray you on your steed,
> Proud and contending as a kingly Frank?
>
> And carven – neither Ghibelline nor Guelph –
> In the imperial chamber, you are shown:
> A silent artist who surpassed himself
> And waits bemused for God to do his own.[43]

It is perhaps not surprising that 'der Bamberger Reiter' came to hold a mystical significance for Claus von Stauffenberg. Not only was the statue an evocative embodiment of the chivalric values to which he subscribed. It also bore a positively uncanny physical resemblance to himself – as if he, in the flesh, did indeed represent God's attempt to rival the work of the unknown medieval sculptor. In George's circle, and later, in the army, friends would tease him by calling him 'der Bamberger Reiter'. Even Sir John Wheeler-Bennett, the eminently unmystical British military historian, was struck by the resemblance between man and statue. In *Nemesis of Power: A History of the German General Staff in Politics*, Wheeler-Bennett published, side by side, photographs of the statue and Claus von Stauffenberg. If one did not know better, one would have no doubts whatever that Stauffenberg had been the sculptor's model.

# 6

## *The New Reich*

Whatever personal chord it may have touched in him, 'der Bamberger Reiter' did, in fact, portend something of Claus von Stauffenberg's destiny. On 1 April 1926, at the age of nineteen, he entered the regiment in which his uncle had served: the 17th Bavarian Cavalry, also known as the Bamberg Cavalry and with its depot in that town.

Having been so drastically reduced in size by the Treaty of Versailles, the Reichswehr was all the more stringent in its training programmes. Candidates for officers' commissions had first to serve in the ranks as ordinary soldiers, and the young aristocrat did not always find this congenial. 'For our kind,' he wrote in a letter to his father a few weeks after his induction, 'it is not easy to play among the common people for long periods.'[1] He also stated that he had never expected the early phases of his military service to be enjoyable; and there was never any question of his failing to 'stick it out'. He was to be promoted to lance-corporal on 18 August 1927; to NCO on 15 October 1927; to sergeant on 1 August 1928; to staff-sergeant on 1 August 1929; to second lieutenant on 1 January 1930, and to full lieutenant on 1 May 1933.

Among other things, his association with the Bamberg Cavalry allowed Stauffenberg to indulge his love of horses.

He had a real passion and an inborn skill for riding and handling horses. When he was billeted on a farmer, he one day came across a young mare among the draught-horses, 'an enchanting personality', as he put it. He bought the mare, trained her to perform the passage and levade and won a prize with her in the difficult dressage test.[2]

In later years, he was to buy shares, along with his father-in-law, in a foal named Jagd, which he chose from a stud farm and trained personally. He was to become one of Germany's most prominent horsemen, standing as a candidate for the country's Olympic dressage team. And a decade later, as war drew nearer, he was to prepare for the Staff College in Berlin two markedly different papers that reflected the contradictory aspects of his character, one oriented presciently towards the future, the other rooted firmly in tradition and the past. The first of these papers was a striking and revolutionary advocacy of the deployment of paratroops in a combat rôle – something unheard of at the time, yet soon to be a cornerstone of the most advanced military thinking and implemented by the Wehrmacht in such theatres as Holland and Crete. The second paper, with an archaic chivalry verging on quaintness, passionately advocated and tried to rationalise the continued use of mounted cavalry in contemporary warfare.

In October 1927, as a candidate for a commission, Stauffenberg was posted to the infantry training school in Dresden, where he first met his later co-conspirator, Merz von Quirnheim, and began to learn Russian. In 1928, he received a new posting, to the cavalry school at Hannover, where only the most highly rated sergeants were sent. During the winter of 1927–8, he travelled frequently to Berlin, where he would meet Berthold and Alexander and attend poetry readings at Stefan George's apartment.

At the cavalry school in Hannover, he first met one of his future divisional commanders, Major (later Lieutenant-General) Friedrich-Wilhelm, Freiherr von Loeper, who, on the basis of his glowing reports, nominated Stauffenberg course leader. In this capacity, he quickly earned the confidence of both colleagues and superiors.

> He was an expert at settling differences, acting as a go-between and smoothing out quarrels; he looked for and found the good side to everybody and had an extraordinary knack of making the best of everything.[3]

And again, his fierce tenacity and concentration of will displayed itself. He himself had originally wondered whether the illnesses which had debilitated him in childhood might impede his military career. Some of these ailments still occasionally recurred, and as late as 1931, he was compelled to spend time at a spa hospital. All the same, he refused to let this deter him, forcing himself to an athletic standard far surpassing that of more robust colleagues, one of whom reported:

> I have often heard Stauffenberg putting forward his views in the officers' mess, generally to the more junior officers. In most cases he would take the floor at once and lay down the law. This came easily to him, for he was intellectually clearly far ahead of his listeners. Being supremely self-confident and undoubtedly some-what inclined to show off, he liked the sound of his own voice. Nevertheless his audience enjoyed listening to him.[4]

The official confidential report by his squadron leader, compiled in October 1933, is particularly illuminating:

> A reliable independent character, capable of making up his own mind and taking his own decisions. Highly intelligent and of above average ability, both tactically and technically.
>
> Exemplary in his handling of NCO's and men and absorbed in training and raising the standard of his mortar platoon.
>
> Unexceptional in his relationships with others. Shows great interest in social, historical and religious matters . . .
>
> As against these outstanding qualities, mention should be made of certain minor deficiencies and weaknesses. He is well aware of his military ability and intellectual superiority and is therefore apt at times to adopt a somewhat overbearing attitude towards his fellow officers, frequently evidenced by a sarcasm, which, however, never leaves hurt feelings.
>
> He is somewhat sloppy in his dress and bearing, and as a young officer, should take more care of his appearance and give an impression of greater energy. He is rather susceptible to throat infections, which means that his powers of physical resistance are sometimes affected. He fights off illness with energy and determination.

If he goes on as he is, there is every prospect that he will do very well.[5]

Stauffenberg passed his officer's exams with honours and also received a special ceremonial sabre 'for outstanding achievements'. On returning to the 17th Cavalry at Bamberg, he was commissioned second lieutenant on New Year's Day of 1930. The restricted size of the Reichswehr meant that advancement was inevitably slow. Training – especially after the National Socialists rose to power – became more arduous, and the insistence on professionalism more severe. Officers were schooled to discharge duties appropriate not only to their rank, but also to those one or even two above. When Germany's armed forces began dramatically to expand, this principle would be turned to account. Officers would automatically move up one or even two grades, and be already groomed for their new responsibilities. The military machine thus had a built-in capacity to increase in size and to take in substantial quantities of fresh recruits while maintaining maximum efficiency in the chain of command.

In 1933, Stauffenberg returned to the cavalry school at Hannover for an advanced course in equitation. He would ride four horses every day, two from the school and two of his own. He concentrated especially on dressage; and in 1935, he took first place in his compulsory military equitation class, beating members of the team which would go on to win a gold medal in the 1936 Olympics.

By this time, he had married. Bamberg had not only initiated him into the military. It also brought him together with his future wife. In 1930, he had met and become engaged to Nina, Freiin von Lerchenfeld, a member of the old Bavarian aristocracy whose distant relations included the Battenbergs (subsequently the Mountbattens). Nina's father, Gustav Freiherr von Lerchenfeld, was very much a man of the world, having served as consul-general in Shanghai, Warsaw and Kovno (now Kaunas in Lithuania). Before the First World War, he had also served as royal chamberlain of Bavaria.

On 26 September 1933, Stauffenberg and Nina von Lerchenfeld were married in the church of Saint Jakobs in Bamberg. She was seventeen at the time, he twenty-six. When she asked him why he had chosen her, he said 'he had soon noticed that she would be just the right mother for his children'.[6] He and his father-in-law became close friends. He was not above teasing his mother-in-law, to whom he quoted Frederick the Great: 'For an officer, a wife is a necessary evil. Warriors ought not to marry, but during times of peace the needs of the family and the offspring must be met.'[7] In Stauffenberg's case, these needs emphatically were. He proved a doting father, taking a simple boyish pleasure in his children. There were to be five of them: Berthold (born in 1934), Heimeran (1936), Franz Ludwig (1938), Valerie (1940) and Konstanze (born in 1945, after her father's death).

*

After the abortive 'Beer House Putsch' of 1923, the National Socialist Party seemed to have vanished from the political arena, but by the end of the decade it was in full resurgence. In the 1928 elections, the Nazis obtained a marginal twelve seats in the Reichstag. Two years later, this number was increased to 107, and in July 1932, it rose to 230 out of nearly 650. The Nazis could no longer be ignored, and the aged President Hindenburg had no choice but to invite them to join the government. Hitler's response to this invitation was predictably exorbitant. He asked that he himself be appointed chancellor, and requested a number of ministries for his party. Hindenburg refused, giving Hitler an angry lecture which was then made public. This fiasco damaged the National Socialists. So, too, did a groundswell of apathy and Hitler's public defence of five storm troopers who had murdered a Communist. In the elections of November 1932, the National Socialists lost thirty-four seats and some two million votes.

By January 1933, however, it was clear that a coalition government could not be formed without involving political extremists, either the National Socialists on the right, or the Communists on the left. Hindenburg was asked to dissolve the Reichstag again and call a new election, this time banning both the National Socialist and Communist parties. To the increasingly senile old president this seemed too draconian a measure, and he refused. The army remained officially neutral, but behind its non-partisan façade it was badly split: few, if any, of its personnel were pro-Communist, but attitudes towards the Nazis ranged from zealous support to equally virulent antipathy and hatred.

Franz von Papen, the country's political *éminence grise* and former chancellor, concluded that stability would be impossible to establish in Germany unless Hitler received the chancellorship he desired. But Papen also hoped to contain the Nazi upstart and force him to share power. On 30 January 1933, therefore, in accordance with Papen's recommendations, Hitler became chancellor in a coalition cabinet. Papen himself became vice-chancellor; and he and his colleagues were now convinced the Nazis could be checked. 'We have framed him in,' one said, alluding to Hitler. As the historian Gordon Craig wryly observed: 'The remark should be included in any anthology of famous last words.'[8]

On 3 February, Hitler met with the military high command and, in a lengthy speech, maintained that Germany's armed forces would function most effectively under the 'strictest kind of authoritarian state leadership'. As an incentive to them, he promised to remove all restrictions imposed by the Treaty of Versailles. In the meantime, the Nazis had, under Goering, wrested control of the police, which allowed their thugs and 'goon squads' to operate with a semblance of legality.

On the following day the new chancellor-cum-Führer persuaded the increasingly malleable President Hindenburg to issue a decree which banned all newspapers or public meetings presuming to criticise the government. On 17 February, Goering issued a decree forbidding the Prussian police to interfere with the activities of Nazi paramilitary formations such as the SA and SS. Three days later, Hitler met a group of prominent businessmen and industrialists, and told them the impending elections, scheduled for March, would be the last for ten, perhaps for a hundred, years.

A week later the Reichstag 'mysteriously' burned down. It is now generally accepted that this act of arson was perpetrated by Nazi agents-provocateurs, but at the time it was easily enough attributed to Communist agitators, against whom Hitler now had a plausible excuse to move. By the following morning, more than four thousand Communist functionaries had been arrested, along with numerous intellectuals and professional people hostile to the régime. Hindenburg was persuaded to sign yet another decree, suspending the rights of citizens and authorising the government to assume power in any of the republic's federated states. German citizens could now be arrested simply on suspicion and imprisoned without trial. Concentration camps began to proliferate across the country for anyone who expressed dissent.

The elections of 5 March 1933 were, as historians have accurately said, 'dominated by terror'. Not surprisingly, given the prevailing intimidation, the National Socialist Party won a majority. Yet it is worth noting that the Communists still took nearly five million votes and obtained eighty-one seats in the Reichstag. Although the Nazis had 288 seats, this was only 43.9 per cent of the vote, and the other parties held 359 seats. In other words, the majority of German citizens voted against the National Socialist Party.

But the Nazis were now not to be stopped. On 23 March, with its Communist deputies all either dead or in concentration camps, the Reichstag was dragooned into passing the notorious 'Enabling Act'. By this act, it became 'constitutional' for the cabinet to frame laws without the approval of the Reichstag. Legislative and executive powers were now effectively merged, and Hitler was voted dictator. He had absolute and ostensibly 'legal' power to do as he wished with Germany. It had taken him less than two months to destroy the last vestiges of the country's experiment in democracy. According to a cabaret joke at the time:

> Members of which choral society earn individually more than Caruso: Reichstag deputies – they perform once a year, sing two songs (the national anthem and the 'Horst Wessel Lied') and receive twelve thousand marks each.[9]

In July 1933, the new régime signed a concordat with the Vatican. In the same month, another law was passed, making National Socialism the only legal party in Germany. To attempt to establish another would be punishable by a minimum three years' imprisonment. Hitler's authority was now beyond any possibility of challenge. Yet for his more grandiose designs, he needed the armed forces. It was to them that he began to turn his attention.

*

During the early years of his military career, Claus von Stauffenberg was, in many respects, less the single-minded professional soldier than the typical 'Renaissance man' he had been in the past. He read copiously, in a number of fields: military history, general history, politics, philosophy, psychology, economics, art and literature. He became fluent in Russian and English. Although no record exists of him having formally studied French, he appears to have known the language well. He continued to attend lectures and concerts, and maintained his ongoing apprenticeship to Stefan George. During 1930, while engaged in specialised military courses at Döberitz, he still contrived to attend readings and recitations at George's Berlin apartment. 'I had the greatest poet of the age as my master,' he said to Nina.[10] It was through George that the seeds of what would become Stauffenberg's antipathy to National Socialism were planted in his mind.

As Nazism gained first support, then power, in Germany, certain of George's poems came increasingly to be seen as prescient. Among the most important of these was a short lyric composed even before the First World War. Inspired by a famous painting of Signorelli's, 'Der Widercrist' ('The Antichrist') was eventually to become a mantra for Stauffenberg's circle of conspirators. Yet, as early as the 1920s, when Hitler first suddenly embarked on his quest for control of Germany, the poem could already be seen as prophetic; and George, as well as certain of his disciples, openly proclaimed it to be so.

'He comes from the mountains, he stands mid the pines!
We saw it ourselves! He transforms into wine
Clear water, and trafficks with dead men!'

Oh could you but hear how I laugh in the night!
My hour is now struck, my snares are all sprung
And fish fill my nets, thickly swarming.

Wise men and dullards, the mob, frenzied, reels,
Tramples the cornfields, tears up the trees.
Make way for the flock of the Risen!

No wonder of heaven but I can't perform.
A hair's-breadth impure, but you'll not note the fraud
With your stunted and stultified senses.

In place of the arduous and rare I invoke
The Facile; from compost I make things like gold,
And perfumes, and nectars, and spices.

And what the great prophet renounced I extol:
An art without ploughing or sowing or toil
Which yet drains the soil of its essence.

The high Prince of Vermin extends his domains;
No pleasure eludes him, no treasure or gain.
And down with the dregs of rebellion!

You cheer, mesmerised by demoniac sheen,
Exhaust what remains of the honey of dawn,
And only then sense the débâcle.

You then stretch your tongues to the now arid trough,
Mill witless as kine through a pasture aflame,
While fearfully brazens the trumpet.[11]

George himself was hardly a conventional Christian. If anything, he was positively hostile towards conventional Christian theology, but he acknowledged a profound validity in the Christian emphasis on self-sacrifice; and he had no reservations about availing himself of Christian imagery and metaphor. The Antichrist in the poem derives in part from the figure in Revelation 19:20:

And the beast was captured, and with it the false prophet who in its presence had worked the signs by which he deceived those who had received the mark of the beast and those who worshipped its image.

He also derives from the similar figure, the archetypal 'false prophet' known as Simon Magus, who appears in Acts 8: 9–24, as well as in the writings of Church Fathers and later Christian tradition. There is evidence to suggest that the original Simon, or the prototype on whom he is based, was in fact an early Gnostic; and one Church Father, Epiphanius, accuses him of being the founder of Gnosticism. In Christian scripture and tradition, he is described as the first heretic, and appears as a self-proclaimed Samaritan wonder-worker and messiah. A charismatic individual with a following of his own, he is, like Peter but in his own more sinister way, a 'fisher of men', whose souls swarm into his net. He offers Peter money for the gift of healing by the laying on of hands. In other words, he attempts to purchase the power of the Holy Spirit for venal purposes, whence the sin known as 'simony' derives. He also casts doubts on Jesus and openly questions Peter's authority as apostle. The encounter, in later sources, culminates with Simon challenging Peter to a kind of duel, each having to match the other, miracle for miracle. At first, Simon actually does outperform Peter, and the wonders he works are indeed impressive. Unlike Peter's, however, they stem not from any divine power but, through mere sorcery, from a more questionable, if not altogether demonic, source. To that extent, they are sullied, tainted, 'a hair's-breadth impure'. They are ultimately manifestations of what George calls 'das Leichte' ('the facile'): the spiritual equivalent of the ersatz or spurious. Dazzling though they may be, they are only the products of trickery, of legerdemain, of 'hoax' or 'fraud'. They appeal to the eye, to the surface of consciousness, but have no more profound validity.

Thus does Simon Magus figure in scripture and Christian tradition. His attempt to challenge Christian authority and usurp it with his own establishes him as the archetype or prototype of the 'black magician' and 'Antichrist', a 'rôle model' for such later would-be necromancers and 'black magicians' as Aleister Crowley. The Antichrist in George's poem, the embodiment of trickery and fraud, offers a form of 'facile', pre-packaged, boil-in-the-bag, television-dinner style salvation and redemption – surrogate, specious and, to that extent, intrinsically evil. He is a demagogue, seducing his followers down a path of meretricious spiritual power that will lead them, as well as himself, to destruction.

By 1933, it was already apparent how dangerously Hitler conformed to the pattern – apparent to George, at least, and to others with eyes to see. (Thomas Mann, for example, had already published his minatory story 'Mario and the Magician'. Hermann

Broch was already at work on the novel subsequently to be published in English as *The Spell*.) As the decade progressed and the Nazis consolidated their position, George's poem became ever more apposite. By 1944, its ominous prophecy had already been effectively fulfilled, and the apocalyptic cataclysm of the closing stanzas was only too obviously imminent.

George had always decreed that politics were alien to art – and, by extension, inimical to the life of the spirit and to the very essence of humanity itself. His attitude towards the Nazis, however, sometimes appeared inconsistent, and this allowed a few members of his circle to support them, though the majority – including, of course, the number of Jews among them – did not. Ultimately, George was hostile to the new régime. Whatever it had in common with the 'renewal' he had advocated was superficial, spurious, 'a hair's-breadth impure', the work of a false prophet; and the political reality of the Third Reich was as divorced from the spiritual Reich he had envisioned as Simon Magus's ersatz miracles were, in Christian tradition, from Peter's.

> George found nothing great in Hitler as he did in Caesar or Napoleon. He was repeatedly disparaging about the National Socialists. In 1931 or 1932, he said that if National Socialism came to power, everyone in Germany would have to go about with a noose around his neck, so that whenever a person was not wanted he could immediately be hanged. To the comment that the Nazis were a dreadful lot, he replied: 'Henchmen are never very pleasant people.'[12]

George's sometimes equivocal disapproval, however, did not deter the Nazis from hailing him as a spiritual precursor and trying to co-opt him, much as they did Nietzsche. He was repeatedly mortified and outraged to find his name, certain of his poems, aspects of his thought, and a number of his personal symbols – the swastika, for example – being appropriated by the Nazis and utilised for their own propaganda purposes. He was no less indignant when he received overtures from Goebbels, inviting him to become the Party's 'official poet'.

In October 1928, George published what he declared to be his most important and prophetic book of poems, *Das Neue Reich* (*The*

*New Reich*), which undertook to evoke a realm of culture and the spirit very different from the one the Nazis had in mind. A month later, he convened a meeting of his circle and regaled his disciples with a personal recitation intended to sum up his life's work. The occasion had a distinctly valedictory atmosphere to it, a sense of leavetaking and farewell. It was also suffused with admonitions, omens and portents for the future. At this assembly, George himself read his last two great hymns, 'Burg Falkenstein' ('Falkenstein Castle') and 'Geheimes Deutschland' ('Secret Germany'). The second of these is an inordinately dense, opaque and impenetrable work. There have been suggestions that it contained a sort of clandestine legacy, coded instructions or covert programme for members of the circle. This seems unlikely but, given George's tendency to incorporate levels of significance accessible only to his own initiates, it would be rash to draw too definitive a conclusion. In any case, and whatever the work's 'sub-text' might or might not be, it clearly meant something very special to Stauffenberg. Fifteen years later, amid the throes of war, it was the title of this poem that he conferred on the conspiracy. In all probability, too, the title of this poem was the last phrase on his lips, flung defiantly into the faces of the firing squad.

In 1931, as the Nazis advanced towards absolute power, George effectively expatriated himself, obtaining premises in Minusio, in Switzerland, near Locarno on the Italian border. Minusio was originally intended to be no more than a winter refuge, but George began to spend more and more time there. By 1933, he had become, to all intents and purposes, an exile, returning to Germany only for brief visits.

In May of that year, a Nazi press statement spoke grandiloquently of the 'great tasks' poets would be called upon to perform. George was specifically mentioned as exemplifying the solidarity poets could display with the State by giving expression to the spirit of the new Germany. At the same time, George was approached discreetly through an intermediary and asked if he would preside over, or at least participate in, a poetic academy. If he were amenable, an official invitation would be issued publicly, acknowledging his rôle as a spiritual and cultural precursor of National Socialism. George replied with a characteristically lofty ambiguity:

I in no way deny the ancestry of the new national government and do not dispute my spiritual contribution . . . The laws of the spiritual and the political are certainly very different – where they meet and where the spirit rises to the general good is an exceptionally tangled phenomenon. I cannot put words into the mouths of those in government about what they think of my work and how they value its significance.[13]

As for becoming associated with a poetic academy, he refused with cool aloofness, adding that 'I have for almost half a century presided over German poetry and the German spirit without an academy. Had there been one, I would probably have been opposed to it.'[14]

He had intended to celebrate his sixty-fifth birthday that year with his sister, in his home town of Bingen, on the Rhine. Fearing some sort of 'official recognition' from the régime, however, he abandoned his plans and slipped quietly away from his sister's premises four days early, on 8 July. He celebrated his birthday on the 12th in the seclusion of his Berlin apartment. Still intent on avoiding Nazi acclamations, he then departed, earlier than usual, for Minusio.

In the autumn of 1933, George's health began to decline rapidly, and by the beginning of winter he was on his deathbed. Calling his closest disciples to him, he voiced his fear that, on his death, members of the SS or some other Party representatives might appear, might try to claim his body, bring it back to Germany and turn his funeral into some sort of state occasion. The Stauffenbergs were requested to prevent this from happening.

George died on 4 December and his burial was scheduled for two days later. Claus von Stauffenberg arranged a roster for the funeral vigil. He ensured that he, his brothers and a dozen or so friends, including some military colleagues, maintained a permanent round-the-clock watch over their mentor's bier, to keep all official German representatives away.

In the middle of the cleared chapel the oak coffin stood on a stand. At the head there was a laurel wreath whose leaves were arranged in Roman style. On the left and right there were three laurel trees, that grew over the coffin. In the corners of the bare chapel the friends kept a vigil for the dead, which is customary in Tessin; following the instructions of Claus von Stauffenberg, they took turns. In front of the chapel, to the left and right of the entrance, two laurel trees were planted. On the evening of 5 December, the friends came to the chapel, to see the dead man once again. By his forehead there were two laurel tree branches; by the left hand was some gold jewellery. As people stepped in, they laid flowers down in front of the coffin. The deceased was separated from the living by the laurel trees.[15]

George's anxieties about official Nazi attempts to take over the occasion appear to have been justified. Certainly there were some enquiries by 'strangers' who, it now seems clear, were Party representatives; and the German consul in Lugano, some seventeen miles away, contacted the mayor of Minusio to discover the time of the burial. On what seem to have been the Stauffenbergs' instructions, the mayor was told the burial would be at three in the afternoon. It took place, in fact, at eight-fifteen in the morning. When the régime's representative arrived, he was too late to give an oration, too late to do anything save lay a wreath with a large swastika on the grave. A woman member of the George circle covered the swastika with an armful of roses. Someone else cleared the roses away. Shortly afterwards, the swastika was removed by an unknown hand.[16]

Theodor Pfizer, the Stauffenbergs' boyhood friend and confidant, left a succinct account of the proceedings.

all three (brothers) belonged to Stefan George's close circle and were gathered at his death-bed on the 4th of December, 1933. They were duty-bound beyond the demands of their own wishes and questions, beyond those of their careers and of the family, to the 'Secret Germany'.[17]

*

By 1933 – the year of the Nazis' seizure of power and of George's death – Stauffenberg had begun increasingly to distinguish himself in the army. Reports spoke of his extraordinary affability and friendliness, his capacity to inspire trust in everybody, his expertise at settling differences, acting as intermediary and resolving quarrels. He was often described as saving a situation with his uninhibited and infectious laugh. He could also be overbearing and witheringly sarcastic.

As might be expected, in many things he was conservative, but he attached no intrinsic value to something simply because it happened to be old and hallowed. When circumstances seemed appropriate, he could also display passionate support for the new and untested. In 1935, an aerodrome was built near the cavalry school at Hannover, depriving the troopers of their accustomed training area. A proposal to move the school to a site near Berlin elicited angry objections and protests: it would be contrary to tradition and would diminish the school's reputation. Yet Stauffenberg vigorously endorsed the move. Attached though he was to the cavalry and its place in military history, he recognised the future importance of air power and arranged his priorities accordingly.

Like most professional armies, the Reichswehr – the army of the Weimar Republic – had forbidden any political stance or activity, any membership of a political party, even the right to vote. It is questionable whether Stauffenberg would ever have belonged to a party anyway. 'He builds his own party,' a colleague observed of him. He saw the Reichswehr as more than just a military instrument or a school for future leadership. It was also, he felt strongly, an essential component in the structure of the republic, a guarantee of the country's security and honourable reputation. To that extent, he believed German soldiers had to be, if not politically active, at least politically aware. Like most members of his caste, he found it difficult to muster any great enthusiasm for the increasingly enfeebled republican government. Yet he regarded his obligation to serve the community as binding, without any explicit display of irony or scepticism, and this placed him at odds with adherents of the old imperial order, pining for the deposed Hohenzollerns and sneering at the Weimar flag as 'black and red mustard'. When visiting relatives in Franconia, Stauffenberg would make a point of wearing his uniform. He knew it would be thought outrageous for a member of his caste to serve as an officer in a republican army. Many of them believed with his own father that the government was one of usurpers – that the King of Bavaria had not abdicated voluntarily, but been forcibly deposed by revolutionary elements. Stauffenberg had no compunction about playing the iconoclast with such entrenched attitudes.

When Hitler became chancellor in 1933, there were predictable public manifestations of both antipathy and support. Stauffenberg's biographers have been consistently embarrassed by a contemporary report citing his involvement in a pro-Nazi street celebration in Bamberg. He was in uniform at the time, apparently on the way to a dinner. According to some accounts, he got caught up in the excited and enthusiastic mob and was jostled – or let himself be jostled – to the front of the procession. According to others he assumed a position at the head of the procession deliberately. Such behaviour, of course, was not just unseemly for an officer in uniform. It was also a flagrant breach of the Reichswehr's official proscription of political activities.[18]

In the context of the time, such behaviour on the part of a 26-year-old officer is understandable enough. In 1933, the most vociferous opposition to National Socialism came from militant leftists, who opposed it not because they truly understood it, but because it was an ideology hostile to their own. Of those not blinkered or constrained by any ideology, only a very few prescient individuals – Thomas Mann, for example, and Hermann Broch – could have any real inkling of what was to come. So far as most Germans were concerned, National Socialism offered a welcome promise of a return to law, a salutary antidote to the dithering weakness of the Weimar government, a prospect of economic recovery and a bulwark against the insidious encroachments of Communism. The horror of the Russian Revolution and civil war were no more than a decade and a half in the past; and the Soviet Union under Stalin was no very inspiring example to Germany's battered and precariously established middle class. What was more, National Socialism could still, at that date, make a potent appeal not just to the country's young, but to the most intelligent and best educated among them. Freud and particularly C. G. Jung had elicited great interest and sympathy among the generation of Stauffenberg's contemporaries; and the new sphere of depth psychology constituted an exciting and hitherto undiscovered world, many of whose governing principles – the insistence on cultural and spiritual rebirth and renewal, and the importance of the language of symbolism – on the face of it appeared to mesh with those of National Socialism. Similar themes were also being stressed by literary figures such as Hesse, Broch and Mann, who drew liberally on Freudian and Jungian thought. While the political Left propagated sterile cerebral concepts addressed to the rational intellect alone, Nazism trafficked in a skilful manipulation of symbols, which struck deeper, more resonant chords than any theoretical abstractions. The language of symbols was sonorous, evocative, puissant, eliciting a response from beyond the threshold of rationality. It spoke to the heart and the nervous system, as well as to the head. It seemed to offer a lofty and exalting poetic truth; and poetic truths can only too easily be confused with political truths – as demonstrated, for example, by rhetoric about a 'united Ireland' in Ulster today.

Thus, a generation of young men and women could be duped with a readiness that now appears both inexplicable and culpable. Yet had not Nazism evolved as it did, and culminated in the horrors that have seared themselves into our collective consciousness, its appeal would have been considerable today, not just to louts and skinheads, but to the literate, the thoughtful, the well-educated, the artistically inclined. It is not too extravagant to suggest that the very people who, since the 60s, have espoused Jung, esotericism, eastern thought, comparative religions, folklore and the 'folk soul', would have been seduced by at least certain aspects of Nazism during the late 20s and early 30s. As Mann attempted to demonstrate in *The Magic Mountain* (1924), the mystically oriented sensibility is inherently susceptible, and vulnerable, to exploitation by right-wing totalitarianism.

As a result a number of the future conspirators, including Tresckow, Merz von Quirnheim and Cäsar von Hofacker, found elements in National Socialism they felt they could endorse. So, too, could certain members of Stefan George's circle. In the early 30s, Stauffenberg could say that 'The German people are rebelling against Versailles, and National Socialism endeavours to do away with the misery of unemployment by creating work and instituting other services for the man in the street.'[19]

He hoped the Nazis' acquisition of power 'would mean the end of party political wrangling', and that there might now be 'a firm, straightforward policy' – an impatience and a yearning only too familiar in the Western democracies of today. And he approved, in theory at least, the principle of a dynamic centralised leadership which – in contrast to the dithering and impotence of Weimar – did not shrink from making energetic decisions. There was also a loftier dimension to Stauffenberg's attitude:

> Hitler is capable of putting into words certain basic and genuine ideas which could lead to a spiritual revival. As a result, both the idealistic and the high-minded might indirectly be attracted to him.[20]

According to one of his friends, Stauffenberg 'was stirred by the magnetism this man was able to generate, by his vehemence which made what seemed impossible in a stagnant world suddenly appear feasible.'[21] In spring 1942, the same friend admitted to another confidant, Hans von Herwarth:

> he had initially been quite impressed by Hitler's accomplishments – the re-arming of Germany, the reoccupation of the Rhineland and so forth.
>
> He had been particularly attracted by the fact that all this had been accomplished without armed conflict. By the time I met Stauffenberg, however, he had already become thoroughly alarmed over what was taking place.[22]

Whatever his initial and qualified sympathies for the new régime, Stauffenberg was not blind to the mechanisms whereby it had attained its success. He explained these lucidly and cogently as consisting of three primary factors. First, Hitler had destroyed democracy, but he had done so by ostensibly democratic means, thus rendering powerless the machinery of the State and of party politics. Second, the Western Allies had, at Versailles, provided Hitler with his most persuasive arguments, enabling him to appear as the champion of 'legitimate popular despair'. Third, the National Socialist programme offered an irresistibly attractive alternative to the perceived menace of Communism.

As for Stauffenberg's alleged involvement in the Bamberg street demonstration, the circumstances remain unclear and unconfirmed. Some commentators have denied that the incident took place at all, as have fellow officers in his regiment. Some days after the Nazi triumph in the elections, the subject of street demonstrations was discussed in the officers' mess. It is uncertain whether this discussion referred to an actual and specific occurrence or to a hypothetical situation. In any case, Stauffenberg is reported to have asserted that the citizenry, in such circumstances, would not have understood if an officer simply stood aloof. In the same context, he is said to have invoked the great military leaders of the wars against Napoleon: Scharnhorst, Gneisenau and Yorck von Wartenburg. They, too, had become politically *engagé*. Not only had they acted as instruments of the popular will. They had also tempered, contained, curbed and channelled the potentially anarchic energy that will had unleashed. As always with Stauffenberg, the sense of aristocratic responsibility functioned as a governing principle, a moral imperative. It went hand in hand with a respect for the people, but a mistrust of the mob. As he stated on another occasion: 'Popular guidance is an inescapable and important part of politics, and is not something that can be left to any Tom, Dick or Harry without disastrous consequences.'[23]

Stauffenberg accordingly agreed to direct night exercises by the SA, the *Sturmabteilung* ('storm troopers', or 'brown shirts'). By forcing the SA to expend energy on night exercises, he hoped, if only on the local level, to keep them off the streets and divert them from their customary nocturnal routine of rioting, drinking, bullying, rowdy carousing, destroying property, beating up and even murdering Jews and political opponents. Reducing fat, swaggering and ill-disciplined louts to haggard and panting wrecks by forced marches and rigorous drills was just the sort of thing to appeal to Stauffenberg's sense of humour.

Like almost all professional soldiers at the time, in Germany and elsewhere, Stauffenberg despised the SA. These oafs, he felt, embodied all that was worst, all that was most loathsome and offensive in the German national character. They were also a constant source of embarrassment and even a potential threat to the army. Not, of course, that they could replace the army. They lacked the discipline, the organisation and the military expertise for that. But they fancied themselves to possess those qualities or, at any rate, something else, which might render those qualities superfluous. In consequence, there was a constant antipathy and rivalry between the army and the SA, and a mounting tension. By 1934, each suspected the other of imminent revolt.

In defiance of the limits imposed by the Versailles Treaty, the army had established secret depots and supply bases, concealed from Allied inspectors. Caches of weapons were hidden on various estates. When the SA learned the location of some of these depots, a race ensued, with the SA hoping to appropriate arms and matériel, the army to safeguard them. On at least one occasion, Stauffenberg organised lorries to transfer arms from their depository before the SA could seize them.

In another context, the SA would have been laughable – or, at worst, a noxious nuisance. But the very numbers of SA recruits made them a force to be taken seriously. In 1933, there were 400,000 SA, four times the size of the regular army. A year later their ranks had swollen to two and a half million, and they were everywhere at large in Germany, parading what Stauffenberg and others called their 'shit brown' uniforms. Every city, every town, every village and hamlet had its official Party branch, presided over by an entourage of SA. The brown uniforms were donned by a spectrum ranging from the bourgeois paterfamilias bored with his wife and family to local bullies, thugs and petty criminals. They spent much of their time in pseudo-martial behaviour: farcical parades and marches, campfire rituals, torchlight processions, drills and 'manoeuvres' with shovels and pickaxes. They wallowed in bouts of drinking, raucous 'patriotic' singalongs and contrived sentimental camaraderie. They were also capable of more sinister things: they intimidated political opponents and, under that guise, anyone they simply did not like, anyone with whom they had personal scores to settle. They wrecked shops and other businesses, and 'punished' nightclub owners and cabaret performers who dared to satirise 'the man with the moustache'. In the period immediately preceding and following the 1933 elections, it was not uncommon, at dawn, to find corpses in the gutters, victims of the SA's mob persuasion and retribution.

Until his acquisition of power in 1933, Hitler needed the SA. Even he, however, recoiled from their anarchical activities, their boisterous and shamelessly ill-disciplined reign of terror. They presented a national disgrace, diminishing Germany in the eyes of the world. Yet they were essential in suppressing opposition, mustering (or dragooning) support for National Socialist policies, and eliminating potential obstacles from the Nazi path.

After January 1933, however, the SA became, for Hitler, superfluous and expendable. Indeed, they themselves were now an obstacle which had to be removed. Having obtained power in Germany, the Nazis now needed a more refined, more disciplined precision instrument to consolidate and exercise it. This function was to be performed by the then much smaller but much more efficient, much better educated and indoctrinated SS. And for the dreams of nationalistic expansion already festering in his mind, Hitler needed the army. Wooing the army involved transferring interest and allegiance to them from their greatest rivals, whom they regarded as swaggering bullies.

In February 1934, Ernst Röhm, commander of the SA and Hitler's hitherto loyal colleague, seriously proposed that his organisation be turned into a new 'people's army', of which the regular army and the SS would comprise parts – under his authority, of course. The army found any such suggestion not just repellant but unthinkable, and relations between the SA and the military high command deteriorated further. By summer, the situation had become critical. On 21 June, the high command persuaded Hindenburg, still the nominal head of state and an old soldier himself, to issue an ultimatum to Hitler: unless the prevailing tension was defused, martial law would be declared and authority in Germany would pass to the army. In the days that followed, action against the SA was advocated with intensifying urgency. On the 25th, the army was placed on alert, all leave was cancelled and all troops were confined to barracks. It was obvious that the SA would have to be tamed, reduced to a subordinate status and docility. The result was the Night of the Long Knives.

In the early hours of the morning of 30 June, Hitler and Goebbels flew from Bonn to Munich. A few miles to the south, on the shores of the lake known as the Tegernsee, Röhm and the SA hierarchy were asleep in an hotel, exhausted by the carousing of their summer festival. At dawn, Hitler and an entourage of SS burst into the premises, catching the 'brown shirts' in their beds. Some were taken outside and shot immediately. Röhm himself was brought back to

Munich and a cell in Stadelheim prison, where a pistol was left for him on a table. When he refused to use the weapon – 'Let Adolf do it himself,' he said – two SS officers entered and summarily dispatched him with their own firearms. Among the Nazi leadership, Röhm's homosexuality had long been an open secret. It was now publicly announced as one of several justifications for his execution. A joke quickly became current:

> It is only now that we realise the true significance of Röhm's recent address to Nazi youth: 'Out of every Hitler Youth, a Storm Trooper will emerge.'[24]

At the same time that Röhm and his colleagues were surprised on the Tegernsee, the SS, in a carefully orchestrated and concerted operation, moved against SA functionaries elsewhere in Germany. In Berlin alone, some 150 SA personnel were shot by SS execution squads. Hitler officially announced the total number of deaths as seventy-seven. Exiled sources in Paris put the number at 401. In one of the post-war trials, more than a thousand were said to have died.

Although the SA were the chief victims of the Night of the Long Knives, there were other casualties as well. In what appears to have been a case of 'mistaken identity' – the kind of thing for which the IRA regularly 'apologises' in Northern Ireland today – the music critic of Munich's most prominent newspaper was also shot, because his name happened to be the same as that of an SA official. A number of hostile politicians perished and so, too, did two members of the army's high command, General Kurt von Schleicher, former chancellor and war minister, and General Kurt von Bredow. In eliminating these prominent military figures, Hitler was taking a potentially dangerous gamble, but there was no backlash or mass protest from the army, which thus, to its tarnished honour, became his *de facto* accomplice.

Whatever individual officers may have felt about the deaths of Schleicher and Bredow, there was universal relief in Germany at the effective neutralisation of the SA. Stauffenberg's opinion echoed the sentiment prevalent among military personnel and the middle classes. He described it as 'the lancing of a boil'. For him, as for most other people, the black-clad executors of murder, the Praetorian

Guard of the SS, still seemed too peripheral, and insufficiently numerous, to constitute a serious menace.

A month after the Night of the Long Knives, at nine o'clock on the morning of 2 August 1934, the aged and doddering President Hindenburg died. At noon, an announcement was issued that, 'according to a law enacted . . . the previous day', the title of 'President' had been abolished. This rôle was now to be fused with that of the chancellor, and Hitler would perform both. He would henceforward be known officially as Reich Chancellor and Führer. He would also be commander-in-chief of the armed forces.

In the past, members of the army (on 21 May its name had been changed from the Reichswehr to the Wehrmacht) had taken an oath simply 'to serve the people and the Fatherland honourably and faithfully'. On the day of Hindenburg's death, German soldiers across the country were marched out on parade and formally ordered to take a new oath:

> I swear by God this sacred oath, that I will yield unconditional obedience to the Führer of the German Reich and People, Adolf Hitler, the Supreme Commander of the Wehrmacht, and, as a brave soldier, will be ready at any time to lay down my life for this oath.[25]

The Oxford historian Gordon Craig has described their acceptance of the new oath as 'moral capitulation on the part of the army leadership'.[26] William Shirer elaborated on the consequences of this self-compromise:

> the generals, who up to that time could have overthrown the Nazi régime . . . thus tied themselves to the person of Adolf Hitler, recognising him as the highest legitimate authority in the land and binding themselves to him by an oath of fealty which they felt honour-bound to obey in all circumstances, no matter how degrading to them and to the Fatherland.[27]

Stauffenberg's co-conspirator Axel von dem Bussche stressed the immense significance of the new oath. It was Hitler's recompense for the Night of the Long Knives, a calling in of markers. Having obliged the army by neutralising the SA, the Führer could demand something in return.

Too little has been published about how it came about that Adolf was able to get the oath of personal allegiance when Hindenburg died. Nobody to my satisfaction has yet connected it with the plot of June 30, 1934. Hitler must have known at that time that Hindenburg would die soon, and it was his problem to get the loyalty of the army as Hindenburg's successor. He killed off the SA, thus getting rid of the only body able to compete with the army. June 30th was necessary for Hitler to get the unbreakable loyalty of the army . . . The morning after Hindenburg died, the army was marched out and sworn in without being lectured about the difference between the old oath – to the Constitution – and the new oath – to Hitler.[28]

Bussche described how various individuals contrived to evade the oath. One man with legal training immediately discerned the difference between the old oath and the new, never lifted his hand and thereafter considered he had never sworn. Another escaped swearing the oath by simulating a faint. Ewald von Kleist did actually swear, then promptly swore a second oath vowing to break the first at the earliest opportunity.[29] Such devices are not, of course, without a certain cynical humour, but they also bear testimony to how seriously an oath of the kind demanded from the Wehrmacht was taken. It was a point of honour, a sacred vow made before God as a soldier, an officer, a Christian and a German. To repudiate such an oath was to impugn one's claim to be all of those things.

The oath of allegiance to Hitler was later to become a point of much contention among Stauffenberg's conspirators. Some prospective recruits were actually deterred by it. For others, it made Hitler's removal by assassination all the more urgent, since his death would free the Wehrmacht from all loyalty to the régime. Even Bussche himself felt compelled to rummage through the army's penal code, seeking a legalistic loophole whereby he might circumvent the oath. Stauffenberg, according to Bussche, was rather more offhand and cavalier about the matter:

I discussed this with Claus. He said: 'Well, I am a Catholic and we have a long-standing tradition that tyrants can be murdered. You have it too, but not as strong. Luther says you can kill a crazed leader.'[30]

What was Stauffenberg's own attitude towards the oath? He appears to have deemed it of no relevance. It could not, in any case, supersede the even more sacred oath which he and his brothers had sworn to the principles of Stefan George. The Stauffenbergs 'remained independent; they had had their "Führer" for a long time. They could not fall under Hitler's spell as long as they felt bound to the poet and his Utopia of a Secret Germany.'[31]

If Stauffenberg accommodated himself to the early years of National Socialism in Germany, he seems to have done so less out of total blindness or naiveté than out of a wilful obliviousness and a determination to hope for the best. He recognised clearly enough (and said) that Hitler, without even a pretence to legality, had ruthlessly had old comrades shot when they were no longer of use. And he repeatedly expressed his revulsion for the crudeness and 'ill-breeding' of Nazi leaders, their orgies of hate-filled invective, their guttersnipe jargon, their vulgar demagogic methods.

On 16 September 1934, Stauffenberg and a colleague were sent as representatives of their regiment to attend an official Party Day lecture in Bamberg. The speaker was the notorious Gauleiter (provincial Party boss) of Nuremberg, Julius Streicher, perhaps the most obscenely vicious of Nazi racial theoreticians – a man whose charisma was matched, if not positively exceeded, by his nastiness. Stauffenberg already harboured a personal grudge against Streicher, who had published an attack on Stefan George. At the lecture, Streicher launched into one of his customary pornographic castigations of Jews. So offensive did Stauffenberg find this torrent of rancid rhetoric that he did what, in the context, amounted to the unthinkable. He was a tall man, and conscious of his height. Accompanied by his colleague, he suddenly stood up, left his seat, stalked down the central aisle of the hall and proceeded to the exit. Here he was intercepted and stopped by SS personnel, obviously annoyed at the conspicuousness of his action; but the SS, at this date, could not afford to alienate the army, still less a dynamic and promising young officer of Stauffenberg's social status and aristocratic pedigree. After a brief verbal altercation, he and his colleague elbowed their way past the black-clad minions and out of the premises.[32]

Stauffenberg's thoughts had already begun to move in potentially dangerous directions. Shortly after the Night of the Long Knives, he had had a private talk with his squadron leader. As junior officers they were hardly in a position to do anything themselves. But as Stauffenberg's colleague later reported, they discussed, if only theoretically, the feasibility of deposing National Socialism by force, and the attitude the churches – particularly the Catholic Church – might adopt in such circumstances. The two men agreed that, given its power and influence, the régime could not be overthrown from below, by the populace at large, in a conventional revolution. Any action would have to be implemented from above, by a small high-level conspiracy. Around the same time, Stauffenberg summed up Hitler as

> the typical modern demagogue with an astounding capacity for tub-thumping, a man who frequently merely takes the ideas that come to him and twists them to his own ends, but who is nevertheless capable of simplifying them and making them politically feasible; and is therefore capable of inspiring the mass of the people to devotion and self-sacrifice, even though to their own disadvantage.[33]

Despite his diffidence towards the régime, Stauffenberg had always refrained from criticising it openly. He seems to have felt no such compunction about the Party. But while criticism, even sarcasm and satire, were one thing, action – especially for a man of his youth and as yet junior rank – was another.

# 7

# *The Path of Aggression*

Between 1933 and 1936, Stauffenberg returned to the cavalry school at Hannover. During this period, he prepared for the compulsory military district examination and for an exam in English. Both were mandatory for admission to the General Staff College. Only 15 per cent of those taking the exams ever reached the college, and only a third of these got as far as the General Staff. Stauffenberg was to do both.

In September 1936, just before entering the Staff College, he spent a fortnight in England. The journey – something to which he had eagerly looked forward for years – was subsidised by a grant conferred on him for his scores in his English exam. He visited the Tower of London, St Paul's, Buckingham Palace, the British Museum, Windsor and Eton, and on 7 September, he was invited to Sandhurst, where he met and spoke to a number of cadets studying German.

He was admitted to the General Staff College at Berlin-Moabit at the beginning of October, along with one hundred other young officers. Three months later, on New Year's Day of 1937, he was promoted to captain. Among his colleagues at this time were two who were to play significant rôles in the conspiracy of 1944: Merz von Quirnheim, his associate from earlier military days, and Eberhard Finckh. Life in Berlin also brought him into regular contact with others, both family and friends, who would be involved in later events: Cäsar von Hofacker, for example, and the diplomat Adam von Trott zu Solz.

It was at the General Staff College that Stauffenberg submitted two memorable papers, one of which, awarded first prize as a competition essay, was entitled 'Thoughts on Home Defence against Enemy Parachute Troops'. Throughout the war, this was to remain a basic text for Colonel-General Kurt Student, commander of the Wehrmacht's paratroops from 1938 on. It is the second paper, however, advocating the continued use of cavalry, that reveals most about Stauffenberg's personality.

> The question so often asked today, Should we have cavalry or tanks, is a bad question. The requirement is for cavalry *and* tanks . . . a tactical or strategic breakthrough now being hardly conceivable without the use of tanks in mass. But this does not affect the strategic rôle of cavalry. Looking at the problem quite dispassionately, the extent to which either the horse or the mechanical vehicle is capable of giving us cavalry-type mobility depends upon factors which have only been touched on here; among the most important are conditions on and beyond our frontiers and the fuel supply problem.[1]

In 1937, then, when French and British military thinkers were still questioning the viability of armoured warfare, Stauffenberg regarded it as a self-evident necessity but still argued for the retention of cavalry. Anticipating a war beyond Germany's borders, he foresaw conditions of climate and terrain (in Russia, for example) in which cavalry would still prove its worth. In his mind the logistic problem of maintaining fuel supplies could lead to the immobilisation of armour and so vindicate the existence of cavalry formations.

But the real justification of cavalry for Stauffenberg lay ultimately in the kind of morale or '*élan vital*' it inculcated, the kind of training it had provided for leadership since the Middle Ages. Cavalry had traditionally been the élite of all European armies, the direct descendant of medieval knighthood and chivalry; and although infantry had been the decisive factor on the battlefield for more than three centuries, it was nevertheless the cavalry that most stressed *esprit de corps*, discipline and audacity of command. It had therefore continued to function as it had traditionally – the arm of the service which provided a repository for the sons of the aristocracy, as well as for the boldest, most dynamic and resourceful commanders.

Much was made of the fact that the cavalry leader operated on the same level as his men, not above them like the mounted infantry officer. To be a cavalry leader was, for Stauffenberg, less a utilitarian business than a state of mind, a constellation of spiritual qualities:

> More than any other arm of the service, cavalry is dependent on the quality of its leaders. Without great generals, without real cavalry leaders, cavalry is no more than an expensive impediment. The qualities of a cavalry leader are inborn and are vouchsafed only to a fortunate few . . . Even those fortunate few only rise to full stature in conjunction with their arm of the service; only in their arm are they ultimately inspired to act in the true cavalry spirit – it almost seems as if only a genius in the art of war is capable of recognising the cavalry as the arm designed for major strategic tasks.[2]

While the qualities of the cavalry leader might be inborn, they nevertheless had to be cultivated and refined. This, Stauffenberg insisted, could only be 'the fruit of long training, which cannot begin early enough'.[3]

Stauffenberg of course identified himself with his own idealised conception of the cavalry leader. In an earlier century, he undoubtedly would have become one. Certainly he displayed the traits of gallantry, charisma, panache and audacity associated with the great cavalry commanders of the past – Prince Rupert of the Rhine in the English Civil War, Friedrich von Seydlitz in the wars of Frederick the Great, J.E.B. Stuart and Nathan Bedford Forrest in the American War between the States – but if Stauffenberg exhibited something of their flamboyant style and flair, he exhibited nothing of their impetuous recklessness. His own real forte was to be logistics, the ability to grasp an 'overview' which is the hallmark of the greatest commanders, and the practical, hard-headed business of keeping an army supplied and maintained over long distances.

Whatever his own romantic attitudes towards cavalry and cavalry commanders, Stauffenberg remained in other respects lucid and pragmatic. He frequently criticised the General Staff's mentality, arguing that they concentrated too much on tactics, not enough on logistics, on military economy and technical matters. They seemed to regard war as something conducted in a social, political and economic vacuum – like a boxing match, or like two warriors of legend meeting in single combat, oblivious to the context in which their engagement took place. Stauffenberg endeavoured to counter this blinkered vision by studying on his own, concentrating on material neglected by his instructors. To his extensive reading, he now added Keynesian economic theory and geopolitics. Influenced by Keynes, he began, for a time at least, to ascribe the catastrophes of the twentieth century – the First World War, for example, and the revolution in Russia – to economic factors. He stressed in particular the shift of Europe's industrial centre of gravity from Britain to Germany, and the effect on British markets of Germany's pre-1914 economic expansion. While at the General Staff College, he became particularly friendly with an American exchange officer, the future General Albert Wedemeyer, who, in 1944, would become Chief of Staff to Chiang Kai-Shek and the Chinese army. Stauffenberg and Wedemeyer often invited each other to meals or cocktails at their respective homes. Stauffenberg would practise his English with the American officer, and put to him probing questions about such matters as American steel production and its greater volume than Germany's. He expressed admiration for Roosevelt and the drastic measures adopted by the American president to revive the country's economy after the Depression. In these discussions. Wedemeyer later reported, Stauffenberg often displayed an implicit disapprobation of National Socialist policies.[4] He could hardly, of course, have made any overt statements.

It was noted, however, that he began to grow more reticent, more reluctant about putting his own positions forward. Such, at any rate, was the case so far as contemporary politics were concerned. On the past, he remained loquacious, often slipping historical allusions into his conversation. During a cavalry exercise on the mountain of Hohentwiel, overlooking Lake Constance and the Rhine, he regaled his companions with a vivid description of the far-flung Hohenstauffen empire, 'in the centre of which you are now standing'.[5] His last exercise at the General Staff College again took him to his native region, where he

used the occasion to persuade the group to pay a joint visit to the Imperial cathedrals on the river. He acted as leader. At the end of the trip, he made a speech on the Rhine in which he evoked the region's century-old history. Then, turning to a time when national states would have passed away, he forecast a new rôle for the Rhine as the main artery of Europe. Of the past he spoke not like an intellectual observer but seemed more of a co-actor, one who had been there himself and now was called upon once again to make decisions. Thus his portrayal of the past became a living example for the present.[6]

During this same speech, he cited the ancient antipathy between France and Germany. The Rhine, he prophesied, was a river of destiny, where a decisive battle would be fought for hegemony of the West. He also expressed his fear that the self-inflicted wounds resulting from such a conflict would leave Western Europe morally, ethically and spiritually bankrupt. Western culture, he argued, had not collapsed after the First World War only because the final climactic engagement on the Rhine had been averted. Whether such an engagement could be averted in future was an open and worrying question. And what, he asked portentously, if new developments gave the fledgling great power to the east an opportunity to take a hand in the struggle . . .?

During his stay at the General Staff College, Stauffenberg, through an old associate from Stefan George's circle, made the acquaintance of a scholar and historian, Professor Dr Rudolf Fahrner, who was working at the time on an ambitious biography of Stauffenberg's own ancestor, Field Marshal August von Gneisenau. It was thus inevitable that the two men would have much to say to each other. Stauffenberg was particularly stirred by Fahrner's description of Gneisenau as an officer ready to play a significant rôle in matters of state and governmental reform: 'His was not a spirit prepared to bow to what to others might seem the inevitable; his mind was busy thinking how, by his own exertions, a man might liberate Prussia.'[7] And Stauffenberg made no secret of his desire to model himself on Gneisenau. At the same time he urged Fahrner not to depict the nineteenth-century commander as too conventional a revolutionary, nor as the instigator of nothing more than a popular rising. As always, Stauffenberg insisted on the importance of leadership to impart coherence and direction to unleashed collective energies:

Any revolt against the state and its leaders is no business of the irresponsible mass of the people and should not therefore even be discussed in too wide a circle. If the use of force against one's own state is unavoidable, it must be confined to men conscious of their responsibilities and, even more important, capable of meeting them.[8]

In our own strenuously egalitarian age, such assertions must sound shamelessly and outrageously 'élitist', but a Wehrmacht officers' mess in the '30s was a very different environment. In any case, Stauffenberg's personal magnetism enabled him to get away with statements that would have been offensive coming from others. 'His charm and ease made one forgive his forceful and uncompromising manner; and his ruthless will was made bearable by his cheerful calm, which allowed no pathos . . . he always smiled as he spoke.'[9] But Stauffenberg's charisma consisted of more than just a surface effect.

> What impressed observers most strongly was that he always saw a problem in its entirety and based his judgement of details on this secure foundation. People from quite different walks of life were his close friends. They were all actively involved in intellectual and artistic pursuits . . .[10]

By this time, he had overcome the illnesses which had plagued his boyhood and youth: 'his nerves and health, which he certainly did not spare, were enviable'.[11] He would often work for as long as sixteen hours a day, impressing others by his powers of concentration.

This aptitude for maintaining concentration while dealing with a multitude of things at once was to become one of Stauffenberg's personal trademarks, something on which, throughout his career, colleagues and eyewitnesses consistently and repeatedly commented. A vivid account has been provided by his fellow officer Erwin Topf during the French Campaign of 1940:

> The 'Q' conferences which he held were unforgettable. In general they did not take place at any set time; gradually the section heads, the commanders of special detachments and the liaison officers arrived. Stauffenberg, tall, slim, lively, and a man of extraordinary personal charm, would welcome us all with genuine

infectious geniality; he would make sure that everyone had something to drink, a cigar or a pipe. He would give us the latest information, ask questions and take interest in apparently trivial matters, tell the latest stories covering the whole divisional area from the reconnaissance detachment back to the field bakery, jump from one subject to another, listen to or ask questions of the latest arrivals. This would go on apparently for ages, and none of our questions had been answered, none of our dispositions made for the next day or even for the next few hours, and no orders issued. Then quite casually and conversationally would come the words, 'Well then, I think we'll do it this way.' And then in all its detail out would come the 'Q' order, Stauffenberg with his left hand in his trouser pocket, a glass in his right hand, wandering thoughtfully about the room, stopping at one moment here, at another moment there, and then going back to the map. He did not issue a formal order as one would have expected from a General Staff officer; he was in no sense hide-bound.[12]

Colonel Bernd von Pezold isolated the characteristics underpinning this impressive aptitude for man-management:

He was capable of seeing several moves ahead in the chess game and taking account of all the various alternatives. He was quick to grasp a situation, to sort out the important from the unimportant, and could spot the decisive factor with unerring intuition. He was capable of logical abstract thought and possessed a lively imagination, which, however, never led him to overstep the bounds of practicability . . .[13]

With the rank of captain, Stauffenberg completed his course at the General Staff College in the summer of 1938, his abilities having become known by all senior officers of the Wehrmacht. He was requested by the Organisation Section of the General Staff, but the request was turned down on the grounds that there were already enough 'strong characters' in the section, and his appointment might 'disturb the balance' between it and others. In consequence, on 1 August 1938, he was posted as staff officer in charge of logistics to the 1st Light Division based at Wuppertal, just east of Dusseldorf. His commanding officer was Lieutenant-General Erich Hoepner, later to be one of his most active co-conspirators.

The Light Division was a hybrid formation, a compromise intended to reconcile the intrinsic conservatism of the Wehrmacht's high command with Hitler's insistance on the accelerated expansion of armoured units. It comprised two regiments of motorised infantry, one reconnaissance regiment, one artillery regiment and one tank battalion with supporting arms. Later, on the outbreak of war, this conglomeration would be dismantled, and the Light Division would be reconstituted as the 6th Panzer Division.

Stauffenberg's brief was to organise logistics for the entire division. Since it had never previously had a logistics section, he had to start from the beginning and build one from whatever he could improvise with his own resources. A colleague of Stauffenberg described him at work, with

> the office door wide open, puffing happily away at a black cigar, striding up and down the room, dictating the most complicated reports straight onto the typewriter. Despite frequent interruptions by visitors and telephone, he would continue his report at the precise point of interruption.[14]

On 23 September 1938, the Light Division received its orders for the thrust into Czechoslovakia. Four days later, it moved to its assembly area near the Czech border. The infamous Munich Conference of 29 September removed all barriers from Hitler's path of aggression, and snatched away from the army's high command their justification for overthrowing him. Between 1 and 10 October, German troops proceeded to occupy the Sudetenland. The situation was formalised on 20 November, with Czechoslovakia ceding to Germany 11,000 square miles of territory, with a population of 2,800,000 Sudeten Germans and 800,000 Czechs. A month before, however, on 21 October, Hitler had secretly ordered the Wehrmacht to prepare to occupy the rest of Czechoslovakia as well. This new aggression began on 15 March 1939. Although a flagrant breach of the Munich Agreement, it was accepted as a *fait accompli* by the Western Allies and went unchallenged.

The Light Division crossed the Czech frontier on 4 October. Its objective was to prevent Sudeten Germans from occupying the region on their own initiative, but this was simply a pretence to mask a full-scale invasion. By 9 October, the division had reached the town of Mies, where the German-speaking population welcomed each vehicle with jubilation and flowers. At Nurschan, however, just before Pilsen, the reception from the Czech population was markedly more hostile. It was unclear whether Nurschan belonged to the zone ceded to Hitler's Reich. Pending an answer to this question, a Czech staff officer, supported by the British mediation commission, demanded that German troops leave. The Light Division's command replied brusquely that any areas occupied by its soldiers could not be relinquished, despite the principle of self-determination according to which territory had been ceded.

The area occupied by the Light Division consisted primarily of farmland, where agricultural methods were primitive and there was little literacy, a low standard of living. Even greater poverty prevailed than in the adjacent forests and mountains. As the puny Czech army mobilised for its futile gesture of defiance, all activity in the region came to a standstill. With everything being requisitioned, there was a dearth of horses and vehicles for harvesting and ploughing. Supplies from elsewhere in Czechoslovakia had ceased altogether, and those from Germany arrived only slowly.

As commander of the Light Division's logistics section, Stauffenberg embarked on a programme characteristic less of an invasion than of a modern United Nations aid and relief effort. At the Mies town hall, he called a meeting of divisional officers and local authorities, and forced them to co-operate with each other. There being no yeast available for bread-making, he instructed the division to buy yeast in Germany and deliver it to the local people. He placed a platoon at the disposal of an estate manager to help bring in the potato harvest and store the wheat harvest – a rather humbling experience, one suspects, for swaggering German soldiers intoxicated by dreams of martial glory. He commandeered two trucks from Germany to help breweries in the region distribute beer. For transport vital to the vicinity's economy and population, petrol was supplied at cost price. Stauffenberg also elicited the support of district authorities in taking measures against an outbreak of hoof-and-mouth disease. When a shortage of brown coal threatened a glass factory with a work stoppage and the loss of four hundred jobs, he dispatched the factory manager to obtain coal from Army Group Headquarters in Karlsbad; and he again made the division's resources available for moving it.

In the meantime, butter and milk from the area, destined for Pilsen, were in danger of going bad, and inhabitants of Pilsen were unable to obtain the essentials they required. Here, too, Stauffenberg took measures to alleviate the situation. He distributed safe-conduct passes for working people, thus effectively and single-handedly opening the frontier for supplies, and he arranged, once again, for his own troops to distribute supplies to needy areas.

It was also necessary to crack down on German personnel. Sudeten Germans were desperately in need of German currency – German marks – and the Wehrmacht's officers and men seized the opportunity to purchase goods at shamefully cheap prices. Stauffenberg was indignant at this exploitation. He obtained an order forbidding all large-scale purchases. Commodities already purchased, even by officers of superior rank to himself, had to be returned.

On 16 October, its mission in Czechoslovakia completed, the Light Division moved back into Germany, returning to its base at Wuppertal. Stauffenberg's high spirits were exemplified by his antic handling of the exercise assigned to his section. This exercise – described by one commentator as 'a witty and sarcastic burlesque for the senior officers' – was purely theoretical, involving no actual troops, only paper. It posited a hypothetical armoured force, looking neither to left nor right, driving straight ahead, with single-minded concentration, to the Urals. As logistics officer, Stauffenberg undertook to concoct the most improbable means of keeping the force supplied, culminating in a strategy based on *reductio ad absurdum*. When the force ran out of fuel in the Ukraine (as, of course, it was bound to do), he suggested the immediate capture of Baku, where a land pipeline was laid. His motto for the operation was: 'The eye of their master makes the cows fat.'[15] On one level, this was intended as a zany non-sequitur of the sort now associated with Monty Python, but it incorporated an implicit ambivalence of meaning which must have had more than a few officers scratching their heads in perplexity.

Stauffenberg's exhilaration after the Czech invasion stemmed less from any triumphalist sense of conquest than from the fact that war had been averted – a war for which he, like all other professional military men, recognised Germany was not ready. The 'peaceable' occupation of Czechoslovakia seemed to confirm Hitler's resource-fulness in diplomacy, his capacity to obtain what he wanted through a combination of bluff and negotiation, without having to shed blood.

Hindsight can discern only too clearly how tragically myopic such a view was, but at the time there seemed abundant evidence to support it. In 1935, for example, Hitler had ordered the Wehrmacht into the Rhineland, officially a demilitarised zone. The operation was undertaken by a diminutive probing force, a mere three battalions; and at the slightest indication of French resistance, they were under orders to withdraw at once. According to documents produced at the Nuremberg trials, each German soldier had only been issued with three rounds of ammunition.[16] Yet the bluff had worked. The French, who could easily have thwarted the German incursion, shrank from the prospect of confrontation and did nothing.

The audacious gamble in the Rhineland had been followed, on the night of 11 March 1938, by the annexation – the Anschluss – of Austria. Here again, German aspirations had been fulfilled, German morale and self-respect had been tremendously boosted and war had been averted. Shortly after the Anschluss, Stauffenberg had stated to a friend his conviction that Hitler would not do anything to risk a full-scale conflict. The friend (being in the national defence section of the General Staff and therefore privy to more information) intimated otherwise. Stauffenberg remained adamant, pointing out that everything so far had been managed without recourse to arms. He had no doubts whatever of Hitler's determination not to incur bloodshed:

> a man who was always emphasising that, as a corporal in the First World War, he knew only too well the horrors of war, could not, with his eyes open, head for a war which would in all probability have to be waged against the entire world.[17]

Events in Czechoslovakia seemed only to reinforce this belief. They had, it was true, entailed some precarious brinksmanship, but that appeared only to prove that Hitler had accurately taken the measure of British and French leadership, and knew precisely how much he could get away with.

All the same, Stauffenberg was now beginning to have misgivings and forebodings. He worried that the effortless success of the Czech occupation might go to Hitler's head and lead, on the next occasion, to a serious miscalculation. His general uneasiness was soon to be reinforced by events within Germany. On 9 November 1938, shortly after the Light Division had returned to German soil, there occurred the notorious *Kristallnacht*. Two days before, in Paris, a young Jewish refugee, bent on avenging his father's deportation to Poland, had shot an official of the German embassy. In retaliation, Goebbels arranged for a series of 'spontaneous demonstrations'. Jewish property was to be destroyed. As many Jews as possible were to be arrested on whatever grounds could be contrived. The police were instructed not to interfere with any displays of 'healthy' anti-Semitic sentiment.

Altogether, some 7,500 Jewish shops were looted, 195 synagogues were partially or completely vandalised, and 20,000 Jews were arrested. The murder of Jews went unpunished. Retribution was visited only on those who raped Jewish women, since this violated the racial laws. The insurance money of the Jewish community was confiscated, and the community was fined a billion marks as a penalty for having provoked the disturbance. As Dr Hans Bernd Gisevius, one of the later conspirators, wrote:

> The conclusions that were forced upon every thinking German were grim and depressing indeed. Not a single general had had the impulse to bring out his troops and see to the clearing of the streets. The army leaders had played deaf and blind. The meaning of this is clear. Everyone had long since given up hope that the cabinet would ever do anything. From whom could decent Germans now expect protection if these horrible excesses were followed by others? . . . the cowed middle class stared at the Nazi monster like a rabbit at a snake. A general psychosis had been created, under which the populace was reduced to absolute submission.[18]

Stauffenberg was mortified by *Kristallnacht*. The outrage marked a decisive turning point in his attitude towards the National Socialist régime. To his military colleagues, he commented only on the purely pragmatic repercussions: the damage done to Germany's honour and reputation in the eyes of the world. His primary objections, however, were personal and moral. His own brother, Alexander, was now married to a woman of Jewish ancestry, Melitta Schiller. Jewish members of George's circle, some of them among his closest friends, were now under threat. The government and the Führer to whom he had taken his oath of allegiance were suddenly beginning to appear ugly in the extreme.

While based at Wuppertal during the early months of 1939, Stauffenberg would often invite a circle of junior officers to his quarters where he would organise, conduct or preside over discussions and lectures intended to widen his colleagues' intellectual horizons, In January 1939, the guest speaker at one of these sessions was Dr Rudolf Fahrner, the scholar and historian he had met while at the General Staff College. Fahrner was still at work on his definitive biography of Gneisenau, and this was to be the subject matter of his lecture. Stauffenberg gave a brief introduction which, albeit obliquely, alluded critically to current events in Germany. Fahrner then spoke for two hours. When the presentation had concluded, Stauffenberg, with a laugh, said pointedly of his illustrious Napoleonic ancestor: 'There, you see. Now we have learned how *he* did things.'[19] What he meant by the way Gneisenau 'did things' will become apparent in due course.

Following the lecture, Stauffenberg and Fahrner went outside and walked for a time together in the nearby forest. Fahrner expressed profound anxiety about the situation prevailing in Germany, and particularly about *Kristallnacht* and the intensifying virulence of Nazi anti-Semitism. He probed Stauffenberg for some information on the Wehrmacht's attitude towards such developments. According to Fahrner, Stauffenberg spoke freely about the plans for overthrowing Hitler which had been thwarted by the Munich Agreement. He then spoke of possible alternative plans and enumerated which generals would be prepared to support a coup. He cited Beck as the man around whom resistance would have to coalesce, the key figure to oppose National Socialism from within the Wehrmacht, even though Beck had recently been replaced as Chief of the General Staff. About a number of other senior commanders, he expressed an embittered pessimism, fostered in part, no doubt, by their passivity on *Kristallnacht*: 'you cannot expect people who have broken their spine once or twice to stand up straight when a new decision has to be made'.[20] As for Hitler, Stauffenberg's previous optimism had now utterly vanished. It was clear, he said, that 'the fool is bent on war' and was 'prepared to squander the flower of [Germany's] manhood twice in the same generation'.[21]

★

By the autumn of 1939, of course, all speculation would be swept aside by events, and the Wehrmacht, like the German nation as a whole, would be too flushed with martial success to contemplate any change of course. The spirit of the times is expressed convincingly by Thomas Mann's narrator in *Doctor Faustus*:

> War, then, and if needs must, war against everybody, to convince everybody and to win . . . that was what fate had willed . . . We were bursting with the consciousness that this was Germany's century, that history was holding her hand out over us; that after Spain, France, England, it was our turn to put our stamp on the world and be its leader; that the twentieth century was ours . . .[22]

On 4 September 1939, Hitler's military machine smashed its way almost effortlessly into Poland. Equipped now with 250 Czech-built Skoda tanks, the Light Division was part of Colonel-General Gerd von Rundstedt's Army Group South, striking from Silesia. Rundstedt's forces formed one arm of a giant pincer movement, the other being composed of Army Group North, under Colonel-General Fedor von Bock, moving down the Polish corridor. The Light Division quickly captured Wielun, just across the German-Polish border, then raced east towards the Vistula, parallel to the retreating Poles. At Radom, south of Warsaw, it turned northwards to link up with other German units and encircle seven divisions. In a report of 10 September, Stauffenberg compared the German pincer movement to that of Tannenburg in 1914, when Hindenburg and Ludendorff triumphantly encircled an entire Russian army.

At the same time an ominous shadow hung over the German success. By a crossroads near Wielun, news had first reached divisional headquarters of the Anglo-French declaration of war. Albeit reluctantly, Hitler's bluff had this time been called, and the prospect of full-scale conflict had become reality. The morale of the troops plummeted. Stauffenberg grimly prophesied a struggle of attrition exceeding even that of 1914–18: 'My friends, if we're to win the war, it will depend on our capacity to hold out; for a certainty this war will see out ten years.'[23]

The capture of Wielun provoked the first of many squabbles Stauffenberg was to have with the military hierarchy, and especially with the mentality seeping into the army from the SS. Two women were arrested by a sergeant-major. They had allegedly been signalling with electric torches from the ground floor of a house, directing the aim of Polish artillery on German positions in the town. It was immediately obvious to Stauffenberg that the two women were simple-minded and could not have been doing anything of the sort. Having hidden in the house, they were merely crawling about with their torches, terrified by the barrage. These facts would have become sufficiently clear in any properly conducted enquiry, but the officer in charge only glanced at the women and in an offhand manner instructed the sergeant-major to 'get rid of them'. It is probable that he meant no more than for the women to be taken or chased away, but the sergeant-major interpreted the instruction as a licence to shoot them. Outraged, Stauffenberg began proceedings to have the officer court-martialled, even though he was an old friend.[24] Sloppy slapdash orders and the wanton shooting of civilians might be accepted procedure in the SS, whose infamous *Einsatzkommandos* – 'rapid reaction' death squads – had already begun to operate.[25] Authorised to murder indiscriminately anywhere behind the front lines, they were already provoking revulsion among regular soldiers, but insofar as he could do anything about it, Stauffenberg was not going to countenance such behaviour in the officer corps of the Wehrmacht. The matter was too important in his eyes to make allowances even for personal friendship.

The Polish campaign involved the Wehrmacht's first serious large-scale venture with mechanised formations, and it revealed complications, never made apparent in exercises. Due to inadequate preparation and an excessive reliance on improvisation, operations were beset by an extremely poor supply situation. Had Poland managed to hold out longer, or had she been reinforced, it is questionable how long the German Blitzkrieg could have been sustained. There were other, unforeseen difficulties as well, problems never properly considered by the military planners, such as feeding vast numbers of prisoners or providing the civilian population with sustenance.

For Stauffenberg these matters were a severe test of his organising abilities and aptitude for logistics, and extended his activities far beyond those officially dictated by his rank and position. At the end of the campaign he issued a questionnaire to all ranks, from privates up to the divisional commander, which covered everything from facilities for treating the wounded to possible improvements needed in weapons and equipment. After studying the results of his survey, Stauffenberg synthesised them into a comprehensive report.

After completing his own work, he would always make a point of offering himself to the divisional commander for other jobs. In part, this served an educational purpose for him, enabling him to extend his own spheres of expertise and gain familiarity with a broad spectrum of responsibilities and tasks. He was grooming himself for senior command. At the same time, more as a by-product at first than anything else, he began to find others increasingly dependent on him, prone to confide in him and seek out his advice. He began to assume the rôle that he would perform more and more often during the course of his career – that of 'father confessor' to men far senior in rank and age. And by establishing so close a rapport with his divisional commander, he became probably the best-informed officer in the entire division. Anyone having business with the commander, anyone seeking his ear or desiring a favour, had first to deal with Stauffenberg.

In all this Stauffenberg was not simply pursuing his own personal ambition. Immediately after the Polish campaign, he met his uncle, Graf Nikolas von Üxküll, and one of Üxküll's friends, Fritz von der Schulenburg, deputy president of Upper and Lower Silesia. Üxküll described the ever more alarming situation in Germany. Stauffenberg, he insisted, must do something – must act or, at very least, set about attaining a position from which action would become possible. At the moment, of course, no such action was feasible. With the best will in the world, Stauffenberg pointed out, a mere divisional logistics officer could not very well initiate anything of consequence. Nevertheless, he was left shaken and thoughtful by his uncle's appeal, feeling 'impotence, perhaps also vexation at the thought that this apparently mighty and victorious army was incapable of ensuring that the state maintained reasonable standards of decency'.[26]

No doubt much of the energy he displayed reflected Üxküll's injunction to attain a position enabling him to act. He now began to question whether traditional concepts of loyalty to a state or a government can be valid unless subordinated to some higher ideal; and whether duty towards the nation and allegiance to the state were not only different, but also, in the existing context, incompatible.

In February 1940, the important post of Operations Officer for the division became vacant. That Stauffenberg would be appointed to fill it seemed a foregone conclusion. Somewhat mysteriously, and to everyone's angry surprise, he was bypassed and the position conferred on another captain, Helmut Staedke. For the first few days, Staedke found himself ostracised, confronted by a united front of surly hostility. Despite his own disappointment, Stauffenberg came to Staedke's aid, smoothing things over for him. He displayed a similar generosity towards other colleagues. He spent many evenings helping one young subaltern prepare for the military district examinations. At Christmas, 1939, he relinquished his leave to enable a fellow officer to spend the holidays at home.

*

On 18 October 1939, a week after withdrawing to Germany from Poland, the Light Division had been reconstituted as the 6th Panzer Division. By the following spring, it was poised for the decisive German thrust into France. Together with the 19th Panzer Division under the famous Heinz Guderian, it comprised the 41st Panzer Corps. This corps, along with other units which included one SS division, was part of a detached Panzer army commanded by General Erwin von Kleist, operating under the overall authority of Field Marshal Gerd von Rundstedt.

At four o'clock in the morning of 10 April 1940, the Blitzkrieg began, with German paratroops seizing bridges and airfields in Holland and Belgium. For some five weeks, the bulk of the fighting was concentrated in the extreme west, on Dutch and Belgian

15 The 'Knight of Bamberg', a thirteenth-century sculpture in the cathedral of Bamberg to which Stauffenberg has often been compared.

16 Field Marshal August von Gneisenau with his staff. Hero of the
War of Liberation, 1813–15, he was an ancestor of Stauffenberg's.

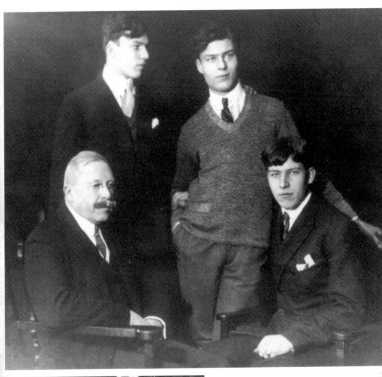

17 Alfred, Graf von Stauffenberg
and his three sons, Berthold,
Claus and Alexander, in 1924.

18 Stauffenberg with his wife,
Nina, at their wedding, Bamberg,
26 September 1933.

19 Stauffenberg on his horse 'Schwabenherzog' during the regimental farewell parade, Bamberg, 1934.

20 On the left, Stauffenberg ridir in a competition, May 1935.

21 Stauffenberg (right) talking Lieutenant-Colonel Coelestin von Zitzewitz and, with his bac to the camera, Eastern Intelligen Chief, Colonel Reinhard Gehle

22 Stauffenberg with his friend and co-conspirator Albrecht Merz von Quirnheim in army headquarters, Vinnitsa (Ukraine), 1942.

23 Stauffenberg recuperating from his wounds at the family home in Lautlingen.

24 Stauffenberg (left) walking with Hitler to a military conference, with the chief ADCs of the army and navy. Vinnitsa, 1942.

25 Stauffenberg meeting Hitler at the East Prussian headquarters,
the 'Wolfsschanze', 15 July 1944. He was carrying a bomb with him but
chose not to explode it.

26 Berthold von Stauffenberg during his trial before the Nazi 'People's Court', 10 August 1944. He was executed the same day.

27 Field Marshal Erwin von Witzleben appearing before the 'People's Court', 8 August 1944. He too was executed the same day.

territory. Then, on 10 May, the Panzer army struck in a direction entirely different from the other German advances. Its tanks and motorised infantry drove south-west, through the Ardennes, which French military planners had deemed impenetrable to armoured formations. The French were caught off guard, and on 13 May, Guderian's division, closely followed by 6th Panzer, broke through their defences at Sédan, the site of Germany's greatest victory in the Franco-Prussian War exactly seventy years before. In a mere seven days, the German armour had swept two hundred miles westwards to the French coast, then swung north to link up with German units advancing through Belgium. Boulogne fell on 25 May, Calais a day later. British lines of communication were cut, and the whole of the British Expeditionary Force was threatened with encirclement. On the evening of 26 May, the evacuation from Dunkirk began and continued until 5 June. Some 338,000 British soldiers were rescued, along with 120,000 French, but more than a million Allied troops were taken prisoner. France was left with only 65 depleted and demoralised divisions to face 140 German. The campaign lasted another fortnight. On 11 June, the French government declared Paris an open city and fled to Bordeaux. On 14 June, German troops goosestepped triumphantly down the boulevards of the French capital. On 17 June, France capitulated and the articles of surrender were formally signed five days later at Compiègne, where the Treaty of Versailles had been signed twenty-two years earlier.

Stauffenberg appears to have been less exhilarated than sobered, even saddened and shaken, by the magnitude and completeness of the French collapse. In a letter from field headquarters on 19 June, he wrote to his wife: 'The French débâcle is frightful. They have been totally defeated and their army annihilated, a blow from which this people is unlikely easily to recover.'[27] Two days later he wrote again, in an even more sombre and meditative mood. France, he mused, had succumbed to a false sense of security after her victory in 1918. A similar fate might easily befall any nation which became too complacent about its accomplishments.

A week from today is the anniversary of the Treaty of Versailles. What a change in so short a time: while rejoicing over our triumph, we should cast our minds back over the three decades through which we have lived and realise how little finality has been reached; abrupt change or indeed a complete reversal of the situation is more probable than even a few years of stability. We must teach our children that salvation from collapse and decay lies only in permanent struggle and a permanent quest for renewal; the greater our past achievements, the more essential renewal becomes. We must teach them, too, that stagnation, immobility and death are synonymous. Only then shall we have fulfilled the main part of our task of national education.[28]

In the middle of the French campaign, Stauffenberg himself had experienced a dramatic change of fortune. On 27 May – a day after his division had captured Calais and the British evacuation at Dunkirk had begun – he learned he was to be transferred from 6th Panzer to the General Staff. This was a significant advancement, and an indication that his merits had been recognised in high quarters, but at first it struck Stauffenberg as 'dismal news'. He had developed a taste for combat against a worthy adversary, yet he, as well as everyone else, was quick to recognise that with the General Staff he was truly in his element. It was with the General Staff that he was to spend the next two and a half years. In this milieu, at the very centre of the chain of command, he was to prove himself. During that time his attitude was to harden and his determination crystallise – Adolf Hitler had to be overthrown.

# 8

# *Operation Barbarossa*

The organisation to which Stauffenberg was posted was OKH, *Oberkommando des Heeres*, the General Staff or high command of the army, officially designated as the Wehrmacht. There was also a distinct, separate, overlapping and often conflicting organisation, OKW, *Oberkommando der Wehrmacht*, the high command of all the armed forces, which did *not* deal specifically with the Wehrmacht as such. OKH was under the supreme command of the Chief of the General Staff – who, when Stauffenberg joined it, was his old friend, Colonel-General Franz Halder, one of the guiding spirits behind the thwarted coup of 1938. OKW, on the other hand, was under the supreme and direct command of Adolf Hitler. In addition to OKH and OKW, there were a number of other chains of command: the SS and the SD; Goering and the Ministry of the Interior; the Foreign Office under Ribbentrop.

> The whole set-up was a chaos of competing authorities, each in its own watertight compartment . . . Hitler was obsessed by a suspicion mania. Instead of a sound, sensible organisation for war, he preferred this total confusion, since it prevented any potential concentration of power in the hands of any one authority.[1]

If the situation seems hopelessly baffling now, it was almost as much so to German officers at the time. One of his colleagues described a lecture Stauffenberg gave to a group of young officers training for General Staff positions. He drew diagrams on the blackboard beside him, detailing the various command organisations and the tangled links of authority and supply between them.

> Before long, his diagram looked like a confused work of abstract art. Stauffenberg paused. Finally, in despair, he asked his audience if any organisation so constructed could possibly win a war.[2]

On another occasion, at the General Staff College, he opened a lecture as follows:

> If our most highly qualified General Staff officers had been told to work out the most nonsensical high level organisation for war which they could think of, they could not have produced anything more stupid than that which we have at present.[3]

The muddled command structure of the Third Reich's armed forces is generally regarded as a major contributing factor to Germany's eventual defeat. It was also to be the bane of Stauffenberg's existence during the two and a half years he spent with the General Staff. Its headquarters, to which he was officially attached, were, for much of the war, frenetically peripatetic. At first OKH headquarters were shunted about between various sites in southern Germany. After the French campaign, they were established at Fontainbleau, near Paris, which enabled Stauffenberg to make frequent trips into the French capital and visit the opera. By October 1940, headquarters were back in Germany, at Zossen, near Berlin, and after the invasion of Russia in the summer of 1941, they were moved to the Eastern Front. Eventually, during the latter phases of the war, they were installed in East Prussia, not far from Hitler's own (OKW) headquarters at Rastenburg.

Stauffenberg was placed in charge of Group II of the General Staff's Organisation Section. The head of the section and his immediate superior was Colonel Walther Buhle, a man he did not particularly like. Subsequently, as a major-general, Buhle was to be transferred from the General Staff to Hitler's own (OKW) headquarters – and to be injured in the blast of 20 July 1944. Among Stauffenberg's colleagues on the General Staff was another friend, Albrecht Merz von Quirnheim.

Stauffenberg's responsibilities involved much travel, both to the front and to support areas in the rear. He had virtually complete freedom of movement, and transport – including aircraft – was made available to him whenever he wished. At the front, he was obliged to maintain ongoing observation of various units and to monitor their battleworthiness, the state of their equipment, supply and morale. In the rear, he had to monitor training programmes in the Reserve Army, to allocate replacements, to find positions for new officers, to shunt recovered casualties back to front-line formations – and to confront the problem, increasingly insoluble as the war progressed, of keeping front-line units properly supplied, reinforced and up to strength. These and numerous other duties kept him incessantly busy. Of all the officers in his section, he is the most frequently cited in the OKH war diary for 1942.

On 1 January 1941, six months after his appointment to the General Staff, Stauffenberg was promoted to major. By this time, he was deeply involved in planning the invasion of Russia, preliminary studies for which had begun as early as July 1940. From the very beginning, he had had serious misgivings about the operation, and worried about Germany's capacity to sustain the requisite military effort on an entirely new front. From a strategic point of view it was more important to him that Britain should be defeated or forced to peace talks before any trial of strength with the Soviet Union began. He considered the plans for the invasion of England to be viable, and believed them to have been abandoned prematurely.[4]

In February 1941, Rommel and the tanks of the Afrika Korps made their first appearance in North Africa, shoring up the crumbling units of Mussolini's beleaguered army. In April, German forces invaded Yugoslavia and Greece, capturing Athens by the end of the month. In May, Stauffenberg visited the Greek capital, as well as Salonika and Crete, which had been taken by German paratroops in accordance with the principles he himself had outlined in his prize-winning paper for the General Staff College. According to Rudolph Fahrner, the possibility of deposing Hitler was again discussed at this time, but Stauffenberg was sceptical about success. The Führer, he observed cynically, 'is still winning too many victories'.[5]

On 22 June 1941, the anniversary of the French surrender, Operation Barbarossa began. In flagrant violation of the non-aggression pact signed with Stalin, 175 German divisions – more than a million and a half men – smashed their way across the frontier and into the Soviet Union. It was a massive, three-pronged offensive along a front of unprecedented length. Army Group North drove towards Leningrad, eventually to besiege that city. Army Group Centre advanced on Moscow, and would come within striking range of the Russian capital. Army Group South swept through the Ukraine towards the Caucasus.

The Red Army was believed to number between 150 and 200 divisions, but during the late 1930s Stalin had purged his officer corps. In consequence, there were few senior commanders left in positions of authority, morale was poor among the troops, training inadequate and discipline slack. The Russians reeled before the speed, mobility and impact of the German offensive. They had 24,000 tanks to the Germans' 3,550, but most were obsolete and 75 per cent of their armour was unserviceable. Despite a numerical superiority of almost three to one over the Luftwaffe, most of the Red Air Force's 8,000 warplanes were hopelessly antiquated and unfit for combat.

By the end of the summer, the Wehrmacht had suffered some 560,000 casualties. The Russians, however, had lost four million killed, wounded or taken prisoner, and were everywhere in retreat. Even so, Hitler and his generals underestimated the Soviet Union's resources, reserves of manpower and resilience. Industrial production, quickly relocated to beyond the Urals, was dramatically increased. New Russian units, previously unknown to the Germans, began to appear, as if from nowhere. After estimating the Soviet strength at between 150 and 200 divisions, the German high command had soon counted more than 360, and fresh ones were constantly entering the conflict. Hans von Herwarth, one of Stauffenberg's subordinates and a cousin by marriage, described how a fellow officer arrived one day with a bottle of cognac and proposed a celebration. 'Astonished, I asked him what in heaven's name there was to celebrate. He replied that he had just heard on the radio that we had just destroyed our minus-100th Soviet division. We drank to our success.'[6]

In August, shortly after Army Group Centre had captured Smolensk, the German advance came to a halt while Hitler and the high command argued about how to proceed. Yet as early as July, and despite the enormous losses inflicted on the Russians, Stauffenberg had received a foretaste of what was to come, finding himself beset by requests for replacements, reinforcements and reserves. These were soon to become unanswerable. By the following year, there would be only a thousand new recruits to replace every ten thousand troops lost. No army could possibly sustain attrition on this scale for long.

Stauffenberg toured the front of Army Group Centre in July, familiarising himself with the situation at first hand. At Smolensk, he paid a call on Guderian, who complained that, had the advance not been interrupted, Moscow could easily have been taken before the Russians regained their balance. He also met Tresckow and Schlabrendorff in Borissov. In August, he made a similar visit to Army Group North.

At the beginning of October 1941, the German advance resumed. Army Group Centre embarked on the thrust which, after ferocious fighting, would carry it to within fifteen miles of Moscow before, on 5 December, the Russian winter brought it to a halt, achieving what the Red Army could not. In the meantime, Stauffenberg's brother, Berthold, was approached on behalf of the civilian 'Kreisau Circle' and asked to sound him out about the prospects of conspiracy. Berthold reported back:

> I have had a talk with Claus. He says that we must win the war first. While it is still going on, we cannot do anything like this, especially not in a war against the Bolsheviks. When we get home, however, we can then deal with the brown pest.[7]

In fact, Stauffenberg was already discussing conspiracy with army colleagues and superiors. Berthold's reply would seem to have been dictated not by reluctance or even diffidence, but by the mistrust and scepticism with which the military plotters regarded the civilians of the 'Kreisau Circle', who had previously confessed themselves to be amateurs, lacking the requisite ruthlessness and expertise.

Stauffenberg's colleague on the General Staff, Major Freiherr

Dietz von Thüngen, has given a vivid description of Stauffenberg at work:

> What was he like? I had some inkling from the reputation which preceded him: 'One of our very best, far above average, his character is his strong point.' This was amply confirmed if one had an opportunity of seeing him at work. I never opened Claus's door without finding him on the telephone, mountains of paper in front of him, the receiver in his left hand, turning over the files with his right, a pencil between his fingers. He always looked happy; depending upon who he was talking to, he would be laughing (that invariably came somewhere in the conversation) or cursing (that generally happened too), or giving an order, or laying down the law; but at the same time, he would be writing, either his great sprawling signature or short remarkably detailed notes on the files. His clerk was usually with him, and whenever there was a pause would take down, post haste, notes for the file, letters or circulars, Claus never forgetting to dictate with almost pedantic accuracy such tiresome accessories to General Staff work as letter heading, reference number and subject. Claus was one of those men who could do several things at once, all with the same concentration. He had an astounding capacity for working through files, in other words, reading them and sifting the important from the unimportant at a glance – an enormous advantage in his type of work. Equally astounding and equally striking were his capacity to concentrate, his clarity of expression and his sudden asides, which invariably hit the nail on the head and frequently took his listeners aback. When I used to visit him he was generally at the end of a twelve-, fourteen-, or even sixteen-hour day filled with telephoning, conferences, visits, dictation, working on files, notes for conferences, etc. He worked at an incredible pace, with unyielding concentration, and yet he appeared just as fresh late at night as he did in the morning.[8]

Again and again in the reports of Stauffenberg's colleagues, one finds testimonies to a charismatic natural authority, which prompted others, even men far senior in rank, to defer to him. According to Hans von Herwarth: 'What surprised me was the manner in which those who surpassed him in rank recognised his natural superiority and yielded to it.'[9]

Stauffenberg's influence among both colleagues and superiors has been effectively summed up by the biographer Joachim Kramarz:

> Young though he was, Stauffenberg soon came to be trusted by everybody. Anyone who got to know him, went to him whenever he wanted to pour his heart out, and this applied not merely to men of his own age and rank; even generals visiting headquarters from the front or from the replacement army would often seize the opportunity of having a talk with him. Whenever Stauffenberg was late for lunch, the word went round: 'He's got some general weeping tears in his office again.' Matters came piling in on him which were really not his responsibility. The fact that he was thereby contravening an order from Hitler did not bother him in the least. He busied himself with anything that interested him, even if outside his official competence.[10]

His position brought Stauffenberg into regular contact with his friend Franz Halder. The two men confided in each other as they could in few others.

> Stauffenberg's personal relationship with Halder was considered as something exceptional by his fellow officers. Major (as he then was) de Maizière, for instance, says, 'Although two or three rungs down the ladder, Stauffenberg was the only one of the organisation section apart from the section head who from time to time did business direct with Halder and with whom Halder would discuss things personally.[11]

To Halder, Stauffenberg was 'magnetically attractive . . . a born leader, one whose sole outlook on life was rooted in his sense of responsibility towards God, who was not prepared to be satisfied with theoretical explanations and discussions, but who was burning to act.'[12] After the war, Halder described Stauffenberg's hardening antipathy towards the régime:

> For hours at a time we would mull over and over possible methods of removing this monster without in the process seriously damaging the army now in contact with the enemy in

fulfilment of its duty to defend the Fatherland, and without destroying the entire structure of the state . . . Later, when Hitler's decision to take the offensive against Russia was becoming ever clearer, and finally in the period when the war was being carried into Russia, our discussions revolved around the question of the way in which military means might be used to remove Hitler from the saddle without turning him into a martyr, and how the party's grip might be broken.[13]

Stauffenberg's hostility towards the régime was now based neither on expediency nor on theoretical political grounds. According to Halder: 'His criticism was based simply and solely upon the revolt of his whole soul against the spirit of Hitlerism.'[14] This point was echoed by Fabian von Schlabrendorff, who stated that 'Stauffenberg's objection to Hitler was fundamentally a spiritual one and in no way based on a fear of impending German military defeat or any other materialistic considerations . . .'[15]

A key factor in the development of Stauffenberg's attitude was first-hand experience of the work of the SS. He had seen the notorious *Einsatzkommando* units performing their grisly tasks in Poland. In France, he had been privy to atrocities committed by other, regular SS and Waffen-SS units, including the murder of unarmed British soldiers who had already surrendered. In a lecture at the General Staff College after the French campaign, he had posed a sarcastic question, then answered it himself: 'What is the difference between an SS division and an army division? Simply that SS divisions have better equipment but no divisional chaplains.'[16]

Whatever the enormities committed by the SS in Poland and in France, they paled beside the carnage wrought by the *Einsatzkommandos* on the Russian front. Enjoying unchallenged authority even a few yards behind the front lines, they went about their murderous business with a zeal that revolted Wehrmacht personnel. Indeed, the scale and intensity of SS savagery began to produce an adverse effect on Wehrmacht morale. In December 1941, a report from Army Group Centre stated that 'the officer corps, almost to a man, is against the shooting of Jews, prisoners and commissars'.[17] SS activities were considered 'a stain on the honour of the German army'. In a statement typical of many others, a commander declared it to be a flagrant violation of 'our concepts of custom and decency that a mass slaughter of human beings should be carried out quite publicly'.[18]

By the winter of 1941-2, OKH had established its headquarters at Vinnitsa, in the Ukraine. A fellow officer, who visited Stauffenberg at his office here, was surprised to see a portrait of the Führer above his desk. Stauffenberg quietly explained: 'I chose this picture. And I put it up so that whoever comes here shall see the man's expression of madness and the lack of any sense of proportion.'[19] Just before leaving, Stauffenberg's visitor asked what could possibly be done about Hitler, what might constitute a solution. 'Kill him,' Stauffenberg replied bluntly.

In July 1942, Hitler paid a personal visit to OKH headquarters at Vinnitsa; and, as plate 24 in this book shows, Stauffenberg was in contact with the Führer. There is no record of what precisely passed between them, or of what Hitler might have said or done to provoke Stauffenberg to an even more intense hatred, but after the visit his statements became markedly more vehement. 'Is there no officer over there in the Führer's headquarters', he exploded one August morning, 'capable of taking his pistol to the beast?'[20] In the autumn, he replied to an officer worried about presenting a report to the Führer: 'The point is not to tell him the truth, but to put an end to him, and I am prepared to do that.'[21] On a morning ride with a colleague, he suddenly burst out in condemnation of the mass shootings of Jews and declared emphatically that such crimes could not be allowed to continue. After that, 'during almost every ride, Stauffenberg spoke of tyrannicide. He cited Thomas Aquinas, who had maintained that in certain conditions tyrannicide was both permissible and commendable.'[22]

It is very likely that Stauffenberg could have been driven to conspiratorial action as early as the summer or autumn of 1942. If he was prevented from being so, it was primarily because he found a constructive, even creative, enterprise into which he could channel both his energy and his antipathy towards the régime. This served to offset his frustrations with Hitler's policies, and to offer an alternative to despair. Had things fallen out differently, it might also have changed the course of the war and of post-war history.

The speed and sledgehammer force of the German advance into

the Soviet Union, coupled with Soviet unpreparedness and initial military incompetence, had yielded huge numbers of prisoners-of-war. The first week of the campaign alone brought in more than 287,000. During the following months, Russian soldiers surrendered not just by thousands or even tens of thousands, but by hundreds of thousands at a time. Soviet armies would capitulate *en masse*, and the tally of prisoners was soon running into millions.

Much of this success could be ascribed to German military prowess, but certainly not all. When the Nazi invasion began, the population of the Soviet Union had suffered cruelly at Stalin's hands and harboured no great love for the Communist régime. In many regions, such as White Russia and the Ukraine, the advancing Germans were hailed by the populace as liberators. And if Soviet citizens were eager to welcome the invaders, so too were many units and elements of the Red Army. During the previous decade, the army, and especially the officer corps, had endured particularly severe victimisation. They had little incentive to fight and die for the dictator who had persecuted them and for the system they despised. Whatever the Nazi tyranny, many felt it could not possibly be worse than what they had already experienced; and the prospect of change seemed to offer a chance of changing things for the better. In consequence, vast numbers of soldiers and officers defected voluntarily.

A more astute German policy could easily have turned these defectors into loyal allies, and also eroded the morale of those who continued to resist. It would not have taken much to turn both the Soviet people and the Red Army decisively against Stalin. At very least, a renewed civil war between 'Whites' and 'Reds' could have been fomented, from which the Soviet system would not have emerged unscathed and Germany could only have benefited. But according to Nazi racial theory, Slavs, like Jews, were '*Untermenschen*', sub-human inferior beings, who could not possibly be regarded as comrades. In his insane prejudice, Hitler insisted:

St. Petersburg must . . . disappear utterly from the earth's surface. Moscow too. Then the Russians will retire into Siberia . . . As for the ridiculous hundred million Slavs, we will mould the best of them to the shape that suits us, and we will isolate the rest of them in their own pig-styes; and anyone who talks about cherishing the local inhabitant and civilising him, goes straight off into a concentration camp.[23]

The savagery with which such pronouncements were acted on transformed potential allies into the fiercest of enemies; and the Nazis irrevocably alienated precisely the people – the Soviet soldiers and citizens – who could have guaranteed their triumph. To the men of the Wehrmacht, the stupidity of the Party hierarchy was blindingly self-evident. Stauffenberg 'was especially outraged at the treatment given to Soviet soldiers who had surrendered or been captured; he spoke about this openly and with passion.'[24]

By the spring of 1942, even Goebbels was beginning to see the errors of German policy. In April of that year, he wrote in his diary:

The inhabitants of the Ukraine were at first more than inclined to regard the Führer as the saviour of Europe and to welcome the German Wehrmacht most cordially. This attitude has changed completely in the course of months. We have hit the Russians, and especially the Ukrainians, too hard on the head with our manner of dealing with them. A clout on the head is not always a convincing argument . . .[25]

Just over a month later, he added: 'Personally, I believe we must change our policies essentially as regards the people of the east.'[26] No such change occurred: Hitler, Himmler and the other members of the hierarchy remained blinded by their own benighted theories. A year later, Goebbels wrote again, almost wistfully: 'We would certainly be able to stir up many of the peoples of the U.S.S.R. against Stalin if we knew how to wage war solely against Bolshevism rather than against the Russian people.'[27]

Despite the strictures imposed by Nazi ideology, the Wehrmacht *did* contrive to accommodate Russian prisoners, to employ them for its own purposes and thus spare them from extermination by the SS. At first they were taken on only in small numbers, and only for non-combat tasks – labour battalions, cooks, drivers and sundry auxiliary services – but gradually the numbers increased, and began to be assigned to combat rôles as well. Battalion-sized units were formed, and these were later expanded into 'legions'. While such units were originally confined to non-Russian Soviet soldiers –

Georgians, for example, Lithuanians, Latvians and Estonians – Russian soldiers were also eventually incorporated. There were attempts, too, to find high-ranking Soviet officers who could be employed as propaganda figures, to induce rank-and-file soldiery to desert and take up German arms. For this purpose, two organisations were established, the Russian Liberation Movement, or R.O.D., and the Russian Liberation Army, or R.O.A.[28] The 'army', of course, did not actually exist in practice, but its mere name gave Russians serving with German forces a sense of unity and identity; and they were further encouraged by being given R.O.A. patches and insignia to sew on their uniforms. By the beginning of 1943, between 130,000 and 150,000 Soviet soldiers (some 176 battalions and thirty-eight independent companies) were enrolled in the Wehrmacht. A key figure in recruiting them was Colonel Reinhard Gehlen, one of Halder's senior aides, then chief of intelligence on the Eastern front and eventually, after the war, head of the West German secret service. Working closely with Gehlen were a number of figures – Tresckow, for example – who subsequently would be involved in the conspiracy of 1944. Among Gehlen's most trusted personal friends was Claus von Stauffenberg.

Stauffenberg's position with the General Staff made him more privy than most to the appalling drain and wastage of German manpower. The statistics were becoming daily more alarming. Infantry companies were being reduced from 180 men to a mere eighty. In January 1942 alone, Army Group Centre suffered losses of 95,000 and received only 10,300 replacements. By the autumn, total losses would exceed total reinforcements by 800,000, and this deficit would soon soar to more than a million. On the basis of such figures, one could calculate and project a precise date at which the entire Wehrmacht would quite simply cease to exist.

The Red Army offered an attractive possible solution for Stauffenberg, who was personally saddled with the responsibility of plugging the gaping holes in Germany's troop strength. Not, of course, that he believed a clear-cut German victory against the Soviet Union was any longer possible. He had no illusions about that now. But he thought it feasible that Russian troops could at least be used as a buffer, and perhaps as a German-sponsored instrument in a civil war that might topple Stalin's régime. If nothing else, the stain on the Wehrmacht might be lessened, a respite might be obtained and an opportunity vouchsafed for Germany to restore her ebbing supplies of manpower. There might also arise some prospect of much more grandiose and ambitious designs.

For Stauffenberg, 150,000 Soviet soldiers in German uniform was only the beginning. He was after something more, and knew well enough that it was there for the taking, if only bureaucracy could be neutralised and Nazi prejudice overcome or circumvented. His first step involved wresting Russian prisoners from certain death at the hands of the SS and obtaining direct authority over them. In the past, such captives, when they were enrolled in the Wehrmacht at all, were enrolled on an *ad hoc* basis by individual units; but as their numbers grew and their need for clothing, arms and equipment increased proportionately, Stauffenberg's section of OKH had a legitimate justification for becoming involved. It was soon in sole charge of 'organising into units all former Soviet soldiers who had volunteered to serve in the Wehrmacht'. By virtue of the 'efforts of Stauffenberg and his staff . . . the volunteers were made the responsibility of army headquarters and not the SS'.[29] When Hitler decreed the recruitment of Russian troops to cease, Stauffenberg managed to get the order modified and, in practice, ignored, to such a degree that the Führer had to issue additional orders in the following months. When yet another order definitively forbade all further recruitment, Stauffenberg had it released to the army command three weeks before it took effect, thus enabling recruitment to be accelerated during the intervening time.

Stauffenberg contrived to circumvent not only Hitler, but also lesser minions of the Reich, such as Alfred Rosenberg, the noxious racial theoretician formerly in charge of Nazi ideological training and now Minister for the Occupied Eastern Territories. Like his master, Rosenberg hated Russians, but he persuaded the Führer to sanction recruitment of non-Russian Soviet soldiers. According to Hans von Herwarth:

Making use of the 'discovery' of the SS that the Cossacks were an independent people, Stauffenberg gave orders that they were exempt from Hitler's ban. We in our turn saw to it that the exception was widely publicised. As a result, thousands of

POW's – many of them Russians – took the hint, identified themselves as Cossacks and left the camps.[30]

At the same time Stauffenberg was engaged in an ongoing struggle to ensure that Soviet volunteers received the same treatment as all other Wehrmacht personnel. A civilian observer speaks of a conference in June 1942, at which Stauffenberg 'gave a masterly exposé, ending with an extempore draft of an instruction laying down equality of treatment for the volunteers'. When Hitler proposed a different coloured uniform for the volunteers, Stauffenberg managed to thwart the idea. Hans von Herwarth reports entering Stauffenberg's office one day and seeing an order on his desk to the effect that all Russian prisoners were to be tattooed with an identification mark on the buttocks. Stauffenberg

> quickly telephoned the general who was in a position to reverse the order . . . I listened in amazement as he pressed his case by assuring the general that, when next they met on Unter den Linden . . . he, Stauffenberg, would challenge the general's identity and require him to drop his trousers to prove he was not a Russian captive.[31]

The order was summarily withdrawn.

By the autumn of 1942, Stauffenberg and one of his colleagues had set up an umbrella organisation called the 'Russian Propaganda Section'. Under the auspices of this section, a training programme was instituted: the 'Russian Leadership Centre'. Its personnel were recruited so as to constitute 'a skeleton officer corps'. Stauffenberg 'set great store by getting the right leaders for these units under his care. He did not want them turned into hired and misused auxiliaries, but to form them into freedom-loving battle groups retaining their own customs and traditions.'[32]

Primarily as a result of Stauffenberg's efforts, more than 800,000 Soviet prisoners-of-war were on active service with the Wehrmacht by 1943. It is interesting to speculate on how he himself may have conceived of deploying them. It has been suggested that he may have regarded them as the nucleus of a potential 'third force', which could be utilised against the tyranny of both Stalin *and* Hitler.[33] If they could have stemmed the tide, or at least stabilised the situation, on the Eastern front, they might then have been turned westwards, against the machinery of the Reich itself. Such a hypothesis is intriguing. It is difficult to believe that something of the sort did not, at one time or another, cross Stauffenberg's mind; and some evidence has been adduced to indicate that he was actually trying to implement, if only in embryo, some such design. But he, along with everyone else, was soon to be overtaken by events. By the end of 1942, the situation on the Eastern front was to have become irretrievable, almost entirely as a result of Hitler's own perversity.

In August 1942, the German 6th Army under Field Marshal Friedrich von Paulus, driving far to the south of Moscow, had pushed the Russians into Stalingrad, strategically sited on the Volga. Early in September, Paulus's troops attacked the city's western suburbs, fighting their way through a desperate house-to-house Russian defence. By mid-October, all but three sectors had fallen. Unknown to the Germans, however, the Russians had been secretly reinforced, and more than a million men were now mobilised in the countryside just beyond Stalingrad. On 21 September, while the Germans were still advancing, the first phase of a three-pronged Russian counter-offensive had begun, striking down from the north. The second prong struck from the south on 1 November. On 19 November, a massive artillery barrage inaugurated the third thrust, in the centre. By 23 November, twenty-two German and satellite Italian, Hungarian and Rumanian divisions – some 300,000 men – had been completely encircled.

A German relief force under Field Marshal Erich von Manstein attacked the Russians from the south on 12 December, fighting to within twenty-five miles of Paulus's encircled army. By now Hitler was at his most hysterical. In September, when things had first begun to go wrong, he had petulantly sacked Halder as Chief of the General Staff and appointed a new commander, Colonel-General Kurt Zeitzler. Although certainly competent enough, Zeitzler was reduced to the status of a puppet and the Führer assumed control himself. Now, in one of his increasingly frequent tantrums, he furiously forbade Paulus to break out of the Russian encirclement and link up with Manstein's approaching relief force. German soldiers could not be seen to retreat. They could only go forward. Without Paulus breaking out to reinforce and support it, Manstein's relief force was defeated and compelled to withdraw, while Paulus remained trapped, the ring of

Russian steel closing tightly on him and his surrounded army.

On 8 January 1943, the Russians invited Paulus to surrender. On Hitler's frenzied orders, Paulus refused, and the Russians attacked again two days later. By 16 January, the German 6th Army had been squeezed into a pocket nine miles by fifteen. In a new crescendo of manic rage, Hitler forbade either retreat or surrender. Every German unit was to fight to the last man, and any soldier who did not die in his tracks was guilty of treason, to be punished accordingly. Against starvation, cold, disease and the ferocity of the Russian onslaughts, such menacing fulminations were puerile. On 31 January, Paulus and a pitiful 91,000 troops of the battered 6th Army surrendered. On 2 February, one Panzer corps which had continued to resist was annihilated. That afternoon, a German aircraft flying over the site of the carnage radioed back that all fighting had ceased. Since November, more than 200,000 German soldiers had perished. Of the 91,000 who surrendered, only 5,000 would ever find their way back to the Fatherland.

Stauffenberg had been a friend and admirer of Paulus. He had corresponded sympathetically with the hapless field marshal about the worsening situation at Stalingrad, and the stupidity on Hitler's part which had produced it. On a visit to Germany in mid-January, he met his colleague Lieutenant-Colonel Werner Reerink, who reported Stauffenberg's reaction to the imminent débâcle:

In the evening Stauffenberg took me for a walk through the Mauerwald, since, as he said, one could talk more freely in the open than in the office huts. He told me the detailed story of the vain efforts by OKH to persuade Hitler to order the breakout from Stalingrad and to save the lives of 300,000 men. OKH had been supported by Goebbels, who had shown himself most sensible – he had been the only party man to take the attitude that the German people must be told the truth about Stalingrad and about the general situation. With Goebbels' help they had almost got Hitler to issue the order for the breakout while there was still time. At the decisive briefing conference, however, Goering had taken the floor with the words: 'My Führer, I guarantee that my Luftwaffe will keep the Stalingrad army supplied.' Hitler had thereupon decided: 'Sixth Army will remain in Stalingrad.'

Stauffenberg was totally and obviously shattered by such irresponsible and treacherous behaviour. He told me this in so many words.[34]

Like most other professional military men, Stauffenberg was severely shaken by events at Stalingrad. Defeat in itself would have been tolerable, but this was more than any conventional defeat, since it could have been averted. An entire German army, which in other circumstances could have retreated and lived to fight another day, had been utterly and pointlessly squandered, solely to appease the Führer's vindictive wrath. In the early days of the war, many Germans, including a good many soldiers, had believed Hitler to be endowed with an uncanny intuitive military genius, an unerring aptitude for the decisive stroke that invited comparisons with Napoleon and Frederick the Great. The Russian campaign had called this belief into question. Stalingrad made it all too clear that the Führer was no more than a bloodthirsty amateur, and a fool whose infantile petulance had to be paid for in German lives. Burdened with the responsibility of making good the appalling wastage, Stauffenberg found it difficult to control his temper. On one occasion, when a number of younger staff officers expressed a desire to get away from headquarters and see action at the front, Stauffenberg retorted:

'What is this sham heroism, going and getting yourselves shot like hundreds of thousands of others "in faithful performance of duty". This is nothing but cowardly evasion, no better than the field marshals who make the excuse of their duty to obey and their "purely military outlook". We have to have something quite different. When, by reason of his office or his upbringing, a man reaches high rank, a moment arrives when the man and the job are identical and no second thoughts can weigh with him; it is his duty to represent the general consensus of opinion. How few there are now who behave that way or even feel that they should do so. We have now got butchers and bakers and candlestick makers dressed up as generals. They draw their pay, do their "duty", put their trust in the Führer and look forward to their next leave. What a way to run a country!'[35]

He then recited Stefan George's 'Verses for the Dead', which invoked a time 'when men of the future are purged of dishonour' and 'men of this nation no longer are cowards'.

Stauffenberg was loved, respected, even revered by the younger officers at OKH headquarters. His magnetism and charisma had often held them in thrall. One can imagine the effect produced by George's harsh, stark and incantatory stanzas – especially in the prevailing sombre atmosphere, the pall rendered ever darker with every fresh communiqué from Stalingrad.

As the plight of Paulus's doomed army became grimly apparent, Stauffenberg became more outspoken. After talking to senior officers about the need to confront Hitler with the reality of the situation, he returned, disappointed. To his colleagues, he reported, with exasperation, that their superiors 'are scared shitless or have straw in their heads'.[36] On another occasion, he attended a lecture for some forty staff officers, given by a civilian functionary, on German agricultural policy in the east. At the end of the lecture, Stauffenberg requested permission to speak, then proceeded to do so for half an hour. The lecturer subsequently reported:

> Feeling responsible for the replacement of troops in the east . . . he was watching the disastrous course of Germany's Eastern policy with horror. We were sowing hatred which would one day be avenged on our children. Any examination of the replacement issue made it absolutely clear that victory in the East was possible only if Germany succeeded in winning over the local population . . . the only thing our policy in the East was likely to achieve was to turn the masses there into Germany's enemies. It was scandalous that at a time when millions of soldiers were staking their lives not one of the leaders had the courage to speak to the Führer openly about such matters, though it might be at the risk of his own life.[37]

The lecturer further commented that no one had dared to mention this in public before.

> I was deeply impressed by Stauffenberg's arguments, especially as they were put forward with such conviction that you felt certain he himself had the courage he demanded of the leaders. I was greatly surprised that it was possible to speak so openly in a

circle of General Staff officers, and even more so at the fact that the chairman of the meeting, far from refuting Stauffenberg's criticism, declared that they all felt the same.[38]

By this time, it appears, Stauffenberg's outspokenness was beginning to attract attention in unwelcome quarters. Although he himself had no great respect for Halder's replacement, General Zeitzler, the general regarded him as 'a good future corps and army commander'. Such promising material could not be spared, and on 1 January 1943, Stauffenberg was accordingly promoted to lieutenant-colonel. Almost immediately, and without being consulted on the matter, he was notified of his transfer to the post of Senior Staff Officer (Operations) for the 10th Panzer Division in North Africa. Zeitzler stated officially: 'I wished to give him experience as a staff officer with troops and in command, in order to prepare him for later command of a corps and an army', but the transfer was also clearly motivated by a desire to get the dangerously forthright and explicit 36-year-old officer away from the Eastern front, where he was 'making waves', and as far distant as possible from the clutches of the SS and SD.[39] Stauffenberg himself recognised the necessity for this. Just before departing for North Africa, he remarked: 'It is time I disappeared from here.'[40] And on reporting to his new divisional commander, he stated that German soil 'was slowly becoming too hot' for him.[41]

After his frustrating and demoralising experience with OKH in Russia, North Africa must have seemed a welcome change for Stauffenberg. It offered the prospect of a 'clean war', waged in a traditional, even chivalrous, style, between professional soldiers and commanders who respected each other as adversaries. Compared to other theatres of operation, there were no serious atrocities. There was minimal interference, at least on the ground, from Party bosses, from politicians and even from the Führer. A few Gestapo personnel operated in cities like Casablanca and Tunis, but there were no SS or SD accompanying the troops and pursuing their murderous activities immediately behind the lines.

Despite these attractive considerations, Stauffenberg appears to have been not altogether free of misgivings, or perhaps just a nagging residual sense of guilt. He threw himself with zest into his responsibilities with 10th Panzer Division, but it was almost as if there were something slightly dishonourable in his transfer – an interruption of his ongoing activities elsewhere, an abandonment of his personal crusade, an attempt to evade his destiny. If, in the eyes of the gods, that was indeed the case, he was soon to be punished for it. Within two months, destiny, in the form of a strafing American P-40, was to catch up with him – and place him, maimed and desperately wounded, squarely at the centre of the situation from which North Africa had seemingly offered a refuge.

# Part Four

———

## THE STRUGGLE FOR THE HEART AND SOUL OF GERMANY

# 9

# *After the War of Liberation*

As Robert Musil has stated, the collective impulses, urges, fears, aspirations, yearnings, dreams and tensions of a people or a culture would, if contained in the psyche of a single individual, produce a frothing lunatic. That, of course, applies to all peoples and cultures. Humanity has long known itself to be its own worst enemy. Nevertheless if the psyche of a 'sane' individual cannot accommodate the spectrum of human experience as a whole, it can still provide, in miniature or in microcosm, some indication of the broader logic governing peoples and cultures. Like individuals, people and cultures pass through periods of collective infancy and childhood, adolescence and youth, maturity and adulthood, senescence and decay. Like individuals, peoples and cultures pass through phases of well-being and maladjustment, health and disease, self-confidence and self-doubt, exuberant energy and apathetic torpor. And like individuals, peoples and cultures can undergo agonising identity crises.

In the half-century since the Second World War, the Third Reich has been explained in terms of many kinds of phenomenon – sociological, economic, ideological, psychological. It was, of course, a combination of all of these. But it was a manifestation of something else as well, something much older, and more deeply rooted, than anything arising from the specific circumstances of the late nineteenth and twentieth centuries. It was a manifestation of – and an attempt to resolve – what might be described as a collective identity crisis, an anxious and long-standing quest for self-definition. The resolution posited by the Third Reich can now be seen as misguided, benighted, demonic and thoroughly inimical to humanity. But the problem that engendered it still exists, and remains unresolved. Germany is still in the throes of a collective identity crisis, still in quest of a viable self-definition. The problem has, if anything, become even more acute with the difficulties thrown up by reunification in 1990. If the Third Reich's putative resolution of the problem proved more destructive and disastrous than anything else, Claus von Stauffenberg offers a more positive and constructive alternative, not just for Germany, but for Western society as a whole. In order to see how and why he does, however, the problem itself must be explored more fully.

*

In the early nineteenth century, Prussia began to exert a significant influence on the rest of Germany, and to challenge Austria for the opportunity, if not the right, to mould and shape German politics and the German collective psyche. The struggle between these two powers extended from the Oder in the east to the Rhine in the west, from the Baltic in the north to the Alps in the south. But it was also a psychological struggle enacted in the mentality of individual Germans, and Claus von Stauffenberg was no exception. He, too, provided an arena for the struggle. The struggle continued on both a personal and a cultural level long after it had been decided politically by the Austro-Prussian War of 1866. Ultimately, Austria and Prussia can be seen as metaphors (what T. S. Eliot calls 'objective correlatives') for a polarity in the German collective psyche. Whatever happened on the battlefield or at the negotiating table, Austria and Prussia remained symbolic embodiments of a less tangible, more internalised conflict. In effect, Austria and Prussia were not just geographical or political entities, but also orientations, attitudes and states of mind.

The principle that made Prussia so dynamic a military power in Frederick the Great's time was not nationalism as we know it today, nor even as it existed in other nations at the time. Frederick's soldiers and administrators acted less out of devotion to the state than out of a kind of feudal loyalty to their monarch. Their loyalty was, in effect, not patriotism, but an unquestioning allegiance to a charismatic king. It was not until the Napoleonic era that allegiance was transferred from the sovereign to the state. Prussian (and German) nationalism was, in fact, born out of the conflict with Napoleonic France. That conflict was initially traumatic, then euphorically uplifting – for Germany in general and for Prussia in particular.

Until 1806, Prussia had reposed on the martial laurels won by Friedrich, the 'Soldier King', nearly half a century before. The army of Napoleonic France had proved invincible against Italians, Austrians and Russians, but no one at the time doubted that it would crumble against the Prussian military machine. In the years since Friedrich, however, the Prussian military machine had become slack and lazy, ill-disciplined, ill-led and complacent. It had done nothing to update its tactics or its organisation, nothing to adapt to the new premises and conditions of early nineteenth-century warfare.

On 14 October 1806, the Prussian army engaged the forces of Imperial France in two simultaneous battles. At Jena, the university town adjacent to Weimar and south-west of Leipzig, 53,000 Prussians confronted Napoleon himself and the main body of his army, 96,000 in number. A few miles away, at Auerstadt, some 63,500 Prussians and Saxons engaged a detached wing of the French army, 27,000 strong, under one of Napoleon's marshals. In the two battles, the French suffered some 13,000 casualties. The Prussians suffered three and a half times that number, and another 18,000 were taken prisoner. But Jena and Auerstadt were more than comprehensive military defeats for Prussia. The initially orderly Prussian retreat deteriorated into a total rout; and the army that had so distinguished itself under Frederick the Great disintegrated in headlong flight, abandoning arms, equipment, cohesion and all semblance of martial discipline. By the end of the day, it had ceased to exist as an effective fighting force. Immediately thereafter, other Prussian units surrendered wholesale, and the number of Prussian prisoners soon exceeded 150,000. Towns and fortresses capitulated without resistance; and on 27 October, Napoleon rode in triumph into Berlin, which had been evacuated by the government and left undefended. By mid-November the whole of Prussia was under French control.

The Treaty of Tilsit, signed in July 1807, reduced Prussia to the status of a French satellite – a status similar to that of, say, Czechoslovakia, Hungary or Poland under the post-Second World War Soviet imperium. Prussia was dragooned into a reluctant alliance with Napoleon, and her allegiance was humiliatingly guaranteed by the establishment of French garrisons and officials throughout the country – an arrangement anticipating, albeit with rôles reversed, that which took place in Nazi-dominated France under the Vichy government. The Prussian army was restricted in size to a token 42,000 men.

For all Prussians, the terms of the treaty constituted a mortifying national embarrassment, an ignominious capitulation that shattered national self-esteem. Yet the very intensity of the shame felt attested to a coalescing sense of national identity, something which many Prussians at the time were surprised to discover within themselves.

Stung by his country's abasement, a cavalry major, one Ferdinand von Schill, embarked on his own freelance rebellion. Shortly after the Treaty of Tilsit, Schill formed a partisan cavalry unit, with which he resolved to pursue the war against France independently (just as numerous guerrilla units were shortly to do in Spain). Predictably, Schill's quixotic plans for revolt came to nothing and he died in May 1809, fighting in the streets of the Baltic port of Stralsund, where he had hoped to link up with a British expeditionary force that never materialised. None the less, at a stroke, he became a national hero whose portrait was soon hanging in homes, offices and barracks across the whole of Prussia. He also posed a question which had never arisen in the Prussian military before – whether insubordination, under certain circumstances, might not be justifiable.

Schill's personal martyrdom accomplished nothing, but it paved the way for two subsequent acts of insubordination which were to have much more weighty consequences. These acts were to involve two of Claus von Stauffenberg's ancestors, and came to figure prominently in his mind as august precedents.

At the beginning of 1812, Napoleon began to prepare for his disastrous invasion of Russia. In order to protect his rear, he forced Prussia into an agreement that involved fresh humiliations. The country was obliged to consent to a full-scale military occupation, and was further coerced into making available one corps (nearly half the size of the permitted army) for the French emperor's grand designs. Some 20,000 Prussians were forcibly attached to the French army and ordered to participate, as a covering force, in the invasion of Russia.

In angry reaction to these terms, there took place the mass protest known as the 'Resignation of the Three Hundred'. Led by Gneisenau, Clausewitz and a number of others, three hundred prominent and high-ranking officers resigned from the Prussian Officer Corps – almost a quarter of the corps' total strength. Some of them, like Clausewitz, even fled to Russia and enlisted in the Tsar's service. Although the resignations were not officially branded an act of mutiny, that is what they were.

Prussian defiance did not stop there. Gerhard von Scharnhorst, Gneisenau's colleague, had also attempted to resign. His resignation was refused, but he was allowed to relinquish his position as Chief of the General Staff. As Napoleon's invasion force marched eastwards, Scharnhorst, working within the Prussian military administration, and Gneisenau, acting outside it, undertook to build an entirely new Prussian army: a 'citizens' army' this time, no longer dominated by the old Junker aristocracy, with noble pedigrees no longer being required for commissions and promotion being based, as in France, on merit. Under the very noses of the occupying French, a new, secret and shadowy Prussian army was clandestinely created and mobilised – not a mere guerrilla force, but a full-fledged military machine intended to take the field and meet its adversaries in pitched battle. This process of martial reconstruction was implemented in flagrant breach of all signed treaties with France, and in clear defiance of the government and King Friedrich Wilhelm III.

While Prussia's 'citizens' army' was quietly mustering in his rear, Napoleon continued his advance into Russia. On 7 September 1812, the French Grande Armée engaged the Russians at the bloody Battle of Borodino, depicted by Tolstoy in *War and Peace*. Borodino was technically a French victory but losses on both sides were enormous, and while the Russians could afford such casualties, the invaders – as Hitler was to learn 130 years later – could not. With his maimed and depleted troops, Napoleon entered Moscow a week later, only to find the city – where he had hoped to rest, regroup and replenish his forces – evacuated and set aflame. Deprived of food, shelter and the anticipated respite, he embarked, on 19 October, on his retreat back to France. This retreat lasted through all the depredations of the Russian winter, and was harried constantly by regular Russian units, as well as by partisan guerrillas.

The withdrawing Grande Armée reached Prussian territory in December. Invoking his agreement with the Prussian government, Napoleon requested a Prussian corps to cover his retreat and delay the advance of the pursuing Russians. The corps placed at his disposal was commanded by another of Stauffenberg's ancestors, Hans Ludwig Yorck von Wartenburg.

On 30 December 1812, Yorck negotiated and concluded a secret agreement of his own with the Russians at Tauroggen. Having signed it, he said to the officers of his staff:

'Gentlemen, I do not know what I shall say to the king about my action. Perhaps he will call it treason. If so, I shall carry the consequences.'[1]

Then, acting entirely on his own initiative, without having received any orders or informed his superiors, he officially declared his soldiers to be neutral and withdrew them from all operations. According to one commentator:

'This was the most signal act of insubordination in Prussian history and, in the context of the moment, next door to a coup d'état, inasmuch as it virtually compelled the government in Berlin to take the logical next step and declare war on France.'[2]

Confronted with Yorck's *fait accompli*, Berlin declared war on 16 March. No longer neutral by then, Yorck's corps was already in combat, aligned with the Russians against the retreating French. At the same time, the 'citizen army' raised in secret by Gneisenau, Scharnhorst and their colleagues broke cover, took the field and joined Yorck's regulars, bringing the Prussian deployment up to maximum strength. The combined Russian and Prussian forces, soon to be reinforced by Austrians and Swedes, proceeded to harry the Grande Armée's beleaguered veterans across Germany and back into France. Here, they linked up with Wellington's British army advancing from Spain across the Pyrenees, and forced Napoleon to abdicate.

Prompted by Yorck's audacious action, Prussia had, in effect, undergone a kind of revolution, perhaps unprecedented in European history: it had not been implemented from below, by the masses, nor had it been a palace coup. It had been forged by a unique alliance between the Prussian populace, particularly the peasantry and aristocracy, against their government and their king, compelling the reluctant régime to enter the war against its own wishes. No one was unduly concerned about the legitimacy of the enterprise. According to Prussian nobles at the time, 'we were here before the Hohenzollern'; and this, of course, applied to the peasantry as well. One is reminded of the revolts of Luther's time, when both peasants and Free Knights of the Empire defied the authority of their imperial master, Charles V.

Yorck's independent action and Prussia's subsequent declaration of war inaugurated what became known as the War of Liberation, and it liberated not just Prussia, but the whole of Germany, from the occupying French. It left the country with a new, well-trained and immensely powerful army, reconstructed along the lines defined by Gneisenau, Scharnhorst and their colleagues. When Napoleon, after his first abdication, escaped from Elba and took the field again, it was this army that mobilised first among the continental powers. Commanded officially by the aged Marshal Blücher, but with Gneisenau as Chief of Staff and making the major strategic decisions, it was this army that came to Wellington's aid at Waterloo.

The War of Liberation triggered a wave of euphoria, verging on hysteria, throughout the whole of Germany. This was something the country had never hitherto experienced. For the first time, the focus of loyalty was not the monarch – indeed, the monarch had been defied, circumvented and rendered impotent – but Prussia, and, beyond Prussia, Germany. Prussia and Germany were embraced and extolled with as much fanatical fervour as if they were new discoveries; and service in their cause was espoused with a rapture verging on the messianic. Men of all ages, of all classes, from all quarters of Germany, rallied exuberantly to the colours. The martial traditions of Frederick the Great were revived and whipped up into a *Zeitgeist*. So numerous was the influx of recruits that not even the new and expanded Prussian army could accommodate them. Paramilitary organisations sprang up, composed of over-zealous youths parading extravagant uniforms and protuberant military ineptitude. War fever raged, and not even the rigorous discipline instituted by Scharnhorst and Gneisenau could altogether contain it.

The campaigns of 1813, 1814 and 1815 midwifed the birth of a German nationalism which bore a distinctly Prussian and militaristic stamp. Although Austria had also re-entered the conflict against France, her army had performed lamely all through the Napoleonic Wars, and continued to do so now. As far as the German principalities were concerned, Austria had been relegated to a peripheral rôle. It was Prussia that first rose in revolt, Prussia that fielded the effective soldiery, Prussia that served as the beacon, the tutelary genius, the guiding spirit and principle. It was from Prussia that the greatest energy and enthusiasm emanated, and Prussia that therefore provided the primary inspiration.

Amid the martial hysteria sweeping Germany, one voice was raised in opposition. It was nevertheless a voice which, for more than a generation, had exerted an influence across the whole of Europe and even Britain, a voice which spoke with a godlike authority and had appointed itself the voice of the German people. The voice was that of Johann Wolfgang von Goethe.

It is difficult for us today, in the world of mass media and celebrities of a very different order, to appreciate the magnitude of Goethe's influence and the Olympian status he enjoyed. Cultural commentators and critics invariably compare him to Shakespeare or to Pushkin. Except perhaps for Tolstoy, no literary figure since Goethe has exercised such authority or received such widespread acclaim. His work and thought dominated the whole of European literature for nearly half a century and his influence is discernible in writers as diverse as Byron, Shelley, Poe, Melville, Pushkin, Gogol, Dostoevsky, Chateaubriand and Victor Hugo. While Pushkin was a folk hero to the Russian people (after his death, 32,000 people a day filed past his home in Petersburg), Goethe was venerated with an almost religious zeal. To the German people, he was their universally acknowledged 'Great Man', their claim to fame, their spokesman to the world, their collective voice.

Goethe's influence extended far beyond literature. He was

considered a leading statesman, philosopher, critic and scientist. His work and thought encompassed virtually the whole of human endeavour; and he commanded as much respect from such men as Alexander von Humboldt, the distinguished explorer and scientist, as he did from the artistic world. He has often been described as 'the last Renaissance man'.

Tsar Alexander I had met him and honoured him with the Order of Saint Anne. Napoleon, too, had met him and conferred on him the Cross of the Legion of Honour. He and the French emperor formed their own mutual admiration society. Each saw in the other an image of himself. Goethe was the Napoleon of arts, letters, culture, the life of the spirit, while Napoleon was the Goethe of politics, diplomacy and war. Both were flattered by the comparison.

And Goethe – this imperious Olympian figure in the sphere of the mind – was implacably hostile to German nationalism. His antipathy rested not on conventional social or political grounds, but on grounds of self-definition and national identity.

★

What does it 'mean' to be 'English'? It is doubtful that many Englishmen have asked themselves that question. For those who have, the answer would probably consist of a helpless shrug of the shoulders, seeming so self-evident as to defy verbal formulation. Or it would consist of clichéd and stereotyped traits or characteristics – the 'stiff upper lip', for instance. But these are descriptions of attributes. They do not answer the question of what being English actually 'means'.

For centuries, there has been no need to question the 'meaning' of being English, and the question itself has become meaningless. Being English is something taken for granted. So, too, is being French. Thus, for example, the major English novelists of the nineteenth century – Jane Austen, George Eliot, Dickens, Thackeray, Meredith, Trollope – will examine English society, English manners and mores, and the English character, but they will not probe the nature of the English 'soul'. Similarly, whatever the concerns of Balzac, Stendhal, Flaubert, Zola and Victor Hugo, the French 'soul' is not among them.

Such complacency is not as universal as most Englishmen and Frenchmen automatically and unwittingly assume. There are other cultures and peoples for whom the problem of self-definition has been an incessant source of uncertainty, of anxiety – a matter not unlike that of a youth passing through the familiar 'identity crisis', and tormenting himself with baffling, seemingly unfathomable enigmas. 'Who am I?' 'What is this "thing", this elusive and mysterious "entity", that I call my "self"?' 'What is my true nature?' 'Why am I here?' 'What is the purpose of my existence?' 'How can I determine – if such a thing exists at all – what constitutes my "destiny"?' 'What is the character of my soul, assuming such a thing exists, and how does it differ from other people's?' Such questions may not seem in the least applicable to the fact of being English or French. For centuries, however, they have been of obsessive relevance to the fact of being Russian or German. Unlike Englishmen or Frenchmen, Russians and Germans have consistently been tortured by the 'meaning' of being what they are. The nature of the 'German soul' has preoccupied German writers from Goethe, through Thomas Mann, to Günter Grass and Siegfried Lenz, and the 'Russian soul' has preoccupied Russian writers from Pushkin, through Dostoevsky, Tolstoy and Andrey Bely, to Andrey Bitov today.

At a number of points in their respective histories, Germany and Russia have seen themselves as a kind of frontier. Each has considered itself a demarcation line between conflicting principles – between west and east, between culture and barbarism, between rationality and irrationality. Each has deemed itself an arbiter between these principles, burdened with the responsibility, even the mission, of reconciling and synthesising them. More often than not, this has meant the subordination of one principle to another, which led to grotesque imbalances and disastrous consequences. For the matter cannot be reduced to a simplistic form based – as it usually is – on facile value judgements.

Rationality, for example, can indeed be a positive force, associated with culture, civilisation, sanity, order, moderation, tolerance and humanity. But it also has its negative aspects: aridity, sterility, desiccated legalism, 'soulless bureaucracy', uniformity and a mechanical adherence to logic. 'Sweet reason' can only too easily find its apotheosis in the computer, or in such vacuous utopias as those of *Brave New World* and *1984*.

Conversely, irrationality can be a negative force associated with barbarism, madness, chaos, anarchy, intolerance, a frenzied orgiastic abandonment and 'bestiality'. Yet it has positive aspects, too: tenderness, affection, passion, intuition, imagination, inspiration, vitality, spontaneity, creative energy. None of these things originates in rationality. Only too often it stifles them.

Since Peter the Great's time at the dawn of the eighteenth century, Russia has sought to impose the structures of Western rationality on a people for whom such structures were often alien, even inimical. The revolution of 1917 ushered in a régime that was yet more rational, derivative from alien sources, and out of touch with the reality of the domain it sought to rule. In consequence, Russia's rationality – imported first from French philosophers of the so-called 'Enlightenment', then from Marx – has consistently proved a fragile and brittle thing. Andrey Bely, the greatest Russian novelist of the twentieth century, builds his most important work, *St. Petersburg*, around a single central symbol – Peter the Great's rigorously geometric, rectilinear, logical and systematic city artificially constructed on the amorphous, undifferentiated foundation of a swamp. This metaphor, for Bely, sums up the relationship between rationality and irrationality in Russia, between consciousness and the unconscious, between the régime and its subjects. The façade of ordered and rational Western civilisation rests precariously on a quagmire of something much more instinctive, inchoate, emotional and temperamental – something which can perhaps be dominated by the superstructure of reason, but never ultimately shaped or transformed by it.

Bely was writing on the eve of the Russian Revolution. By that time, Germany had been wrestling with essentially the same problem, the relationship between rationality and irrationality, for considerably longer – since Luther's era at least, if not since the Middle Ages. Germany, after all, was the frontier between the high civilisation of ancient Rome and Eastern 'barbarism'. It was the 'end of the world', or, at least, the end of the European world. What lay beyond seemed as forbidding, as mysterious, as vast, as intimidating, as inimical as the Atlantic, seen from, say, the west coast of Ireland. In his most famous work, *The Demons*, the Austrian

novelist Heimito von Doderer describes the reactions of the
Teutonic mind when first confronted with the seemingly endless
vacancy to the east – the vacancy of the Hungarian plain, the Russian
steppe. The Teutonic mind, Doderer says, is numbed and overwhelmed by disquiet, by an intimation of the numinous, whether
sub-rational or supra-rational.

Even more than Russians, Germans saw their country as a focal
point, the European nerve centre where the currents of East and
West, as well as the characteristics symbolically associated with
each, converged. Among other things, this dictated a different
orientation in gender. Despite the rational structures imposed first
by Peter, then by Lenin and Stalin, Russia remained for her people a
feminine and maternal entity – 'Mother Russia'. Germany veered
towards a masculine, patriarchal and paternalistic collective identity
– the 'Fatherland'. Despite this, for Germany as for Russia, the
irrational continued to lurk precariously close to the surface, liable at
any moment to erupt and usurp dominion. The more urgently the
German psyche endeavoured to distance itself from the irrational,
the closer it approached. Why this should be is a complex matter,
requiring some explanation.

The human creative activity which appeals most obviously to
rationality is philosophy. From classical Greece onwards, philosophy has been seen as a unique adjunct of 'higher' civilisations
based on reason. (Until very recently, philosophy encompassed
science and mathematics, both of which are no longer classified
among the 'Humanities'.)

The human creative activity which appeals most obviously to the
irrational is music. Music is not a unique attribute of 'higher'
civilisations. It plays a prominent rôle in the most 'primitive' and
'barbaric'.

Is it coincidental that Germanic culture, during the formative
eighteenth and nineteenth centuries, should dominate both
philosophy and music? France, it is true, produced Descartes;
Holland and Denmark produced Spinoza and Kierkegaard, respectively – but no European culture can muster a parade of luminaries
to equal Leibnitz, Kant, Hegel, Schelling, Fichte, Schopenhauer and
Nietzsche. Nor can any European culture match, in music, Bach,
Handel, Haydn, Mozart, Beethoven, Brahms and Wagner.

Even *within* the respective spheres of philosophy and music, Germanic culture spans a greater spectrum than any other. No Western philosopher appeals to rationality more than Kant or Hegel. No philosopher embraces and extols the irrational more than Schopenhauer or Nietzsche. No composer is more rational than Bach, and none is more extravagantly irrational than Wagner.

Germanic culture and the Germanic collective psyche are stretched tightly between opposite extremes, the supremely rational and the supremely irrational. This spectrum can be visualised as a taut elastic band. From a clinical point of view, such tension, were it situated in an individual psyche, would amount to a state of chronic hysteria – a nervous system so highly strung that it constantly twangs like a banjo string. And when the string, or the elastic band, snaps, the effect is inevitably violent – a recoil to one or the other pole of the spectrum. Thus, every intensification of rationality stretches the continuum more strenuously, rendering it all the more liable to fray, to snap and recoil violently to the opposite extreme, the irrational.

In *Doctor Faustus*, perhaps the most profound and penetrating examination of Nazi Germany so far to have been written, Thomas Mann proposes an alternative model for understanding the problem. Mann maintains that rationality and irrationality need not be seen as opposite poles of a continuum, nor even as existing on a linear continuum at all. The continuum between rationality and irrationality can just as readily be seen as circular – in which case, rationality and irrationality flow into one another. Indeed, it is precisely the most extreme hyper-rationality that lies closest to the irrational.

Above and beyond all schematic models, there lies the phenomenon of the Third Reich itself, which reflects a disquieting mélange, unique in modern history, of rational and irrational. It is precisely this mélange that renders the Third Reich so terrifying and so apparently inexplicable in 'reasonable' terms. At Nazi Party rallies – in the mass hysteria, the ecstatic rapture, the mindless chanting, the torchlight processions, the hypnotic ritualistic pageantry and ceremonial, the rhythmic incantatory rhetoric as mesmerising as a drumbeat – the irrational holds triumphant sway. Rationality attains a monstrous apotheosis in the death camps, where mass murder and genocide are transformed into a mechanical bureaucratic process, a drearily routine matter of engineering, accountancy and book-keeping. Often, too, rationality mantles itself with the irrational fervour, energy and power of a religious appeal, as in Goebbels' cunningly constructed propaganda, the machiavellian manipulation of popular yearning for a messiah figure. And irrationality masks itself with a semblance of rational scientific respectability in Nazi racial theories, in dogma about Aryan superiority, in crack-brained concepts of purity of blood, in an infatuation with 'hollow earth' concepts and Hoerbiger's doctrines of 'fire and ice'. Few institutions in the course of human history have equalled the SS in the smooth-working precision and efficiency of its murderousness. Yet the SS, that epitome of rational methodology and competence, encouraged its personnel to procreate on the gravestones of illustrious Germans of the past, in order that the children thus spawned might somehow 'absorb' something of a dead hero's qualities. So 'rationally' was this bizarre premise spread that the official SS newspaper published lists of gravestones on which copulation was recommended.[3]

If the Third Reich's fusion of rational and irrational is disquieting to the 'civilised' modern Western mind, it is not without precedent in Judaeo-Christian tradition. Indeed, the very precedent it subliminally evokes may have much to do with the disquiet it engenders. For it is precisely in the volatile, mercurial relationship between rationality and irrationality that the Third Reich conforms to traditional Judaeo-Christian concepts of the devil. Christian theologians have never satisfactorily determined exactly who or what their devil ultimately is – what principles he reflects, what energy he embodies. At times, in the history of Christendom, he is the lineal descendant (or reincarnation) of horned, goat-tailed and cloven-hoofed Pan, avatar of 'unregenerate nature', of man's unredeemed 'lower' or 'bestial' self, of anarchy, chaos, orgiastic abandonment, frenzied intoxication. The very word 'Pandemonium' was originally one of the names for hell. Thus does 'Pandemonium' figure in Milton's *Paradise Lost*. But if Pan is one variant of the Judaeo-Christian devil, there is also another – the suave and cunning 'tempter', the sleek master logician, the adept of insidious sophistry and casuistry who could out-Jesuit a Jesuit, the 'fallen angel' who fell originally through the sin of 'intellectual pride'. These conflicting and seemingly irreconcilable identities have characterised the devil throughout the course of Christian theological history. It is these identities that are mirrored by the Third Reich. Thus does the Third Reich figure symbolically in Mann's *Doctor Faustus*. Thus – still symbolically but even more explicitly – does it figure in Luchino Visconti's film *The Damned*.

# 10
## *Culture and Conquest*

Johann Wolfgang von Goethe was born in 1749, seven years after Frederick the Great ascended the throne of the still-fledgling Kingdom of Prussia. He died in 1832, seventeen years after the Battle of Waterloo, when Prussia was solidly established as one of Europe's 'great powers' and already outbidding Austria for the 'heart and soul' of Germany. He did not live to witness the events and personalities that shaped Germany and the German people during the last two-thirds of the nineteenth century. Nevertheless, his life spanned a crucial and formative period of German history; and for much of his life, his position and status enabled him to exert a significant influence on German attitudes and thought. Like Mann a century later, Goethe regarded himself as sophisticated, cosmopolitan, 'European'. At the same time, and again like Mann, he felt himself to be utterly and distinctively German. Both men used their understanding of the relationship between Germany and the world beyond to investigate the qualities of German self-definition and cultural identity, and both were obsessed with the nature of the 'German soul'. For Goethe, the 'German soul' was largely uncharted terrain, inviting exhaustive exploration.

Confronted with the emergence of German nationalism during the War of Liberation, Goethe was alarmed. The German people, he had concluded, could not be trusted with political responsibility. They were unsuited, he felt, for political activity; and nationalism, in their hands, could only be misused. Why should this be so? In part, Goethe believed, because the Germans, unlike other major European peoples, were claustrophobically hemmed in and effectively land-locked. Their outlets to the Atlantic were restricted, and the Baltic was a tamed, domesticated sea. How then, Goethe wondered, could the German people find space in which to expand, extend themselves, reach outwards? In what direction could they hope to aspire, to express and fulfil man's inherent yearning to overreach and transcend himself, to probe new frontiers, to conquer new dominions? For Germany, hemmed in and land-locked as she was, such an impulse, if translated into political terms, must necessarily assume the form of territorial expansion, and this would inevitably lead to militaristic aggression.

For Goethe, there was only one domain in which the German people could safely and validly reach out and extend themselves – the domain of culture and the spirit. Germany, Goethe maintained, was a nation not in any conventional political sense, but in spirit and culture. As an embodiment of these principles, the German people could be a beacon to the entire world, surpassing even the achievements of France, believed at the time to be the *ne plus ultra* of civilisation. If the German people's energy and resources were translated into political reality instead, they could be dangerous. If they were converted to a political reality oriented towards petty nationalism, they could be more dangerous still. And if nationalism were embraced under the aegis of Prussian militarism, the results would be catastrophic – not immediately, perhaps, but unquestionably within the span of a century.

Translated into modern terminology, Goethe felt that German nationalism, especially if pursued through Prussian militarism, could not possibly accommodate the spectrum encompassed by the German collective psyche – the spectrum running from the irrational to the hyper-rational. By all means, he insisted, let Germany and the German people lead the world in philosophy, in music, in the arts, in creative endeavours that served to express and transmit culture and the spirit. Let rationality and irrationality contend with each other, cohabit, remain in opposition or achieve equilibrium in that sphere. Let Germany establish a cultural and spiritual imperium analogous to the political imperium of Napoleonic France; but for her own sake, as well as for that of the civilised world, Germany must not attempt to compete in the arena of politics and war.

France, under Napoleon, aspired to European, if not world, domination, but Napoleon was no Hitler, and his aspirations were tempered by moderation, by adherence to a rigorous legal code, by a sense of responsibility and by humanity. Should Germany develop aspirations to political domination, Goethe questioned whether they would be so tempered. The Germans, he feared, would prove incapable of controlling themselves, incapable of self-restraint. In consequence, he saw the energies released by the War of Liberation as tantamount to a genie escaping from a bottle – a genie that would assume a form similar to Frankenstein's monster.

In retrospect, of course, one can appreciate Goethe's foresight. One can also recognise how his insistence on spiritual and cultural leadership, if allied to social and political ambition, could themselves become pernicious, providing a foundation for a theology of racial supremacy. At the time, however, Goethe's pronouncements only threw many educated Germans into a quandary, and fostered an incipient collective schizophrenia.

In 1813, when the War of Liberation erupted and a new Prussian army rose phoenix-like from the remnants of the old, Goethe was already in his sixty-fourth year. For more than a quarter of a century, he had been a minister, then '*Geheimrat*' or Privy Councillor, of the tiny Duchy of Saxe-Weimar-Eisenach, a minor principality in itself, little more than a Ruritanian city-state. But Weimar was closely associated with the powerful Kingdom of Prussia, and Goethe's influence extended far beyond Weimar itself – to Prussia and beyond, to the whole of Germany. As a result he loomed even larger in German consciousness than had Frederick the Great sixty years before.

When the armies created and led by Yorck and Gneisenau took the field, they found themselves pitted not just against the French, but against the voice of Goethe – the voice of a veritable oracle and demi-god. On the one hand, then, Germans were confronted by the authoritative voice of their collective father-figure, admonishing them and offering his own idealised vision of a nation and people dedicated to culture and the spirit. On the other hand, they were seduced by the feverish hysteria of war and its promises of martial glory, a newly discovered collective identity, a nationalistic self-definition based on prowess at arms, an exhilarating atmosphere of fraternity and solidarity. Many Germans, and not just the well-educated, were faced with a painful moral dilemma; and whatever the choice they made, they were to be haunted by guilt and self-recrimination for the path not taken.

In the end there could only be one conclusion. Goethe's voice was drowned out by the intoxication and militaristic euphoria sweeping the country; and for Germany's youth at the time – a generation he prided himself on having shaped and moulded – he was supplanted as 'rôle model' by the likes of Gneisenau and Yorck. Young Germans of 1813 no longer dreamed of becoming great composers, poets or philosophers, but only of becoming great soldiers, great warriors. The achievements of the Prussian army during the last two years of the Napoleonic Wars, while not perhaps as dazzling as later commentators claimed, were still impressive enough to justify pride and self-congratulation. Goethe's indifference to such things was perplexing and often offensive. A few actually dared to accuse him of treason. Even old friends and protégés were upset. One, for example, a Prussian officer, visited him in the autumn of 1813, shortly after the triumphant Battle of Leipzig, and found that

> there was, frankly, one thing that did not now greatly appeal to me about Goethe, and that was his lack of patriotic enthusiasm about our recent brilliant victories and the expulsion of Napoleon from Germany. Towards all this he maintained a remarkably cool and critical attitude, and even waxed very eloquent in the praise of the Emperor Napoleon's many brilliant qualities.[1]

Stung by criticism, Goethe replied, but in a characteristically haughty and ambiguous way that did little to appease his detractors:

> Don't think for a minute that I am indifferent to great ideals such as freedom, the nation, the fatherland. No; we carry these ideals within us; they are part of our nature, and no man can divest himself of them. Moreover, I am deeply interested in Germany. It has often been a bitter grief for me to think of the German people, so praiseworthy in its individuals and so pitiful as a whole.[2]

More than anything else, Goethe seems to have felt embittered, seeing himself deposed as the unofficial potentate presiding over German thought. The German people seemed to him like wayward and unruly children, defying the sage advice of their self-appointed but universally acknowledged father. Prompted less probably by paternal solicitude than by petulance and spite, he flaunted his personal power by pulling strings and ensuring that his own son, August, was banned from service in the field. August suffered grievously in consequence, incurring accusations of favouritism, weakness and cowardice. The opprobrium visited upon him by his now uniformed, booted and spurred contemporaries drove him to alcoholism and an early death. For this and for everything else, Goethe never really forgave the German people. During the remainder of his life, he was to be accoladed as a titan throughout Europe, but his relationship with Germany was to constitute a state of armed neutrality.

His legacy, however, was to endure. During what remained of the nineteenth century and during the first decade of the twentieth, German artists and thinkers repeatedly invoked the ideal of a nation dedicated not to political or territorial ambitions, but to culture and the spirit. Among the most prominent early exponents of this ideal was a Jew, Heinrich Heine (1797–1856). After Goethe and Hölderlin, Heine was the greatest German poet of the nineteenth century. In the years following Goethe's death, he assumed his predecessor's unofficial mantle of national bard. Even more than Goethe, Heine saw himself as a 'citizen of the world' – indeed, it was he who coined that phrase – and spent much of his life in exile. Like Goethe, he immersed himself in scrutiny of the 'German soul' and its relation to Western culture, to Western civilisation and Christianity. And like Goethe, Heine issued repeated warnings about the dangers of German, and especially Prussian, nationalism.

In one famous passage, Heine inveighs against the uniquely Germanic demagogue-thinker who 'will be terrible because he allies himself with the primitive powers of nature, can conjure up the demonic forces of ancient German pantheism'.[3] Such a figure, he warns, will kindle 'that lust for battle which we find among the ancient Germans and which fights not in order to destroy, nor in order to win, but simply in order to fight'.[4] Christianity constitutes a bulwark against this dangerous impulse, but a fragile one.

Christianity – and this is its finest merit – subdued to a certain extent that brutal Germanic lust for battle, but could not destroy it, and if some day that restraining talisman, the Cross, falls to pieces, then the savagery of the old warriors will explode again, the mad berserker rage about which the Nordic poets have told so much. This talisman is decaying, and the day will come when it will sorrily disintegrate. The old stone gods will then arise from the forgotten ruins and wipe the dust of centuries from their eyes, and Thor will at last leap up with his giant hammer and smash the Gothic cathedrals.[5]

Stressing the distinction between the world of the mind and the world of politics, Heine goes on to admonish the rest of Europe:

Don't smile at the visionary who expects in the realm of reality the same revolution that has taken place in the realm of the intellect. The thought precedes the deed as lighting precedes thunder. German thunder is of course truly German: it is not very nimble but rumbles along rather slowly. It will come, though, and if some day you hear a crash such as has never been heard before in world history, you will know the German thunder has finally reached its mark . . . A play will be performed in Germany compared with which the French Revolution might seem merely an innocent idyll . . .[6]

\*

Goethe's ideal – cultural and spiritual achievement taking precedence over politics and nationalism – was promulgated by Heine and others not just in Germany, but in Austria and the old Habsburg imperium as well. For most of Germany, however, and especially for Prussia, the first intoxicating draught of nationalistic fervour had proved addictive, and there could be no going back. In the aftermath of the Napoleonic Wars, the Prussian army grew into the largest and most powerful military machine in Europe west of the Russian frontier; and, having redressed the humiliation of Jena and Auerstadt with such victories as Leipzig, it proceeded to deck itself anew with the laurels of Frederick the Great's time. Yet nationalism in Germany was now no longer dependent solely on emotional fervour and the instinctual solidarity fostered by war. It was beginning to evolve a persuasive rationale, to establish itself on a solid, respectable and imposing philosophical foundation.

When Goethe first embarked on his literary career in the 1770s, his closest friend and collaborator was the writer, aesthetician and philosopher Johann Gottfried Herder (1744–1803). Herder developed in the young Goethe a pantheistic love and reverence for nature and the natural world. He opened Goethe's eyes to the beauty, power and resonance of folk tales, folk songs and folk poetry. He extolled Shakespeare, Homer and the Ossian poems of James Macpherson, and developed a concept for which he coined the term '*Volksgeist*', usually translated as 'folk soul'.

For Herder, history was not shaped or determined by a human agency. It was the working out, and manifestation, of divine or cosmic principles or laws. These expressed themselves through the folk soul of cultures and peoples. The folk soul was a people's collective soul and destiny. Its relationship to the divine was ultimately analogous to that of the individual soul. It constituted a connecting link and conduit between heaven and earth. Through the folk soul, mystical energies, the *vertu*, the ordained destiny with which the cosmos had impregnated a particular soil could find expression in the human spirit and thence return to the cosmos, thereby closing the circle and creating – or attesting to – universal harmony. As Herder conceived it, the process amounted to a mystical or spiritual equivalent of photosynthesis.

Every people, according to Herder, had its own unique and distinctive folk soul. He did not presume to extol any one folk soul over another; for Herder, this would have seemed as absurd as ascribing an intrinsic superiority to a particular individual soul. So far as Herder was concerned, each folk soul was valid; each possessed its own traits, its own propensities, its own strengths and weaknesses, its own generic qualities; and if he himself had any personal sympathies for a specific folk soul, it was for England's, not Germany's. Essentially, Herder's conception of the folk soul was not significantly different from what this book has called 'national identity' or 'the collective psyche', except that Herder attached to his conception a sacred, mystical, divinely ordained character.

If Herder accorded no intrinsic superiority to the German folk soul, other people could – and the War of Liberation offered grounds on which to do so. Herder was dead by that time, and in no position to object when his conception was appropriated and conscripted on behalf of nationalism, chauvinism and a xenophobia hostile to anything foreign. When it was yoked to these things, the conception of the folk soul provided a seemingly respectable philosophical foundation for theories of racial supremacy. Goethe's ideas were vulnerable in the same way. Despite his insistence on the universality of culture, he himself could be cited as proof of the supremacy of Germanic culture. With the nationalistic self-confidence engendered by the War of Liberation, Germanic culture, as a manifestation of the Germanic folk soul, was soon being trumpeted as superior to others. And if, as Goethe maintained, the Germans were a people uniquely qualified to reflect or represent culture and the spirit, that too constituted a claim to superiority.

Out of this arose the nineteenth-century cult of '*das Volk*' ('the People') and an elaborate '*Volkische*' ideology. *Das Volk* did not mean 'the masses' in any socialist or Marxist sense. Neither did it imply socialist or Marxist class distinctions. And it entailed something diametrically opposed to the materialism of socialist and Marxist thought. The War of Liberation allowed *das Volk* to be put forward as an heroic collective entity, cosmically or divinely ordained to manifest the power of the folk, fulfil a national destiny and shatter the yoke of Napoleonic tyranny. The 'people' denoted by *das Volk* were thus imbued with a numinous quality, a mystical dimension, a status mantled with the sacred. In *das Volk*, nationalism acquired a religious mandate and ratification.

> Idealized and transcendant, the Volk symbolized the desired unity beyond contemporary reality . . . The Volk provided a more tangible vessel for the life force that flowed from the cosmos . . . Volkish thought made the Volk the intermediary between man and the 'higher reality'.[7]

Unlike the urban proletariat exhorted to unite by Marx, *das Volk* were essentially rural and deeply rooted in the sacred national soil, to which they were inseparably bound by the folk soul.

The landscape thus became a vital part of the definition of the Volk . . . Man was not seen as a vanquisher of nature, nor was he credited with the ability to penetrate the meaning of nature by applying the tools of reason; instead he was glorified as living in accordance with nature, at one with its mystical forces.[8]

In other words, the relationship between *das Volk* and the soil harked back to an archaic, atavistic and pre-Christian symbiosis – the volcanic pagan energy which, as Heine had warned, lurked latent beneath the brittle crust of German society, and was liable at any moment to erupt. For the adherents of '*Volkische*' ideology, however, this energy was not destructive, but laudably dynamic, an assertion of strength, durability and solidarity.

What was more, the essentially 'rooted' nature of *das Volk*, the symbiotic rapport between people and soil, rendered 'rootlessness' reprehensible. If rootedness in the soil was a virtue, lack of roots had necessarily to be seen as a vice, testifying to lack of harmony, to something alien and artificial, to a disruption of the mystical natural order. Rootlessness became synonymous with restlessness and was stigmatised as a threat to '*Volkische*' stability. Foreigners were one embodiment of this threat. The migratory urban proletariat was another. There were also, of course, Germany's Jews, emancipated relatively recently and now prospering. In '*Volkische*' ideology, the Jew was the very incarnation of rootlessness. The 'Wandering Jew' could only too easily be identified as the natural adversary of '*das Volk*', the inimical outsider and stranger, the unwelcome intruder. Thus the ground was prepared for later anti-Semitism.

Prompted by an identity crisis similar to Germany's, and equally seeking a post-Napoleonic self-definition, Russia was experiencing the same developments. A comparable version of the folk soul was being extolled, and a mystical rapport between people and soil exalted. Hostility was displayed towards foreigners, 'alien' influences were deplored, and a uniquely national 'purity', in this case Slavic, was sought. And in Russia, too, the seeds of anti-Semitism were being sown. The '*Volkische*' movement in Germany, also know as pan-Aryanism, had a counterpart in Russia known as pan-Slavism. Like their contemporaries in Germany, adherents of pan-Slavism disseminated a kind of racial supremacy, and ascribed to their people a sacred 'mission' of 'world historic' import. Among the most prominent exponents of pan-Slavism were the mystical philosopher Vladimir Solovyov and, of course, Fyodor Dostoevsky.

In Germany, the leading early exponent of '*Volkische*' ideology was Wilhelm Heinrich Riehl, whose expositions, published between 1857 and 1863, exerted a considerable influence. But Riehl was soon overshadowed by figures of much greater artistic consequence. There was, for example, Richard Wagner, who proclaimed himself a proponent of pan-Aryanism and whose operas often focused on characteristically '*Volkische*' themes – works such as *Tannhäuser* and, of course, *The Ring*, which drew extensively on Germanic legend, saga, folklore and pagan tradition.

The propagators of pan-Aryanism and '*Volkische*' ideology eagerly conscripted figures of the recent past as well – Goethe's contemporaries from the beginning of the century and luminaries of German Romanticism. Thus, Herder was repeatedly invoked, even though he would have disapproved. Another such posthumous recruit, who would also have disapproved, was the great Romantic poet and essayist Friedrich, Freiherr von Hardenberg (1772–1801), better known by his pen name, Novalis. There were also the eminent philologists, scholars, antiquarians and collectors of folklore, the brothers Jacob Ludwig and Wilhelm Karl Grimm, whose systematic collection of folk and fairy tales, published as the War of Liberation erupted in 1812 and 1813, remains, even to this day, the supreme work of its kind. Like Herder, the Grimm brothers did not really exalt the German '*Volk*' or folk soul over any other, but they issued such pronouncements as: 'The eternal, invisible, towards which every noble spirit must strive, is revealed in its purest and most distinct form in the totality, that is, in the idea of a Volk.'[9] These pronouncements provided vital sustenance to the more nationalistic and xenophobic '*Volkische*' ideology of the mid-nineteenth century.

Later works were also press-ganged into '*Volkische*' service. One such was *Wanderings through the March of Brandenburg*, a three-volume collection of travel sketches, anecdotes, folk tales and historical reflections published between 1862 and 1882 by Theodor Fontane. With the possible exception of the Austrian Adalbert Stifter, Fontane, a Prussian of Huguenot descent, was the greatest German-language novelist of the nineteenth century – a figure who warrants comparison with Turgenev and Flaubert. It would be difficult to find a man more temperamentally hostile to '*Volkische*' attitudes: Fontane was signally unmystical and regarded '*Volkische*' pantheism with an indifference verging on disdain. He deplored nationalism, loathed militarism and despised xenophobia. He condemned the creation of the German Empire after the Franco-Prussian War. He practised and extolled an urbane cosmopolitan tolerance. He prided himself on his own French origins and even pronounced his surname in the French fashion, keeping the 'e' at the end silent. Notwithstanding all this, *Wanderings through the March of Brandenburg* became a bible of the '*Volkische*' movement.

In addition to literary figures past and present, the '*Volkische*' movement could muster some impressively lofty and weighty philosophical support, including Georg Wilhelm Friedrich Hegel (1770–1831). Hegel was contemporary with German Romanticism, with figures such as Novalis, Schelling and Hölderlin, and was personally acquainted with the latter two. He knew Goethe, and although they did not often agree, they regarded each other with a cordial mutual respect.

Hegel is probably best known today for his exposition of 'the dialectic', and particularly the 'dialectic of history', which was appropriated and adapted by Karl Marx, but there were other aspects of Hegelian thought that lent themselves readily to nationalism and '*Volkische*' ideology. Heine had warned that only Christianity, 'the talisman of the Cross', stood between civilisation and atavistic Germanic barbarism. Hegel, however, was hostile to Christianity, which he described as 'the product of an alien race and out of harmony with the Germanic soul'.[10] He wrote a life of Jesus, whom he depicted as nothing more than a moral teacher, eminently mortal. But what most endeared Hegel to later proponents of pan-Aryanism and '*Volkische*' ideology was his theory of history.

The theory had elements in common with Herder's concept of the folk soul. For Hegel, history was ultimately a manifestation of metaphysical principles, 'the self-actualisation of spirit' – or, more specifically, what Hegel called the 'World Spirit'. The men who shaped history – Alexander, for example, Caesar, Frederick the Great and Napoleon – were 'used as instruments of the World Spirit'. And the World Spirit, working through history, was the ultimate and definitive arbiter, transcending all human systems of ethics or morality. According to Hegel: 'The actual fate of each nation constitutes its judgement.'[11] In other words, there is no morality except for what is, the *fait accompli*. Thus, 'if one nation succeeds in conquering another . . . its action is justified by its success'.[12] At any given historical moment, Hegel further maintained, there was only one dominant people, a people who reflected the workings of the World Spirit and served as its instrument. Such a people would have a brief span of pre-eminence and would then decline. The people ordained for pre-eminence in his own time, Hegel believed, were the Germans.

Hegel went even further. He also yoked the concrete entity of the people, '*das Volk*', to the more abstract concept of the State, and thus to nationalism. The State, for Hegel, was not an abstract artificial structure imposed on, and presiding over, the people within it. It was, rather, a tangible manifestation of the people, their collective will and folk soul. Each people's folk soul, or 'national spirit', when embodied in the State, was 'a phase or moment in the life of the World Spirit'.[13] And because the State reflected the World Spirit, it enjoyed the prerogatives traditionally reserved for the divine. The State therefore took precedence over all individual rights. True freedom existed only when the individual's aspirations and desires concurred harmoniously with those of the State, and 'the will of the State must prevail over the particular will when there is a clash between them'.[14] In effect, Hegel contrived to deify the State. He even described it, on one occasion, as 'this actual God' – in other words, as the only palpable embodiment of a divine principle in the phenomenal world.

On this basis, Hegel also justified war as the supreme arbiter in disputes between states resulting from the abrogation of treaties and international law. War was therefore both 'rational and necessary'; the means whereby the World Spirit asserted its will in history. From this Hegel could go on to assert that war

> is the chief means by which a people's spirit acquires renewed vigour, or a decayed political organism is swept aside and gives place to a more vigorous manifestation of the Spirit.[15]

It is easy to see how Hegel could be used to reinforce the

nationalism fostered by the War of Liberation and the burgeoning '*Volkische*' movement. He provided one of the chief ingredients of a heady and intoxicating cocktail with which National Socialism would later inebriate the German people.

Yet among its ingredients were some that did not mix altogether palatably. Inevitably, contradictions here and there occurred. '*Volkische*' ideology was rural in its orientation and enamoured of the past. It was hostile towards industrialisation, which was nevertheless essential to the war machine that would soon weld Germany into a new imperial unity. When industrialisation produced victories against Denmark, Austria and France, '*Volkische*' ideology therefore contrived to accommodate it.

★

In the wake of the War of Liberation, Goethe's and then Heine's ideal – a nation dedicated to culture and the spirit – was disastrously undermined. It was now one of two self-definitions contending for the 'heart and soul' of Germany. The other was based on nationalism, militarism, '*Volkische*' ideology and pan-Aryanism, and an espousal of political unity and the Hegelian cult of the State. After the wars of Bismarck's era, it was this second self-definition which emerged triumphant – at least externally. With Prussia's dramatic defeat of Denmark, Austria and especially France, the struggle for Germany's 'heart and soul' effectively ended, at least in the sphere of politics. The new German Empire – the Second Reich – was created, and the monster feared by Goethe, Heine and others came into being.

Yet the Prussian political apparatus of the new imperium was ultimately only a superstructure, artificially imposed on something much less unified and homogeneous than its façade suggested. Behind this superstructure, the old identity crisis persisted. Many Germans felt themselves less 'German' than Bavarian, Swabian, Hannoverian or Saxon. There were also deep-seated divisions between the Protestant north and the predominantly Catholic south, which continued to look to Vienna as its real capital rather than Berlin. And Goethe's ideal of a nation dedicated to culture and the spirit was kept alive and propagated by such literary figures as Fontane, Theodor Storm, Wilhelm Raabe and, especially, the

Swabian Eduard Mörike, whom Stefan George and the Stauffenbergs
esteemed almost as much as they did Hölderlin.

For outsiders, as well as for Germans themselves, a single unified
self-definition and national identity remained elusive. In the aftermath
of the Franco-Prussian War, it was easy enough to characterise
Germany by a spiked helmet, but developments in the south were
running counter to this image. While Bismarck was making war in the
north, Ludwig II, King of Bavaria, was encouraging art. Regarded as
an effete fool and probably mad, Ludwig nevertheless subscribed
passionately to the Goethean ideal of a nation dedicated to culture and
the spirit. While Prussia burgeoned with steelworks and armaments
factories, Bavaria bloomed with fairy-tale castles, enchanted grottos
and the supreme temple to high '*Kultur*' at Bayreuth. Under the
patronage of Bavaria's monarch, *Kultur* became, in effect, the official
state religion, Wagner's operas assumed the status of religious rites
or festivals, and Bayreuth became a pilgrimage centre. It was not
uncommon, during the late nineteenth century, for educated Euro-
peans (and especially educated Britons) to describe themselves as
'Wagnerian' in precisely the same way that their predecessors might
have described themselves as 'Christian'. *Kultur* became a creed. In
France, it assumed the form of '*l'art pour l'art*', 'art for art's sake', but the
focus of it all, even for its most assiduous French apostles, was Wagner
and Bayreuth. And whatever Wagner's own pan-Aryan orientation,
his art was perceived at the time less as a testimony to Germanic
supremacy than to that of culture and the spirit.

Given the contrasting and conflicting values of Prussia and
Bavaria, the question of what it 'meant' to be German remained
unresolved. What constituted the more accurate, more profoundly
valid reflection of 'the true Germany'? Was it the material progress
of increasingly industrialised Prussia, with her cult of blood and
iron, her strategically organised railway system, her state-of-the-art
artillery and awesomely efficient war machine? Or was it the
cultural and spiritual Mecca of Bavaria, with her rival cult of
religio-aesthetic rapture, her lofty aspirations to the numinous, her
investiture of art with a dimension of the sacred and supernal?
Neither outsiders nor Germans themselves were altogether sure,
and not even Ludwig's mysterious death, probably at the hands of
Bismarck's agents, did much to resolve the dilemma.

It is true that Wagner's music, so fervently embraced and patronised by Ludwig, contained many elements later adopted, embraced and revered by Hitler and National Socialism. But Ludwig, certainly, had no interest in seeing these elements translated into politics; and it is doubtful that Wagner, despite his pan-Aryanism, did either. Of course, that did not spare him from being posthumously conscripted, as was the philosopher Friedrich Nietzsche. Yet Nietzsche, too, repudiated politics, especially in so trivial and contemptible a form as nationalism. The Nietzschean 'Ubermensch' or 'superman' was hardly a political figure; and the transformation or revolution he represented was one of spirit and consciousness, not of political institutions or geographical frontiers. For Nietzsche, as for Goethe, transformation was of paramount importance; but Nietzsche's conception of transformation, like Goethe's, had nothing whatever to do with bureaucracy or the machinery of the Hegelian State.

# 11
## Myth and Might

For most English-speaking readers today, and especially for those who fought it, the Second World War was probably as close as one can imagine to a just war. It had a clearly discernible and defined justification and sanction. Moral issues were starkly delineated. There was no question of who was right, who wrong. Distance in time has, of course, rendered certain Allied actions and policies – the bombing of Dresden, for example – difficult, if not impossible, to condone; but except for the occasional warped would-be historian, no one has attempted to excuse or 'rehabilitate' Nazi Germany.

If the Second World War was indeed a just conflict, it was so because it constituted a moral contest, a crusade against madness and recognisable 'evil'. General Eisenhower could title his account *Crusade in Europe* without seeming guilty of pretentiousness, portentousness or rhetorical hyperbole. To the extent that Nazi Germany could be seen as embodying and incarnating the potential madness and 'evil' of all mankind, that madness and 'evil' became endowed with form; and once something is endowed with form, it can be opposed. One knows what one is fighting *against*, and this clarifies and crystallises what one is fighting *for*. If one knows what one is fighting for, the fight is meaningful and justifiable.

By incarnating madness and 'evil' within itself, the Nazi régime, paradoxically, 'redeemed' the rest of the Western world into sanity and virtue. This, with typical Olympian irony, Thomas Mann demonstrates in *Doctor Faustus*; and other writers, from George

Steiner in England to Jorge Luis Borges and Carlos Fuentes in Latin America, have since picked up the theme. It took Nazi Germany to teach us the meaning of atrocity and outrage. It took Auschwitz and Treblinka to remind us of what we as human beings are capable of perpetrating, despite our veneer of civilisation, and to make us wish to disown such propensities. Nazi Germany rendered us, albeit only temporarily perhaps, a degree or two more moral, more decent – a degree or two more sensitive to such things as, for example, 'ethnic cleansing' in what used to be Yugoslavia. To that extent, and however uncomfortably the recognition may sit with us, we are in Nazi Germany's debt.

If the Second World War made sense and rested on some moral basis, the First World War did not. On the contrary, the First World War was the most terrifyingly insane conflict in the whole of modern European history, not excepting the Thirty Years War of 1618–48. It was insane in its causes (or lack thereof), its motivation (or lack thereof), and the policies (or lack thereof) that precipitated it. It was pre-eminently insane in its conduct. On the opening day of the Battle of the Somme on 1 July 1916, more than a hundred thousand British and French soldiers, forming three lines fifteen miles long, clambered out of their trenches. Each bearing sixty pounds of equipment on his back, they then proceeded not to charge, not to duck or dodge, but to march, as if on parade, into the face of machine guns firing more than a hundred rounds per minute. By the end of the first day – the single most costly day in the history of the British Army – 57,470 had fallen. By the end of the battle, the toll on all sides amounted to a million and a half. The territory gained at this price came to an average, along the front, of five miles – five miles of mud, of shell craters, rubble and devastated fields.

This was insanity, and the insanity was repeated at Verdun, at Ypres and Passchendaele, at Gallipoli, on the Russian and Italian fronts. Never had mankind engaged in such wholesale and mindless slaughter to so little purpose, with so little to show for it. And while this orgy of carnage enacted itself, arms merchants and munitions manufacturers in Britain, France and Germany were negotiating business deals and trade agreements with each other, keeping the blood flowing because it was profitable to do so.

There have been numerous evocations of the First World War's madness. Some of the best, and most penetrating, can be found in Hermann Broch's novel *The Sleepwalkers*, first published in 1931.

The unreal is the illogical. And this age seems to have a capacity for surpassing even the acme of illogicality . . . it is as if the monstrous reality of the war had blotted out the reality of the world. Fantasy has become logical reality . . . An age that is softer and more cowardly than any preceding age suffocates in waves of blood and poison-gas; nations of bank clerks and profiteers hurl themselves upon barbed wire . . . Amid a blurring of all forms, in a twilight of apathetic uncertainty brooding over a ghostly world, man like a lost child gropes his way by the help of a small frail thread of logic through a dream landscape that he calls reality and that is nothing but a nightmare to him.[1]

The madness of the First World War achieved the scale it did because it consisted, as Broch says, of 'a blurring of all forms'. In effect, and in contrast to that of the Second World War, the madness had no form. In the Second World War, Nazi Germany incarnated and gave form to human madness. In the conflict of 1914–18, the madness was rampant, diffuse, omnipresent, devoid of shape or contour – like the clouds of poison gas sifting insidiously over the trenches. The madness was everywhere, suffusing everyone and everything, extending from hapless soldiers in their dug-outs to army commanders in their châteaux, corporate executives in their boardrooms and heads of state in their offices. No one side, in the First World War, could exercise a monopoly on guilt. Despite all the propaganda, there were no clearly defined villains or culprits. Everyone was to blame – and, therefore, no one was entirely to blame. The conflict has generally, and not inaccurately, been seen as the culmination of a subterranean dynamic inherent in Western civilisation – the consummation, so to speak, of a long-standing, long-evolving collective European death wish. It was all the more traumatic by virtue of what had immediately preceded it.

On the eve of the war, during the first decade of the twentieth century, Western society appeared to have reached a zenith in its development. Never before had a culture achieved such a degree of opulence, luxury, refinement, cosmopolitanism and sophistication.

Never had optimism been greater or more unqualified. 'Civilisation' had conferred seemingly inestimable benefits on Western Europe and was now, under the aegis of imperialism, bringing those benefits to more 'benighted' sectors of the globe. Medicine was making such strides as to foster belief in the eventual eradication of all disease. Science was opening dramatic and exciting new vistas on past, present and future. Psychology was promising to eliminate all disorders, maladjustments and 'abnormalities' of the mind. Technology was advancing at a pace that would transform the entire world of human activity. Travel had attained the level of comfort and extravagance embodied by the 'Orient Express' and the great ocean liners, and the conquest of the air was imminent. '*Kultur*' had imparted taste, sensitivity and discrimination to social life. Education was becoming ever more widespread. Across the entire Occident, a complacent sense of order and stability prevailed. In every sphere of human endeavour, it appeared that things could only become better. A fervent, unquestioning belief in 'Progress' and its bounty constituted, in effect, the dominant religion of the age.

In fact, however, the most apposite symbol of the age was the *Titanic*. The faith reposed in 'Progress' culminated only in the horror of 'the war to end all wars'. The conflict of 1914–18 was not only the most appalling bloodbath in Western history. It was also the single most profound and traumatic betrayal of faith, of hope, of optimism, of aspirations and expectations. Everything that had previously seemed to promise so much proved treacherous, not serving to improve man's lot, but to augment his capacity for destructiveness. Civilisation, despite its refinements, had led to the primitive barbarity of the trenches and to abattoirs like the Somme, where men died as if on an assembly line, regardless of class, calling, aptitude or educational background. Science and technology had led not to an improvement of the human condition, but to Zeppelins, to explosives raining from the sky, to combat aircraft, tanks, submarines and ever more efficient engines for killing – as well as to the ultimate nightmare of poison gas, a weapon so terrifying even Hitler was to shrink from employing it. Religion, which plumed itself on bringing enlightenment to the 'heathen', proved unable to curb the bloodlust of its own devotees. As Heine had prophesied, cathedrals such as Amiens were indeed pulverised by Thor's hammer, disguised as Krupp howitzer shells.

Since the Thirty Years War, certain 'rules of warfare' had been observed. Among other things, civilian populations were supposed to be exempt from the depredations of conflict. Now, in flagrant repudiation of everything 'civilisation' was alleged to stand for, the world's great cities and their populations comprised a new front line. The bombs dropped on London by Zeppelins did scant damage and caused few casualties, but the mere fact that an urban centre could become a target for aerial bombardment introduced a dimension unknown in war since the seventeenth century – and established a new precedent which Hitler would ruthlessly exploit.

In the cataclysm of the First World War, virtually an entire generation of young men fell. The casualties inevitably included many of the best and brightest, the most original and imaginative, the most highly educated, the most qualified for future leadership. Altogether, more than 65 million men had been engaged in combat. More than half were killed, wounded or 'missing'. The British Empire lost 2 million, Austria-Hungary 5 million, France 6 million, Germany 8 million, Russia as many as 2 million. When the war was over, there were 2 million demobilised, maimed and often unemployable veterans wandering in the streets of Britain and her dominions; 3.6 million in Austria; more than 4 million in France, and another 4 million in Germany's fledgling Weimar Republic.

Those who survived became known, not inaccurately, as the 'lost generation', chronicled by such writers as Hemingway and Scott Fitzgerald. For this generation, the betrayals of the First World War had left nothing in which to believe any longer, no authority worthy of honour. The result was not just disillusion. It was what Broch depicted in *The Sleepwalkers* as an utter and total 'disintegration of values'. The optimism and confidence, the certainty and complacency of 1914 had given way to a vista of emptiness, apathy and relativism. Robert Musil, Broch's compatriot and contemporary, succinctly characterised the prevailing mood as 'a relativity of perspective verging on epistemological panic'.

In Germany, the 'disintegration of values' was particularly pervasive and debilitating. However appalling their losses, the Allies could at least muster rhetoric to congratulate themselves on

what purported to be victory and claim substantial war reparations. Russia had lost her reigning dynasty and imperial status; but
she had at least the illusion – like a rainbow arching beyond the
horrors of revolution and civil war – of a new and bright future in
which to believe. Austria, too, had lost her reigning dynasty, but a
sizeable portion of her former population – in Poland, Hungary,
Czechoslovakia and Yugoslavia – could find hope in independence
and freshly formed democratic republics, however artificially
contrived.

Germany had no such solace. Europe's most recently created
imperial power – so recently created she had not yet had time to
take her status for granted, had still been glorying in that status –
was now bereft of her ruling dynasty and imperial splendour. The
Weimar Republic, whose very name was intended to embody
Goethe's old ideal of a nation dedicated to culture and the spirit,
offered little palliative, little to replace what had been lost. For one
thing, the new republic was not accepted by Germans because it was
less an organic development than an artificial construct: a dictated
and imposed national identity, based on foreigners' conceptions of
what Germany was supposed to be. It reflected other people's ideal
of Germany, in an environment that militated against idealism of
any kind. And the Weimar Republic could not cope with the apathy,
the numbness, the privation, the starvation, the ruined infra-
structure, the dingy greyness that prevailed. For Germany, there
appeared to be no future, illusory or otherwise, and the present
entailed extreme hardship, which was only intensified by soaring
inflation and economic depression of such proportions as virtually
to wipe out the middle class, the traditional bulwark against
extremism. To exacerbate the situation further, there were crippling
war reparations to pay.

There were other humiliations as well, less tangible perhaps, but
none the less devastating to the country's morale. As both soldiers
and civilians recognised, Germany's military machine had acquitted
itself impressively enough – as well as those of its adversaries, if not,
indeed, better. That had not, however, prevented defeat; and defeat,
seemingly inexplicable, had to be ascribed to someone or something, thus fostering a quest for a scapegoat.

Equally baffling was the fact that Germany, in the eyes of the world, was held solely responsible for the cataclysm – as if Germany alone had instigated it, as if Austria and Russia, Britain and France, had been altogether innocent. Certainly Germany had been guilty of a serious transgression in violating Belgian neutrality, and her ruling dynasty made mistakes. But the ruling dynasty had paid for their mistakes with their throne, and the country as a whole had paid for the 'rape of Belgium' with casualties exceeding those of the Western Allies. So far as the causes of the war were concerned, Germans felt themselves no more culpable than the conflict's other belligerents. The débâcle had begun, after all, with a dispute between Austria and Russia. Russia had declared war on Germany, not Germany on Russia. Given these circumstances, it seemed monstrously unfair that Germany alone should have to bear the weight of the world's opprobrium.

These factors converged to engender a national crisis. Contrary to the assertions of many historians, this crisis was not simply economic, social or political, nor even a combination of these. It was, in fact, Germany's old, long-standing and deep-rooted collective identity crisis – the crisis of collective self-definition, collective self-assessment and self-esteem, collective orientation, direction and purpose. But now, with the collapse of the institutions that had previously masked or sublimated it, that crisis no longer smouldered in the background, beneath the surface or behind transient façades. It dominated the foreground of German consciousness.

In the wake of the First World War Germany required not just a social, political or economic palliative, still less an idealised and somewhat saccharine conception of Weimar imposed by foreigners. The country needed an entirely new *raison d'être*, an entirely new sense of purpose, direction and self-definition. Such needs can seldom, if ever, be fulfilled by political, social or economic programmes. Such needs cannot even be satisfactorily fulfilled by ideologies. But such needs have traditionally been fulfilled by religions. This, ultimately, was what National Socialism offered.

Great is the anguish of the man who becomes aware of his isolation and seeks to escape from his own memory . . . And in his fear of the voice of judgement that threatens to issue from the darkness, there awakens within him a doubly strong yearning for a Leader to take him tenderly and lightly by the hand, to set things in order and show him the way . . . [2]

Thus Broch wrote prophetically in 1929. And thus, in a drama only too familiar today, does the lonely self-alienated youth – in the throes of an identity crisis, fearing responsibility, seeking meaning, purpose and direction for his existence – find illusory solace and a supposed sense of 'belonging' in one or another sect or cult, presided over by a self-appointed guru or messiah figure. Thus does one fall prey to the likes of Charles Manson in California, Jim Jones in Guiana, David Koresh in Waco and, on a much more cataclysmic scale, Adolf Hitler.

★

Under Mussolini, Fascism in Italy never amounted to more than a political ideology. It made no attempt whatever to activate, channel and exploit the religious impulse, but contrived instead a 'live-and-let-live' accommodation with the Catholic Church, according Rome certain prerogatives and then proceeding to implement its own purely secular programmes. To that extent, Italian Fascism may have had a qualified, abstract intellectual appeal for more simplistic minds, but it made no corresponding emotional appeal. It offered only a superficial vainglorious nationalism, a crude jingoistic imperialism and a pompous façade of grandeur and splendour. There was little in all this to elicit a visceral response from hearts or souls. Hearts and souls were left to the custody of the Church. As a result, Italian Fascism, compared to other mass movements of the period between the wars, was puerile, often laughable. While not underestimating its more sinister aspects, Thomas Mann could depict it farcically in 'Mario and the Magician'.

In Spain, Franco's kind of Fascism was more sophisticated. It took pains not just to reach an accommodation with organised religion, but to align itself explicitly with organised religion. Franco's movement was therefore more than a mere ideology. It yoked itself to the religious impulses and yearnings of the Spanish people, or at least many of them, and could thereby arrogate a kind of divine sanction or mandate. Spanish Falangists did not tacitly assume that God was on their side. Through such organisations as Opus Dei and El Cristo Rey, they dragooned Him into being so, attaching Him inseparably to Franco's cause. Franco could thus present himself as a latterday crusader, engaged in an enterprise ordained and endorsed by heaven. By tapping the reservoir of religious energy, Franco could appeal to hearts and souls in a way that Mussolini could not. This imparted to his movement an impetus and a vicious fanaticism that Mussolini's never displayed.

In Germany, National Socialism sought more than an Italian-style accommodation with organised religion, or even a Spanish-style alliance. It sought nothing less than to supplant organised religion and become, in effect, the official state religion of the 'new order' Germany aspired to impose. Any film of the crowds at a Nuremberg rally, chanting 'Sieg Heil!' with hysterical rapture, reveals something more potent at work than just political commitment – it is the dynamic of an evangelical church or a revivalist meeting. This imparted to National Socialism in Germany a demonic power and hypnotic appeal that neither Italian nor Spanish totalitarianism could achieve.

In the essentially religious, carefully orchestrated and choreo-graphed spell cast by Hitler and the Nazi hierarchy, hitherto irreconcilable opposites were reconciled – as they could be only under the auspices of a religion. The German propensities for both irrationality and hyper-rationality were fused in a single all-encompassing and all-embracing euphoria. In a warped fashion that would have appalled Goethe and Heine on the one hand, Gneisenau and Yorck von Wartenburg on the other, Germany became what all of them had sought to make her: a political and nationalistic entity which, at the same time, embodied culture and the spirit. This fusion, of course, perverted, distorted and diminished its contributing components. Political and nationalistic impulses were reduced to their lowest common denominator, a crude tyranny, swaggering braggadocio and brutal self-aggrandisement. Culture, as Broch stated, was reduced to the level of kitsch; and the spirit, though energetic enough, was a malevolent one. It took the form of what Stefan George called '*das Leichte*' ('the Facile'): the spurious and illusory miracles performed by that false prophet, the Antichrist.

Fourteen years before Hitler came to power, C. G. Jung had issued a warning that echoed Heine's:

> As the Christian view of the world loses its authority, the more menacingly will the 'blond beast' be heard prowling about in its underground prison, ready at any moment to burst out with devastating consequences.[3]

Three years after Hitler's accession as Chancellor, Jung sought to explain the subterranean dynamic behind the Nazi phenomenon by invoking, metaphorically, the ancient Teutonic pantheon:

> We are always convinced that the modern world is a reasonable world, basing our opinion on economic, political and psychological factors. But if we may forget for a moment that we are living in the Year of Our Lord 1936 . . . we would find Wotan quite suitable as a causal hypothesis. In fact I venture the heretical suggestion that the unfathomable depths of Wotan's character explain more of National Socialism than all three reasonable factors put together.[4]

Again, Jung was echoing Heine:

> No, memories of the old German religion have not been extinguished. They say there are greybeards in Westphalia who still know where the old images of the gods lie hidden; on their death-beds they tell their youngest grandchild, who carries the secret . . . In Westphalia, the former Saxony, not everything that lies buried is dead.[5]

Until March 1933, '*Volkische*' ideology, specifically as it had been disseminated by the Nazis, was banned by both the Lutheran Church in Germany and by the universities. With the Nazi accession to power, this ban was lifted. In a lecture that summer, a Tübingen theologian asked whether the church was ready 'to interpret a great turning point in German destiny as coming from the hand of God, and to take a creative part in it'.[6]

Other theologians responded with zest, claiming 'It was their mission, entrusted to them by God, to interpret to the German Volk that prevenient action of God and at the same time to help shape it in unconditional solidarity with the Volk.'[7]

According to a prominent ecclesiastical spokesman and leader at the time:

> If the Protestant church in genuine inner solidarity with the German Volk . . . wishes really to proclaim the gospel, then it has to take as its natural standpoint the circle of destiny of the National Socialist movement.[8]

On 22 July 1933, the annual Bayreuth festival culminated with a production of Wagner's most loftily spiritual opera, *Parsifal*. Immediately after this production, Hitler gave a major radio speech, announcing his plans to create a united Reich Church. At a synod two months later, on 27 September, the church was officially established, with a fervid Nazi, Ludwig Müller, as first Reich Bishop. A liberal Protestant newspaper dared to satirise the event:

> Church service. The opening hymn has ended. The pastor stands at the altar and begins:
> 'Non-Aryans are requested to leave the Church.'
> No one moves.
> 'Non-Aryans are requested to leave the Church immediately.'
> Again all remain quiet.
> 'Non-Aryans are requested to leave the Church immediately.'
> Thereupon Christ comes down from the altar and leaves the church.[9]

For publishing this, the editor of the newspaper was arrested and consigned to a concentration camp.

With the establishment of the Reich Church, Hitler himself became increasingly invested with messianic qualities. In March 1934, pastor Herman Grüner wrote: 'The time is fulfilled for the German people in Hitler. It is because of Hitler that Christ . . . has become effective among us. Therefore National Socialism is positive Christianity in action.'[10] In the same year, a text was prepared for study and memorisation by schoolchildren, invoking the abortive *Putsch* of 1923:

> As Jesus set men free from sin and hell, so Hitler rescued the German people from destruction. Both Jesus and Hitler were persecuted; but, while Jesus was crucified, Hitler was exalted to

Chancellor. While the disciples of Jesus betrayed their master and left him in his distress, the sixteen friends of Hitler stood by him. The Apostles completed the work of their Lord. We hope that Hitler may lead his work to completion. Jesus built for heaven; Hitler for the German earth.[11]

At first the Reich Church paid at least nominal obeisance to established Christianity, but it was not long before even this was left behind. Wilhelm Hauer, Professor of Indology and Comparative Religions and founder of the so-called 'German Faith Movement', proclaimed in print that the epoch of Christianity was now over and only 'German faith' remained. Hauer was echoed by Alfred Rosenberg, the Party racial theoretician, who wrote: 'The longing to give the Nordic race soul its form as German church under the sign of the Volk mythos, that is for me the greatest task of our century.'[12]

As a religious creed, Nazified paganism quickly took root. Doctor Langermann is not the only example of a former evangelical pastor conducting the funeral of an SS officer and speeding the deceased, in full dress uniform and jackboots, not to any Christian heaven, but to Wotan's Valhalla with the words: 'May this God send the nations of this earth clanking on their way through history. Lord bless our struggle.'[13]

Under SS auspices, schools called 'Napolas' were established for the education and indoctrination of selected members of the Hitler Youth. In his novel *The Erl-King*, Michel Tournier evokes the way in which, at these 'Napolas', future SS personnel celebrated Christmas:

All the Jungmannen were gathered in the armory around a glittering Christmas tree, for the ceremony of the Yule Festival. It was not the birth of Christ that was being celebrated, but that of the Sun Child, risen from his ashes at the winter solstice. The sun's trajectory had reached its lowest level and the day was the shortest of the year: the death of the sun god was therefore lamented as an impending cosmic fatality. Funeral chants celebrating the woe of the earth and the inhospitableness of the sky praised the dead luminary's virtues and begged him to return among men. And the lament was answered, for from then on every day would gain on the night, at first imperceptibly but soon with triumphant ease.[14]

It was as a religion, then, not as any conventional political ideology, that National Socialism was to sweep through Germany and elicit fanatical adherence from the German populace.[15] Under National Socialism, the gods of the ancient Teutonic pantheon would indeed emerge anew, asserting a self-arrogated supremacy over Judaeo-Christian tradition and theology. Wotan – the 'berserker, god of storms, wanderer, warrior, Wunsch and Minne God, lord of the dead, Einherier, dead hero of Valhalla, magician' – would once again gust through the German collective psyche like the raging wind from which his original name derived. And, as Heine had prophesied, Thor would arise anew and, with his mighty hammer, smash the Gothic cathedrals. Nazi Germany would be the only state in modern Western history to rest ultimately not on social, economic or political principles, but on spiritual, even magical, ones. The spirituality, however, was warped, malevolent and demonic, and the magic – if magic can be defined as a metaphor for the manipulative relationship between consciousness and will on the one hand, and external phenomena and people on the other – conformed to the traditional tenets of so-called 'black magic'. It was the magic which had first entered Christian thought through the biblical figure of Simon Magus, the Samaritan 'Antichrist', whose miracles, while ostensibly matching Peter's, remained 'a hair's-breadth impure' and therefore intrinsically rotten.

*

The religion – or, to be more accurate, the ersatz or surrogate religion – of National Socialism drew its vital sustenance from a number of diverse quarters. There was the nationalism fostered by the War of Liberation, which was augmented, and decked out with imperial grandeur, by Bismarck's victories against Denmark, Austria and France. There was pan-Aryanism and '*Volkische*' thought, which embedded Goethe's ideal – a nation and people dedicated to culture and the spirit – in a mystical, pantheistic and specifically nationalistic context. There was also Hegel, who provided a lofty philosophical sanction for yoking the actual entity of *das Volk* to the abstract conception of the State. Other influences were at work as well in the years immediately preceding and following the First World War. All of them furthered the establishment of National Socialism on a religious foundation, and enabled it, thereby, to offer an apparent palliative and resolution to Germany's collective identity crisis.

There was, of course, literature, both past and present. Figures by now enshrined as 'classics' were either quoted out of context or suborned in their entirety. Such was the fate that befell Goethe, Schiller and Herder, Hölderlin, Novalis, Heinrich von Kleist, Theodor Storm. Heine could be conveniently disparaged and dismissed. He was, after all, they felt, a 'rootless' Jew, and his self-imposed exile only accentuated and confirmed his 'rootlessness'. Of more recent figures, Theodor Fontane was (when ostensibly relevant) also appropriated, as was Nietzsche. And Oswald Spengler's opus, *The Decline of the West*, could be seen, even by its title, to herald the end of 'decadent' European civilisation and the advent of a new, apocalyptic and 'full-blooded' dispensation.

In a somewhat bizarre fashion, popular culture also contributed, conflated with what purported to be earnest scholarship. Germany's landlocked inability to expand geographically or territorially had prompted Goethe to advocate a different kind of expansion or extension – into cultural and spiritual domains – but the absence of a frontier continued to foster a sense of claustrophobia. This became increasingly acute with the creation of the German Empire after the Franco-Prussian War. The very name of the new imperium could not but ring slightly hollow, simply because it existed in name only. The German Empire was not, strictly speaking, an empire, because it lacked the colonies and dominions which justified imperial status. By 1871, virtually every quarter of the globe worth annexing had already been acquired by other powers; and Germany's belated scramble for overseas possessions produced very little, apart from South-West Africa. Such as there was did not lend itself to the kind of romantic grandeur on which the very concept of empire depended.

In Britain, successive generations of youths read G. A. Henty or, were they more literate, Kipling and Robert Louis Stevenson, and dreamed of exotic adventures in the South Seas, in Africa, in the Raj, at the Khyber Pass on the North-west Frontier. The death of General 'Chinese' Gordon at Khartoum was the British equivalent of Custer's at the Little Big Horn; and Britain had, moreover, such triumphs as Rourke's Drift and Omdurman on which to plume herself. In the empire on which 'the sun never set', there was plenty to appease one's hunger for the exotic.

France, too, could wax romantic about adventures, explorations and conquests in remote, mysterious and seemingly enchanted places. North Africa, for example, supplied France with an ample diet of such material; and thus the mystique of the Foreign Legion could enflame the popular imagination. In Russia, the Caucasus had performed a similar function, inspiring, among others, Pushkin, Lermontov and Tolstoy. There was also, as the nineteenth century unfolded, the Far East, Mongolia and the Chinese frontier. And like the British, the Russian imagination was stirred by the misty mountain fastnesses of Afghanistan and the Khyber Pass. As for Austria-Hungary, the yearning for exoticism could be to some degree satisfied within the empire itself, where a diverse spectrum of races, cultures, traditions and peoples provided the cultivated Viennese mind with an inexhaustible source of glamorous mystery.

For Germany, the trappings of empire had no arena in which to parade themselves. German schoolboys sought some imperial extension of the country on which romantic fantasy could be projected, and they found nothing. For want of anything else, they turned in what today may seem a bizarre and improbable direction – the 'Wild West' of the United States. They did so under the influence and auspices of a man named Karl May.

May is unknown in the English-speaking world. Measured by aesthetic standards, he was little more than a hack, and does not even qualify for inclusion in reference works on German literature. In Germany, however, and indeed throughout central Europe, he was the most successful bestselling author of his era, casting a spell over successive generations of youth. Even today, he is still widely read.

May's massive corpus of work (amounting, in some editions, to more than sixty volumes) was produced during the last third of the nineteenth century and the first decade of the twentieth. His most popular books, derivative of Fenimore Cooper and the 'dime novels' then current in America, were westerns – precursors, in many respects, of the novels of Zane Grey and the more recent Louis l'Amour. In these texts, May's own specifically Teutonic conceptions of justice, law and order were dramatised against the landscape of the American West. In a milieu today associated with John Wayne and Marlboro Country, cowboys and Indians addressed each other in German.

By modern standards some of May's work might appear offensive. In fact, he was much more humane, 'enlightened' and sympathetic to the plight of the Indian than most of his American contemporaries. He was also a pacifist, and vehemently opposed to imperialism – both Germany's and everyone else's. In itself, his influence on the German collective psyche may have been detrimental to literary taste and discrimination, but it was otherwise harmless. It was, however, to become entangled with a much more pernicious influence – that of Heinrich von Treitschke.

Treitschke was a very different kind of writer. Among his contemporaries, he passed for an eminent and distinguished historian, with seemingly impeccable academic credentials. Unlike May, he was not read by every German schoolboy. For the most part, he was read only in the universities, but his ideas – in even more partisan and simplified form – filtered out from there. Among his major works was *Das deutsche Ordensland Preussen*, an evocative history, engorged with purple prose, of the medieval Teutonic Knights in Prussia and the Baltic. His orientation, in this and other works, was aggressively pan-Aryan, '*Volkische*', nationalistic and racist. This is made clear in the analysis by D. Seward:

> Reading Treitschke's *Das deutsche Ordensland* one immediately recognizes his interpretation's influence on the architects of the Third Reich. He spoke of 'the formidable activities of our people as conqueror, teacher, discipliner of its neighbours', of 'those pitiless racial conflicts whose vestiges live on mysteriously in the habits of our people' . . .[16]

Seward observes that the Teutonic Knights were portrayed by Treitschke as 'medieval stormtroopers'. As such, they were later 'canonised' by the Nazis and adopted as icons by the SS. The knights' crusade in Prussia and the Baltic was depicted as Germany's great imperial adventure. Indeed, Treitschke credited them with having established the governing principles of the imperial policy later adopted by Europe's major powers. Yet in fact the activities of the Teutonic Knights were to be echoed most approximately by those of the settlers and the United States Cavalry in the American west.

The crusades in Prussia and the Baltic may indeed have constituted a 'great imperial adventure'. But for German youths of Treitschke's era, that adventure, unfortunately, lay centuries in the past. Through Karl May's work, it found a contemporary analogy. In the prairies, deserts and mountains of the American west, white Anglo-Saxon Protestants were pursuing their 'manifest destiny' and, in the process, exterminating the indigenous native population in their path. Why, then, could Germany not have her own 'manifest destiny', which sanctioned her conquest of the 'inferior' races to the east? The United States was only re-enacting what the Teutonic Knights had done in the past. With this contemporary parallel to validate them, why could not a new generation of Teutonic Knights follow in the footsteps of their predecessors? Thus did Treitschke's romanticised depiction become conflated, in the popular mind, with the mass appeal and familiar settings of Karl May. This was to be a significant impetus in the Nazi '*Drang nach Osten*', the 'drive to the East'.

The coalescing religion of National Socialism was to draw further sustenance, in the years just before and after the First World War, from figures of much greater literary stature than either Karl May or Treitschke. One of these was Hermann Hesse. Like May, he was a pacifist, violently opposed to German militarism and to the conflict of 1914–18. He was also fervently anti-Nazi, and prominent on the list of authors whose books the Nazis burnt when they came to power. Nevertheless, in such works as *Steppenwolf* and *Narziss and Goldmund*, German youth between the wars found both their personal and collective identity crises powerfully mirrored and dramatised. In the earlier novel *Demian*, they found what seemed a tangible incarnation of the Nietzschean 'superman'. For his readers at the time, Hesse appeared to offer the same solutions to the problem of self-definition that he did to the alienated youth of the 1960s.

Utterly different from Hesse, but equally influential, was Ernst

Jünger. During the First World War, Jünger had enlisted in the ranks, earned a field commission and established a reputation for heroic exploits as a leader of élite storm troops. He survived the conflict and emerged as one of Germany's most frequently wounded, and most highly decorated, soldiers. Although loftily contemptuous and hostile towards National Socialism, he was to serve in the Second World War as one of the Wehrmacht's most admired and respected officers. In such works as *Storm of Steel* (1920), Jünger expounded a creed of macho martial mysticism that readers today might associate with the Samurai of Japan. He endorsed a Samurai-like fusion of sensitivity with hardness, resilience and tenacity. In prose of an incandescent, almost visionary intensity, he extolled the fraternal 'bonding' of men in combat, and, even more, the transforming effects of danger, stress, violence and physical suffering. He was neither political nor nationalistic in any conventional sense, but war became for him a kind of supernal rite of passage through which men fulfilled themselves and established contact with the numinous. He embodied, in effect, the quality Heine had described: 'that lust for battle which we find among the ancient Germans and which fights not in order to destroy, nor in order to win, but simply in order to fight.'[17] It is not therefore surprising that, despite his disdain for them, Jünger was adopted as an icon by the SS.

Although diametrically opposed in sensibility, temperament and *Weltanschauung*, Hesse and Jünger both exerted a profound influence on German youth between the two world wars, but there was another literary figure whose influence, and artistic stature, was appreciably greater. Knut Hamsun was not even German, although as a Norwegian he could still officially be classified as 'Nordic' and Aryan. Hamsun was one of the half-dozen or so most important cultural influences of his age. Although subsequently eclipsed by some of his disciples, his work contributed decisively to the transformation of prose fiction in the twentieth century; and as a prophet, he was considered by his contemporaries to equal Nietzsche, many of whose attitudes he shared. Since the 1890s, Hamsun had been advocating a pantheistic 'return to nature'. In novels with such evocative titles as *Pan*, *Mysteries*, *Vagabonds* and *The Road to the Open*, he depicted a sequence of alienated and solitary wanderers living in mystical communion with the unsullied and untainted wilderness. In 1920 he won the Nobel Prize for his most popular (if not best) work, *Growth of the Soil*, a sustained prose hymn to the rhythms of the earth and the cycle of the seasons – with which, he insisted, humanity had to place itself in accord.

For the youth of Stauffenberg's generation, Hamsun's work represented the apotheosis of the novel as both art and prophecy. For the *Wandervögel* in particular, his work was a manifesto, a credo, a bible. His attitudes and values were, again, only too easily pressed into service by National Socialism – and, in Hamsun's case, with his consent. Although an old man at the time, and verging on senility, he applauded the Third Reich and subsequently welcomed the German invasion of Norway. For this transgression, he was blisteringly castigated and stigmatised after the war, and only narrowly escaped punishment as a collaborator. Not until the 1960s was his artistic reputation rehabilitated; but even today, in Scandinavia, a residue of odium attaches to his name.

\*

Different though they were, writers such as Hesse, Jünger and Hamsun all put forward an essentially 'religious' or, to be more accurate, 'spiritual' vision which lent itself to appropriation and exploitation by National Socialism. The youths who read and revered them, such as the *Wandervögel*, were youths in quest of a religious answer to problems of meaning, purpose, self-definition, and individual and collective identity. The otherworldly yearnings of these youths rendered them particularly vulnerable to National Socialism's allure. Their religious energy could be channelled into the National Socialist cause and could thereby impart to it an intensified religious dimension.

The *Wandervögel* were officially founded in a Berlin suburb in 1901, initially as a 'hiking association for schoolboys'. In the beginning, they comprised a centralised organisation with an hierarchical structure. As the movement proliferated, however, it also fragmented. Eventually there were some forty separate *Wandervögel* associations and numerous splinter groups. The 'New Pathfinders', the *Wandervögel* cadre to which the Stauffenberg brothers belonged, had been founded in 1920. Unlike most, it included Jewish members. In 1913–14, 92 per cent of all *Wandervögel* chapters had no Jewish members, and 84 per cent had clauses explicitly forbidding the admission of Jews.[18]

In *The Erl-King*, one of Michel Tournier's characters vividly evokes the spirit of the *Wandervögel* in the aftermath of the First World War:

The Wandervögel movement, named after the migratory birds, was first of all an act by which the younger generation cut loose from its elders. We didn't want anything to do with the defeat, the poverty, the unemployment, the political agitation. We threw back in our fathers' faces the sordid heritage they were trying to fasten on us. We refused their ethic of expiation, their corseted wives, their stifling apartments stuffed with drapes and curtains and tasselled cushions, their smoky factories, their money. We went around in little groups with our arms linked, singing, in rags but with flowers in our battered hats, our only baggage a guitar over the shoulder. And we discovered the great pure German forest with its fountains and its nymphs. Thin, dirty and lyrical, we slept in lofts and mangers and lived on love and cold water. What united us first and foremost was belonging to the same generation. We kept up a sort of freemasonry of the young.[19]

In many respects, the *Wandervögel*, with their 'earth mysticism' and idealism, anticipated the hippies of the 60s and the so-called New Age Travellers of today, except that they were primarily middle-class and did not pursue their activities on a full-time basis, only on weekends and holidays. Bands of *Wandervögel* would embark on the kind of diversions familiar enough to our own epoch: camping and hiking forays into the mountains and forests, nights spent convivially around campfires, folksinging, storytelling, poetry reading. At the simplest level, they advocated an even then clichéd 'return to nature'. The more sophisticated of them embraced a kind of romantic pantheism and a strikingly modern insistence on ecology and environmental conservation. '*Volkische*' ideology figured prominently in the *Wandervögel* movement, and there was much talk of Herder's 'folk soul', of pagan Germanic culture, of the mystique of the German forest and its nurturing power, as well as of the need to reconcile spirit and nature, and to establish a new basis for man's relationship to his environment and the natural world around him.

At their best, the *Wandervögel* could be a positive and healthy force. They included in their ranks a number of future thinkers and cultural figures, as well, of course, as the Stauffenberg brothers. They espoused a number of values and attitudes which would be found congenial today. They offered a respite, even if only temporarily, from the dire social and economic conditions that prevailed in Germany, and they represented a positive alternative to hard-line left-wing agitators who sought to foment in Germany a Russian-style revolution. Yet it is also easy to see how the *Wandervögel*, in their youthful idealism and gullibility, could be co-opted for purposes more sinister than they themselves recognised at the time.

Shortly after the Nazi accession to power, all youth movements, including the *Wandervögel*, were subsumed into a single, all-encompassing organisation, the Hitler Youth. Unlike its more bohemian predecessors, the Hitler Youth stressed obedience, hierarchy and discipline, and incorporated a specifically martial dimension. Uniforms were worn, activities were expanded to include marching and drill manoeuvres, and a military-style command structure was introduced. A new aggressiveness supplanted the old pacifism, as exemplified by the organisation's official song:

> Who'er against us stands
> Shall fall beneath our hands.
> Our lives and loyalty,
> Our Führer, are pledged to thee.[20]

There were also lectures in 'racial biology', and other such typical National Socialist preoccupations. The diffuse, more or less inchoate religious gropings of the earlier *Wandervögel* were not only reinforced, but also given a sharper, more specific, focus. Members of the Hitler Youth were initiated into neo-pagan rituals and taught, quite explicitly, that Hitler was the representative on earth of the divine.[21] Service to Hitler, and to Hitler's Germany, was invested with a sacred and consecrated status.

\*

If the *Wandervögel* anticipated developments of the 60s, so, too, did another element in the air immediately preceding and following the First World War. This, too, helped National Socialism to establish itself as a surrogate religion. Freud, Jung, Adler and Otto Rank had only just opened up the vast, new and uncharted territory of depth psychology and the unconscious. The vistas it afforded were as revelatory, and as exciting, as those following the discovery of America in the late fifteenth century. In those first heady days, psychology was able to arrogate to itself the status of a legitimate and recognised science, with all the prestige and credibility that science enjoyed. But if the psychologist was deemed analogous to the discoverer of a new continent, the true 'conquistadore' of the unconscious was the artist. Not just individual figures, but whole schools – the Surrealists in France, for example, and the Expressionists in Germany – attempted to hurl themselves into the unconscious as if into a welcoming pool. When they surfaced, they triumphantly proclaimed the unconscious to be a conduit to the numinous. Through such figures as the Surrealists and the Expressionists, psychology was made to converge with religion, and to open out, like a funnel, into a specifically religious domain. There thus arose a preoccupation with the mystical or numinous experience as a psychological phenomenon, and with what, during the 1960s, would come to be called 'altered states of consciousness'. As in the 1960s, this preoccupation was to receive an added stimulus and impetus from drugs.

Drugs were not, of course, unique to Germany. Nor were they in any sense new. Ergot had been used across Europe since pre-Christian times, and was an integral component of the medieval *Walpurgisnacht* or 'Witches' Sabbath'. Addiction to opium, in the form of laudanum, had been common in England since the early nineteenth century, when Coleridge, De Quincey and James Hogg both cursed it and drew upon it for inspiration. Absinthe had long been familiar in France and, following French conquests in North Africa, had been complemented by hashish. Both figured prominently in the works of Nerval, Baudelaire, Rimbaud and Verlaine; and both, by the end of the century, had become inseparable from

Parisian cultural and bohemian life. Morphine was prevalent across the whole of Europe, and not even Sherlock Holmes was proof against it. Cocaine, too, was everywhere, and included Sigmund Freud among its devotees. But the drugs that began to appear in Germany at the beginning of the twentieth century were altogether different in kind; and the experience they offered lent itself very specifically to a religious interpretation.

During the second half of the nineteenth century, Germany, like most other European countries, sent successive waves of emigrants across the Atlantic. Since the explorations of Alexander von Humboldt in the early years of the century, Germany had felt a particular affinity with Latin America, which had, after all, first been colonised by the conquistadores of the Habsburg emperor Charles V. In consequence, many German settlers found their way not to the United States, but to Mexico and points south. Many of them, too, formed themselves into tightly knit sects, cults and religious communities there. It was not the 'hippies' of the 1960s who 'discovered' mescaline and promoted the active ingredient of the peyote cactus around the world. It was, in fact, the German settlers of the late nineteenth and early twentieth centuries. By the end of the First World War, mescaline was readily available in Europe, and especially in Germany. Among the best-known experimenters with the drug was Hermann Hesse. It is now generally recognised that *Steppenwolf* reflects, fairly explicitly, his experience with mescaline. In the novel, the drug experience converges with a kind of spiritual or religious experience, and as a result *Steppenwolf* became as much a 'manual' for Germany's alienated youth between the wars as it did for America's alienated youth of the 1960s.

As in the United States of the 1960s, drugs were used between the wars in Germany to induce an 'altered state of consciousness' with a distinctly religious tinge. It was in precisely this domain that National Socialism manipulatively trafficked.

*

In *The Magic Mountain*, published in 1924, Thomas Mann repeatedly stresses the ease with which the mystical sensibility and so-called 'esoteric' thought can be exploited by totalitarian interests – and, indeed, can themselves become totalitarian. Once again, Mann was far-sighted. The mystical sensibility and esoteric thought were very influential in Germany between the wars. Like so much else, they were skilfully redirected and channelled into the swelling mainstream of National Socialism, and imparted to National Socialism something of their own character, energy, and orientation. They played, in fact, a significant rôle in establishing Nazism as an ersatz or surrogate religion.

During the post-war trials of the International Military Tribunal at Nuremberg, material relating to the influence of esoteric thought on National Socialism and the Nazi hierarchy was deliberately suppressed, and has been lost to the record. According to one of the British prosecutors, the late Airey Neave, large bodies of existing evidence were too bizarre to be admitted: they would have permitted too many high-ranking Nazi Party members to plead insanity and thereby escape retribution on grounds of diminished responsibility.[22] There was also a general recoil, by the Western democracies and the Soviet Union, from the very nature of the evidence itself. The Western democracies, after all, and even more so the Soviet Union, could at least claim to represent the principle of reason, the supremacy of rationality. So flagrant an eruption of the irrational as the Third Reich represented was uncomfortable, disturbing and potentially dangerous. For the world to be made aware of the sheer potency of the irrational, on so awesome a collective level, would have been to open a Pandora's box of incipient ills for the future. And it would have been profoundly unsettling, for citizens of both the Western democracies and the Soviet Union, to confront too blatantly what precisely they had been up against. After all, its latent power resided within themselves, within all humanity, as much as it did within the German people. It may perhaps have been more difficult to tap, to mobilise and channel, but it was none the less there.

In consequence, for a generation of post-war historians and commentators, the rôle of esotericism in the rise of Nazi Germany was never accorded the attention it deserved. Instead of being assessed and explored as what it was, the religious dimension of National Socialism was nervously dismissed by such facile formulations as 'mass madness', 'mass hysteria' and 'mass hypnosis', and then subordinated to theories of economics, sociology and so-called political science. A few novelists attempted to address the matter honestly. Thomas Mann and Hermann Broch, both of whom had been among the first to warn against the religious principle at work in Nazi Germany, performed the most comprehensive autopsies of it in such works as *Doctor Faustus* and *The Guiltless*. They were later followed by Michel Tournier in *The Erl-King*, by some of the Latin American novelists and by George Steiner in *The Portage to San Cristobal of A.H.* But historians chose deliberately to ignore the entire issue for more than twenty years. When it was finally acknowledged, it was acknowledged by 'fringe' historians, who, with dubious 'facts' and luridly spurious theories, swung the pendulum wildly in the opposite direction.

In 1960 there appeared in France *Le matin des mages* by Louis Pauwels and Jacques Bergier. This book, published three years later in Britain as *The Dawn of Magic* and in the States as *The Morning of the Magicians*, became an international bestseller and one of the most influential works of its time, especially for the youth of the era. Hitching a ride on the prevailing *Zeitgeist*, Pauwels and Bergier posited an elaborate conspiracy theory of history, which rested ultimately on 'occult' or esoteric principles. In the course of their exegesis, they depicted National Socialism and the Third Reich as essentially 'occult' or esoteric phenomena.

During the decade and a half that followed, the tantalising hints and snippets of evidence assembled by Pauwels and Bergier were woven into elaborate cosmic dramas, the most famous of which perhaps was *The Spear of Destiny* by Trevor Ravenscroft. But Ravenscroft's book was only one in a chain reaction of exegeses, which still continues today. Thus Nazi Germany has been interpreted in terms of alchemy, astrology, satanism, ritual magic, theosophy, anthroposophy and virtually every other such system that might come to hand.

For the most part, these interpretations toppled headlong into crankiness, if not certifiable dementia – when, that is, they were not flagrantly and perhaps cynically invented or fabricated, as many of the 'facts' on which they rested demonstrably were. In the resulting miasma, it became increasingly difficult to distinguish fact from the wilder reaches of fantasy, which gave more sober orthodox historians fresh grounds for ignoring the subject entirely. Yet while most accounts of esotericism in relation to the Third Reich were arrant nonsense or worse, there lay neglected behind them a tenuous thread of validity. Only recently has this been seriously examined. Dr Nicholas Goodrick-Clarke's 1985 study, *The Occult Roots of Nazism*, constitutes a landmark of scholarship in the field.

It is not uncommon today to speak of the French 'occult revival' of the nineteenth century. The term is accurate enough, because the phenomenon it designated comprised a reaction to the so-called (and, some would argue, misnamed) 'Enlightenment' of the century before. In Germany, however, there was no need to 'revive' the 'occult', because it had never really died out, never even gone so very deeply underground. On the contrary, it had remained an ongoing theme, a recurring leitmotif, in Germanic culture.

Esotericism had reached one climax in Germany during the first half of the seventeenth century. This was the era of the famous 'Rosicrucian Manifestos' and what the late Dame Frances Yates has called the 'Rosicrucian Enlightenment'. By the end of the seventeenth century, while rationalism was taking authoritative hold elsewhere, an updated version of 'Rosicrucian' thought was being propagated by the philosopher Gottfried Wilhelm Leibnitz. During the eighteenth century, Germany was a hotbed for the more mystically and esoterically oriented forms of Freemasonry. Under Frederick the Great's successor, Friedrich Wilhelm II, the entire Prussian administration and government bureaucracy was the most notoriously 'Rosicrucian' in Europe.

What is now known as the Romantic Movement originated in Germany during the 1770s under the auspices of the young Herder, Goethe and Schiller. Initially called '*Sturm und Drang*' ('Storm and Stress'), romanticism was to sweep across to England, then to disseminate itself throughout the rest of European culture. Goethe himself was later to repudiate romanticism, at least nominally and in theory. In practice he was to remain more or less romantic in orientation and temperament for the rest of his life; and even after his nominal repudiation of it, romanticism was kept vigorously alive in Germany by a new generation, including Novalis, Hölderlin and E. T. A. Hoffmann.

German romanticism – as *Faust* most clearly demonstrates – was

28 Torfelsen, a rocky outcrop high above Lautlingen, which was
a favourite retreat for Stauffenberg.

29 The village of Lautlingen, in the Swabian Alps south of Stuttgart.
Schloss Stauffenberg lies in the centre.

30 Schloss Stauffenberg, the family home for over three
hundred years, now a museum dedicated to music.

31 The Altes Schloss in Stuttgart where Stauffenberg
lived as a child. His father, Senior Marshal to the last king of
Württemberg, held an apartment there until 1918.

32 The poet Stefan George in 1899.

33 Stefan George and the 'Cosmics', July 1900. From left: Alfred Verwey, George, Ludwig Klages, Alfred Schuler and Karl Wolfskehl.

34 Stefan George with members of his circle in the gardens of Heidelberg Castle, 1919.

35 Stefan George in 1928.

36  Stefan George with Claus and Berthold von Stauffenberg,
Berlin, 1924.

37  Stefan George, Berthold von Stauffenberg and
Cajo Partsch in 1933.

38 The courtyard of the former army headquarters, Stauffenbergstrasse, Berlin, today a museum of the German resistance to Hitler. To the left is the entrance to Stauffenberg's office; to the centre, the site where he and his companions were shot on the evening of 20 July 1944.

39 The execution room at Ploetzensee prison, Berlin, where conspirators were hanged from rope attached to the meat-hooks.

steeped in 'occult' or esoteric thought. It also yoked 'occult' or esoteric thought to other influences that were to play key rôles in subsequent German history. Through philosophers such as Schopenhauer and Johann Gottlieb Fichte, the tradition of German mysticism – now labelled 'Idealism' – was made philosophically respectable and integrated with romantic attitudes. Gothic medievalism and a more empirical mysticism were introduced by Novalis; classical mythology was integrated by Hölderlin; the corpus of Germany's legend, fairy tale and folklore was integrated by the brothers Grimm; and a distinctive kind of pantheistic nationalism was integrated by '*Volkische*' ideology. By the mid-nineteenth century, these elements had fused and comprised the single most identifiable strand in Germanic culture. The symbolic figure who embodied them all, the tutelary genius presiding over the German collective psyche, was Faust. He is, of course, perhaps the supreme metaphor for the whole of modern Western civilisation, but he also remains uniquely German, uniquely identified with Germany. Thus does his twentieth-century avatar function in Mann's *Doctor Faustus*.

During the mid to late nineteenth century, Faust seemed for many people, German and otherwise, to have become incarnate in the person of Richard Wagner. In European cultural circles, Wagner was seen not just as 'the Master' in a musical context, but as a master magician, a supreme artistic alchemist who, according to the poet Stéphane Mallarmé in France, had transmuted and fused the entire spectrum of the arts and of human endeavour into a new, higher, unprecedentedly lofty spiritual unity. Wagner effectively founded a new religion based on '*Kultur*', and this became the official state religion if not of Germany as a whole, then certainly of Bavaria and the south.

In *The Flying Dutchman*, Wagner offered his own variation on the Faust story. In *The Master Singers*, he evoked a Germanic tradition extending from the Hohenstauffen emperors and the high Middle Ages to the Lutheran Reformation and the Free Knights of the Empire. In *Tannhäuser* and *The Ring of the Nibelungen*, he plundered Germanic myth, legend, folklore and fairy tale. In *Lohengrin* and *Parsifal*, he drew on Wolfram von Eschenbach to place the mysteries of the Grail in a new Germanic context, which was very different from that of, say, Tennyson's contemporary *Idylls of the King*. Not only did Wagner shake and stir this heady cocktail of themes. He also added to it the distinctive ingredient of pan-Aryanism – an insistence, implicit and sometimes explicit, on the uniqueness and ultimately the supremacy of Germanic thought, blood, tradition and cultural heritage.

In the wake of the Second World War, Wagner has frequently been stigmatised. Even today, he remains a source of controversy. Heated debate has raged in Israel about whether his music can be played there. To some extent, this is understandable. Wagner was certainly anti-Semitic, and his music offered inspiration to Hitler and other members of the Nazi hierarchy, who annexed as much of him as they could to their cause.

Yet Wagner's pan-Aryanism had nothing to do with political institutions or with government. It was much more spiritual, metaphorical and symbolic, much more otherworldly. In many respects, too, it was a response to other, rival, 'isms' then in the air. In Britain, complacent mutton-chop-whiskered Victorians were gamely shouldering the 'white man's burden' of imperialism and colonialism; and others, of the British Israelite Society – precursors of today's Christian fundamentalists – were arrogating to themselves an even more sanctimonious supremacy as 'God's chosen'. Across the Atlantic, America's white Anglo-Saxon Protestants were zealously promulgating, against Mexicans and Indians alike, what they ultimately regarded as less the country's than their own 'manifest destiny'. To the east, pan-Slavism was rampant, from Petersburg down through Serbia, Bulgaria and the Balkans. Indeed, at the beginning of the twentieth century, pan-Slavism was considered a greater threat to Western Europe than pan-Aryanism. The perception was not altogether askew. It was from the revolver of a pan-Slavic agitator that the shots which precipitated the cataclysm of 1914 rang out in Sarajevo.

In his temperament and many of his attitudes, Wagner was not the most endearing of human beings, nor the most sympathetic to modern thought. He was, however, an artistic genius, and probably the single most important figure in nineteenth-century musical history. Yet if he cannot unequivocally be blamed for the noxious uses to which a later generation put him, neither can his influence on that generation be altogether dismissed. Wagner not only revitalised certain key elements of esoteric tradition. He also infused those elements, and that tradition, with a uniquely and specifically Germanic character. He himself may have disdained nationalism as a political phenomenon, but, inadvertently or otherwise, he helped to establish for that phenomenon a spiritual, quasi-religious, framework, and thereby imbued it with a new and more profound justification. Perhaps more than anyone else, Wagner furnished the sanction whereby the ideal of Germany as a nation devoted to culture and the spirit could be translated, and twisted into political terms. He also provided a conduit whereby important aspects of esotericism could be channelled into National Socialism, thus imparting to National Socialism a mystical impetus.

Except for Wagner, however, esotericism in late nineteenth-century Germany was a more or less peripheral or subterranean phenomenon. In France, the so-called 'occult revival' had been gaining momentum for years. The Franco-Prussian War, the fall of the Second Empire and the collapse of external social and political institutions had engendered a period of national soul-searching, and an attending uncertainty about meaning, purpose and direction. A vacuum had been created, and a multitude of sects and cults prospered because they offered a prospect of filling it. During the period of the *fin-de-siècle*, esotericism was able to weave itself into the very fabric of French culture at the time. It was particularly evident in the 'school' of French symbolist literature exemplified by Mallarmé and the playwright Maurice Maeterlinck, and in the music of Debussy.

Germany, in contrast, had entered a period of social stability. The newly created empire offered a façade of certainty and national self-confidence. External institutions appeared to be established on a solid and unshakeable foundation. Industrialisation diverted outwards the energies which, in France, were focused on national introspection. Esotericism, therefore, played a relatively minor rôle in the national consciousness. Nevertheless, it was there and, albeit quietly, thriving. For not even the external institutions of the new imperium could altogether resolve the collective identity crisis. Nor could they altogether replace the spiritual sustenance provided by organised religion – which, faced with the challenge of Darwinian thought, was itself under serious threat and undergoing its own crisis of confidence.

In 1888, two English esotericists, Dr William Wynn Westcott and S. L. MacGregor Mathers, created the supposedly 'Rosicrucian' and magically-oriented Order of the Golden Dawn, a secret society that was to include such figures as Arthur Machen, Algernon Blackwood, Aleister Crowley and, most significantly, William Butler Yeats. Mathers later declared his organisation to have been devised, shaped and inaugurated in accordance with a blueprint received from an unidentified 'seeress' living in Ulm. The Order of the Golden Dawn was supposed to have been an essentially Germanic conception and, so Mathers implied, intended to complement other, similar secret societies which were already operating in Germany.

Yet a full half-century before the Golden Dawn traces of Germanic esotericism were seeping into British culture. Edward Bulwer-Lytton, one of the most popular 'mainstream' and typically nineteenth-century English novelists, was steeped in esoteric and 'Rosicrucian' thought. Although best known for such lumbering bestselling potboilers as *The Last Days of Pompeii* (with its oft-satirised opening sentence), Lytton also produced a number of 'occult' works: *Zanoni*, for instance, and the rather less sonorous *A Strange Story*, which he himself considered much more important. It was in his mantle of 'Rosicrucian' and esoteric propagandist that Lytton adumbrated his concept of 'Vril', a mysterious potency, *puissance* or *vertu* in the blood that might engender the supposed race of the future – a race of superior human beings, a master race of supermen. This concept, which was later to be of enormous influence among pre-Nazi esoteric sects in Germany, now seems to have originated in Germany in the first place. Lytton, in other words, was not its true author, but only its conduit.

Whatever the shadowy Germanic influences that so affected Lytton and Mathers, they were eclipsed, or perhaps subsumed, by much more public and prominent esoteric prophets whose work and teaching stamped European culture as a whole, but assumed a specific and distinctive character in Germany. During the last quarter of the nineteenth century, Theosophy, created by Helena Petrovna Blavatsky, swept Europe with an impetus and energy comparable to that of Wagner or Nietzsche. Wagner may have created a religion of his own, but few people at the time would explicitly have acknowledged it to be such. Theosophy, on the other hand, did announce itself as a full-fledged organised religion – or, rather as the definitive and supreme synthesis of all religions, the universal and all-encompassing ultra-religion of the future. It thus posed a challenge and a threat to existing faiths that generated considerable alarm. With its declared foundations in what purported to be 'esoteric Buddhism', its hierarchy of 'secret masters' and its all-embracing scope, Theosophy offered a complex framework that incorporated all other creeds within itself. It exerted an appeal for eminent cultural figures like Yeats, Conan Doyle and even Stefan George. It established its primary foothold in Britain, where it survives today, but it was no less popular on the continent. In the summer of 1884, the first Theosophical Society was founded in Germany. By the turn of the century, there were similar societies across the whole of the German and Austro-Hungarian empires. Once again, a few far-sighted artists divined a potential danger. In the early novel *Young Törless*, published in 1906, Robert Musil depicts a proto-Nazi youth exploiting the tenets of Theosophy for psychological manipulation and domination.

In Austria and Germany, Theosophy spawned a number of particularly noxious progeny, sects with a '*Volkische*', pan-Aryan and viciously anti-Semitic orientation. Among other things, these sects – collectively known as 'Ariosophy' – imparted a further esoteric and religious dimension to National Socialism, and helped provide a cosmology and a specious justification for Nazi racial theoreticians. According to Dr Nicholas Goodrick-Clarke:

> The Ariosophists . . . combined German *volkish* nationalism and racism with occult notions borrowed from the theosophy of . . . Blavatsky, in order to prophesy and vindicate a coming era of German world rule.[23]

In order to disseminate their skewed vision,

> the Ariosophists founded secret religious orders dedicated to the revival of the lost esoteric knowledge and racial virtue of the

ancient Germans, and the corresponding creation of a new pan-German empire.[24]

Three Ariosophist sects, and the personalities associated with them, were particularly influential.

In 1905, a renegade Cistercian monk, Adolf Josef Lanz, assumed the spuriously noble title of Jörg Lanz von Liebenfels and began publishing, in Vienna, a fervently anti-Semitic journal called *Ostara*. Two years later, in 1907, Liebenfels founded a cranky racist secret society dubbed '*Ordo Novi Templi*', the Order of the New Templars. On Christmas Day of that year, having purchased a small castle overlooking the Danube, he raised his order's flag – bearing a swastika – above the tower.

Among *Ostara*'s most assiduous readers and avid devotees was the young and then destitute would-be painter, Adolf Hitler, who is known to have met with Liebenfels at the journal's offices in 1909.[25] The New Templars also exerted an influence on Heinrich Himmler and, through him, on the SS. Many SS rites and ceremonies, and much of the pseudo-archaic 'runic lore' with which SS personnel were indoctrinated, derived, directly or otherwise, from Liebenfels's loathsome organisation. Among his beliefs was that of a universal psychic energy animating the cosmos, which had as 'its most perfect manifestation [the] blond-haired blue-eyed Aryan'. Among the programmes he advocated was a ritualistic immolation of 'racial inferiors' as sacrificial offerings to pagan gods.

One of Liebenfels's closest friends and associates was Guido von List, whom Dr Goodrick-Clarke describes as 'the first popular writer to combine völkish ideology with occultism and theosophy'.[26] In 1908, he created his own Guido von List Society, which overlapped the New Templars in its tenets and included a number of the same members. The membership also included the entire Viennese Theosophical Society. In 1912, certain of List's disciples created another secret society, the '*Germanenorden*' or Germanic Order.

In 1918, a Munich-based faction of the by then moribund '*Germanenorden*' founded a new organisation, known as the '*Thule Gesellschaft*' or 'Thule Society', under the leadership of an adventurer named Rudolph von Sebottendorff.[27] To the beliefs of his immediate predecessors, Sebottendorff (whose real name was Adam Glauer) added the concept of 'Vril' previously outlined by Bulwer-Lytton. Sebottendorff bought and proceeded to edit the newspaper which would subsequently become the *Völkischer Beobachter*, the official organ of the National Socialist Party, and which, by 1921, was owned by Adolf Hitler. Among the members of the '*Thule Gesellschaft*' were such later Nazi eminences as Alfred Rosenburg and Rudolf Hess. The membership also included Anton Drexler, first chairman of the National Socialist Party, and Dietrich Eckart, a demented poet who was one of Hitler's most important early mentors and, from 1921 until his death in 1923, editor of the *Völkischer Beobachter*.[28]

In France, esotericism had acquired great influence in the wake of the Franco-Prussian War, the collapse of existing social and political institutions and the ensuing crisis of faith. It helped to fill the vacuum created by a loss of national self-confidence and offered people something in which to believe. In Germany, the obverse of this situation prevailed. The apparent stability, solidity and – perhaps most significantly of all – novelty of the new social and political institutions fostered national self-confidence, and precluded the need for introspective soul-searching. In consequence, esotericism, though well entrenched, was largely confined to the periphery. In Austro-Hungary, as in Russia, the situation was something between those in France and Germany. External social and political institutions had not yet collapsed, but they were shaky and enervated, lacking in vitality and novelty, and manifestly in a state of atrophy and decay. As a result, esotericism, in both the Habsburg and Romanov empires, was something rather more than a peripheral phenomenon; and thus it was in Vienna, rather than Berlin, that the Ariosophist sects first established themselves. After 1918, however, Germany's condition was analogous to that of France in 1871, if not much worse; and as the kaleidoscope of relative values mutated into ever new configurations, esotericism, especially in the form of Ariosophy, moved inwards from the periphery, closer to the men and principles that shaped developments.

It was suggested earlier in this book that 'magic' might be defined as a metaphor reflecting the manipulative relationship between human consciousness and will on the one hand, external phenomena and people on the other. By that definition, the Ariosophist sects comprise an element of 'black magic' in the religious edifice of National Socialism. But there was also what might be regarded as a 'white magic' counter-current. As Mann said, esotericism and mystical thought have a natural affinity with totalitarianism, and are therefore susceptible to totalitarian exploitation. There are, however, exceptions that prove the rule.

For many commentators, the chief such exception – the primary embodiment of a 'white magic' counter-current to the Ariosophists – was Rudolf Steiner. Born in 1861 in what was then Hungarian territory, Steiner established credibility for himself as a Goethe scholar and the editor of Goethe's scientific writings for a projected definitive edition. From his twenties on, he was also a zealous adherent of Theosophy. In 1906, he became a member of another organisation, the *Ordo Templi Orientis*, or O.T.O., which derived obliquely from the Golden Dawn in England and was subsequently to be presided over by Aleister Crowley.

In 1913, Steiner and an entourage of primarily German disciples defected from Theosophy and created their own rival system, Anthroposophy. Steiner described Anthroposophy as 'spiritual science'. Ultimately, it was a re-vamped and updated variant of Theosophy, embedded in a specifically Christian context. It also stripped Theosophy of many of the tenets that lent themselves to racist interpretation. Not surprisingly, perhaps, Steiner became singled out for vilification and attack by the Ariosophists and, as it consolidated power, the National Socialist Party. Nazi propaganda regularly castigated Anthroposophy as an integral component in the alleged international Jewish-Masonic conspiracy.

On the whole, Anthroposophy tended to exert a beneficent influence. Among its most enthusiastic adherents, sponsors and financial supporters were the family of Helmuth von Moltke, Chief of Germany's Imperial General Staff on the outbreak of the First World War and nephew of the earlier Helmuth von Moltke, architect of victory in the Franco-Prussian War. Another adherent, at least for a time, was the great Russian novelist, poet and aesthetic theorist Andrey Bely. The currency that Steiner's thought enjoyed in such social and cultural circles attests to its influence and its aura of legitimacy and respectability. That aura remains largely intact even today. It has been reinforced by the promotion of Goethe studies, by other literary scholarship, by publishing ventures which have restored to print a number of important but neglected works, and by the network of Steiner Schools in Germany and elsewhere across the world, including Britain.

It is not altogether inappropriate, therefore, to see Steiner as a species of 'white magic' counter-current to the 'black magic' of the Ariosophists and National Socialism. Nor is it inappropriate to compare him in certain respects to Stefan George. But there were important differences between the two men. Steiner actively sought and recruited disciples. Like H. P. Blavatsky, he dreamed of establishing a new religious system, if not, indeed, a new religion. He created a large, widespread and diffuse organisation and, as a necessary corollary of this, was perfectly content to delegate authority. And although he himself was repeatedly attacked by the Nazis, he did not counter-attack. On the contrary, his particular form of mysticism – a latterday variant of German pietist tradition – led him to a sage-like pacifism reminiscent of Gandhi's.

George was much more haughtily Olympian than Steiner, much more aloof, much more fastidiously selective, much more patrician, much more 'élitist'. He did not actively seek disciples; would-be followers had first to petition him, and then pass through a stringent assessment before they were deemed worthy to sit at his feet. Unlike Steiner, George recoiled with distaste from all mass movements, which were, for him, synonymous with the mob. He had no interest in founding an organisation, for, among other things, that would have entailed delegating authority, the very suggestion of which would have been inconceivable to him. There was, and could only ever be, one Stefan George. While Steiner's gentle and accommodating *Weltanschauung* led him to a tolerant pacifism, the much more aggressive George insisted on the necessity for action.

Steiner died in 1927, when the prospects of National Socialism acquiring power in Germany still seemed remote. George died in 1933, when the Nazi accession to power had just become a *fait accompli*. We cannot know how these two men, in their differing fashions, might have reacted to subsequent developments. Both, however, through their respective disciples and protégés, were to oppose the Third Reich from beyond the grave. Yet it was George's influence, operating through Claus von Stauffenberg, that came closest to striking a decisive blow which would have transformed the course of twentieth-century history.

# 12
## *Legislators of the World*

Stefan George was born at a village near Bingen, on the Rhine between Koblenz and Wiesbaden, in 1868. He was thus three years younger than William Butler Yeats, the English-language poet he most resembles, and older than his two great Austrian contemporaries, Hugo von Hofmannsthal and Rainer Maria Rilke, by six and seven years respectively. There was one other child in his family, an elder sister. His parents owned a few vineyards, made their living in the wine trade and were devout Roman Catholics, which George himself would quickly cease to be.

Even as a schoolboy, George is said to have kept aloof from others and displayed a haughty, autocratic personality. He only joined such groups, clubs or student organisations as he could lead or preside over – and, when this was not possible, he would create his own. He began writing poetry at the age of eighteen and in 1887 began to edit his school's literary journal. He left school a year later in order to travel. Like so many important German poets and novelists, he felt magnetically drawn to southern Europe; but if the lure for Goethe, Hölderlin, Heine, Mann and others was Greece or Italy, George – though certainly devoted to the world of classical antiquity – felt a profound affinity for Spain.

In 1888, George visited England. In February of the following year, he visited Italy and then, in March, he made the first of a number of pilgrimages to Paris. Here he became acquainted with many symbolist literary figures, including Verlaine and the dying

Villiers de l'Isle-Adam. Eventually he was introduced, and apprenticed himself, to the arch-mage of '*le symbolisme*', Stéphane Mallarmé, who was also revered as a prophet and near demi-god by such English and Irish artists as George Moore, Arthur Symons, Ernest Dowson, Lionel Johnson, Oscar Wilde and W. B. Yeats. Like them, George fell under Mallarmé's spell, fervently embraced the symbolist aesthetic and adopted aspects of the French master's inscrutable demeanour. In certain respects – an insistence on rigour, discipline and an almost monastic asceticism, for example – George even outdid Mallarmé. In consequence, he contemptuously repudiated the lurid morbidity and 'decadence' – exemplified by the novelist Joris-Karl Huysmans – with which French symbolism was often associated, and which Mallarmé deigned to tolerate. This repudiation imparted to both his work and his personality a hard, uncompromising and frosty edge, which differentiated him from Hofmannsthal and Rilke, his Austrian contemporaries and fellow symbolist exponents.

Yet, like Hofmannsthal and Rilke, George dedicated himself self-consciously, and with a genuinely religious sense of vocation, to the life of the spirit – which meant, of course, the life of Art, in its most exalted, orphic and prophetic sense. George subscribed to the prevailing dictum of '*l'art pour l'art*', 'art for art's sake', but art, for George, as for the other great figures of his generation, was not what it might be for most people today – not just one of many possible and equally valid human endeavours. On the contrary, art was nothing less than a repository for the sacred, a conduit between spirit and the mundane world, a lens into the numinous. For George – as for Rilke, Hofmannsthal, Yeats, Joyce, Mann, Proust and the other monumental poets and novelists of the early twentieth century – art was a mystical vocation, and the artist was a combination of priest, prophet, magus, sorcerer, occult adept, metaphorical alchemist and, ultimately, martyr to his calling. In consequence, the frontiers between art and religion, art and magic, art and the esoteric, were deliberately blurred.

George concurred with Shelley's famous statement that 'poets are the unacknowledged legislators of the world', and resented the fact that they were unacknowledged. He regarded the poet as 'the appointed keeper of the nation's inner strength' – in other words, of its 'folk soul' or true collective identity. The poet, in effect, was not what he is generally understood to be, but something closer to the sacred bards of ancient Wales and Ireland, or the wrathful and chastising prophets of the Old Testament:

> In placid times they say the poet is
> A wingèd child who sings his tender dreams
> And showers beauty on a busy world.
> But when abuses swell into a storm,
> And Destiny pounds at the door his verses
> Ring like a pick on ore . . .
> When all are blinded he, the only seer,
> Unveils the coming doom in vain . . .[1]

And further:

> But in a mournful age it is the poet
> Who keeps the marrow sound, the germ alive.
> He stirs the holy flame . . .
>
> A younger generation rises towards him,
> The youths who, steeled by years of galling pressure,
> Again have honest standards for the probe
> Of men and things . . .
>
> He breaks the chains and sweeps aside the rubble,
> He scourges home the lost to lasting law,
> Where lord is lord again, the great is great
> And where integrity returns. He fastens
> The true device upon the nation's banner.
> Through tempests and the dread fanfares of dawning
> He leads his tried and faithful to the work
> Of sober day and founds the Kingdom Come.[2]

In 1890, George travelled to Copenhagen and again to Paris. In that year, he also produced his first volume of verse, *Hymnen* (*Odes*), a slender volume in an edition of one hundred copies intended for private circulation only. A year later, he produced a second volume, *Pilgerfahrten* (*Pilgrimages*) and visited England again, Munich and

Vienna, where he met and became friends with Hofmannsthal. In 1892 he organised the clique of associates and disciples which was to become known as the '*George Kreis*', the 'George Circle'. In that year, too, there appeared the first issue of *Blätter für die Kunst*, the esoteric-oriented literary and cultural journal which George was to co-edit for the next twenty-seven years. The inaugural issue contained, along with some of his own poems, one by Hofmannsthal. In its subsequent issues, the journal, as much as the manifestos and volumes of poetry that appeared concurrently, affords an accurate and ongoing reflection of George's personal and artistic development.

In 1893, George became loosely associated with an Ariosophist-style cultural school called the 'Cosmics', and with two of their mentors, the racial theoreticians Alfred Schuler and Ludwig Klages. Before long, his relations with them became strained, and plummeted when George, disgusted, walked out in the middle of an anti-Semitic diatribe by Schuler. Associates of both men made sporadic attempts to heal the rift, but George was becoming increasingly incensed by pseudo-scientific blither about 'pure blood' and by anti-Semitism generally. By 1904, his breach with Schuler, Klages and their entourage had become permanent. It is significant that this, rather than any aesthetic disagreement, constituted the grounds for the rupture. But it was an aesthetic disagreement that led, shortly thereafter, to a rupture between George and Hofmannsthal. Or, to be more precise, it was Hofmannsthal's refusal to accord George unquestioning deference and the status of supreme aesthetic potentate.

In the meantime, successive volumes of poetry had appeared in 1893, 1894, 1897 and 1899. And in 1902, in Munich, George had encountered a twelve-year-old youth named Maximilian Kronberger, for whom he conceived a highly idealised, and stylised, affection. Contrary to allegations made at the time, and even today repeated, it seems clear that there was no homosexual relationship between George and Maximilian. In fact, George saw Maximilian on no more than a dozen occasions, and always in public or in the boy's home and in the presence of his mother. But Maximilian came to be imbued by the poet with a portentous symbolic significance – came to represent an epitome of classical Grecian beauty in human

form and, as such, an 'avatar' of divine forces. This fused with a
poignant solicitude and tenderness, very likely paternal in character,
and engendered a passionate attachment – probably the most
passionate attachment of George's life. When Maximilian died in
1904, George was stricken. Maximilian's death – the fragile
mortality of what had seemed so sublime and so supernal –
continued to haunt him for years afterwards. He seems not wholly
to have recovered from the blow until 1924, when, it has been
suggested, the young Claus von Stauffenberg appeared as an 'avatar'
of the same numinous principles formerly incarnated by the boy
who had died twenty years before.

By the first decade of the new century, George was beginning to
publish for, and reach, a wider audience. He maintained a restlessly
peripatetic lifestyle, moving constantly between Berlin, Munich,
Bingen, Vienna, Frankfurt and Heidelberg. In each of these cities he
had a circle of friends who served to insulate him, acting as a buffer
between himself and the world and enabling him to sustain his aloof
stance. The members of each such circle were carefully vetted and
expected to prove worthy of George's lofty expectations. His
relation to them was always that of 'Master' to disciple. They were
obliged to swear an oath of allegiance to the circle and to George
personally. In his book on Stefan George, E. K. Bennett makes it
clear that it was 'not just a conception of poetry which the disciples
were required to share with the Master, but a conception of life'.[3]
It was Hofmannsthal's refusal to accept these terms that led to
his alienation from George.

For three years following Maximilian Kronberger's death,
George published nothing. Then, in 1907, there appeared his
seventh volume of poetry, entitled *Der Siebente Ring* (*The Seventh
Ring*), divided into seven sections. Among other things, this volume
reflected the influence of Theosophy and H. P. Blavatsky, for whom
seven was the supreme sacred number. But *The Seventh Ring* also
marked a dramatic change in George's orientation, something
amounting to a kind of conversion.

In the past, George had shared with Mallarmé and the French
symbolists not only an aesthetic, but also a comprehensive
*Weltanschauung* which encompassed its own metaphysics and ethics.
According to symbolist metaphysics, the material or phenomenal

world was ultimately but a reflection of some other, higher reality – what Mallarmé generally denoted by such words as '*l'azur*' and '*l'idéal*'. Symbolist ethics dictated a complete dissociation of the artist from society. The symbolists did not see themselves as teachers or mentors: their rôle was simply to embody and refract the numinous in the perfect work of art, which need be accessible only to fellow initiates. To this extent, they felt themselves absolved from mundane morality and all social or pedagogical responsibility.

Until the end of his life, George continued to employ symbolist literary techniques, and remained loyal to the underlying aesthetic, but with *The Seventh Ring* he repudiated the accompanying metaphysics and ethics. He now undertook to seek and reflect the sacred, the numinous, not in some ethereal 'other' dimension, but in the actual and mundane world around him. The characteristically intangible images of the symbolists – smoke, mist, clouds, sky and wind – began to disappear from his poetry, and were replaced by motifs that were harder, more solid, more tangible, often with a polished, glazed and brightly enamelled patina. And Maximilian's death seemed to have left him with a legacy of responsibility, of obligation to Germany's young. He appointed himself custodian of Germany's spiritual and cultural future. Abandoning the godlike indifference of the symbolist poet-mage, he assumed the more Platonic or Pythagorean rôle of mentor and teacher. He remained, of course, detached and aloof. He was hardly going to demean himself as a conventional pedagogue. But with the élite, handpicked cadre of youths he admitted to his circle, he felt himself playing a part analogous to that played in Greek myth by Chiron, the centaur who functions as guide, instructor and tutor to such heroes as Aesculapius, Jason, Achilles and Hercules.

In the past, then, George had sought to impart to art, and especially to poetry, a new purity and perfection. After 1907. he sought to impart a new purity and perfection to reality itself – or, more specifically, to Germany's future. '*L'idéal*' of Mallarmé was now no longer to be a remote transcendant principle, but an agent active in the phenomenal world – as what one commentator has called 'a germinating and transforming seed'. According to one of his associates writing at the time, George felt himself entrusted with 'a holy mission which raised him alone above the mass of fellow poets . . . [He] believed fanatically in the advent of a new spirit-filled age and in his special mission to bring it about.'[4]

To this end, his circle had not only to be esoteric initiates. They had also to be mystical warriors, soldiers of the spirit engaged on a spiritual crusade. In this respect, they were heir to the knights in the poem entitled 'Templars', although George meant by the term something very different from the Ariosophist New Templars of Lanz von Liebenfels.

> Once in a Golden Age we merged with all,
> For aeons now the crowd has shunned our call.
> We are the Rose: the young and fervent heart,
> The Cross: to suffer proudly is our art.
>
> On unknown courses, silent and austere,
> We turn the sombre spool, we turn the spear.
> Through coward years our flaming weapon rings,
> We scourge the people and we challenge kings.
>
> We do not join the customs and the bout
> Of those who look askance at us and doubt
> And fear because their hatred never felled
> What with our savage love we caught and held.
>
> Whatever loot our swords and slings have gained
> Pours negligently from our spendthrift hand,
> And though our rage devises harsh decrees,
> Before a child we fall upon our knees.
>
> We veil the flashing glance, the loosened lock
> Which once betrayed the lord in beggar's smock,
> Shyly from forward swarms who on our shade
> – When we are gone – confer their accolade.
>
> We nursed at alien breast and so our sons
> Shall never be the children of our loins,
> They never will be weak, dilute, or old,
> For unborn fires quicken in their mould.
>
> And only one of ours can complete
> The needed change or do the iron feat

To which they summon us when chaos reigns,
Only to stone and curse us for our pains.

And when in wrath the Mighty Mother scorns
To lean and couple at the lower bourns,
Some world-night when her pulses scarcely stir,
Then only one who always strove with her,

Ignored her wishes and denied her will,
Can crush her hand and grip her hair until
Submissively she plies her work afresh:
Turns flesh to god, embodies god in flesh.[5]

The latterday 'Templars' George gathered around him comprised for him a unique kind of nobility and aristocracy of the spirit, not unlike that extolled a few years earlier by Nietzsche, and a few years later by D. H. Lawrence. The status of this élite had nothing whatever to do with social class, caste or background, and nothing to do with race or heritage:

The nobility you long for
Does not hail from crown and scutcheon.
Through their glances men of every
Rank betray their venal fancies
And their raw and ribald prying.
Sons of rare distinction grow from
Anywhere among the people,
And you will discern your kindred
By their frank and fervent eyes.[6]

It was for this nobility, for the sources of their inspiration and for what they were expected to achieve, that the words 'Secret Germany' were first employed. In 1910, three years after the publication of *The Seventh Ring*, one of George's disciples composed an essay on the importance of the circle as the seed from which German renewal would spring:

For what is beginning to stir today beneath the desolate superficial crust is still half a dream, the secret Germany, the only living thing in this time . . . (and) only here put into words.[7]

The essay, which had George's own personal blessing, went on to state that the revitalisation of Europe's culture and spirit could only emanate 'from the secret Germany, for which each of our words is spoken, from which each of our verses draws its life and rhythm'.[8] Another disciple wrote that 'the members of the Secret Germany consider themselves as a "cloister" or an "Order".[9] In *Weimar Culture* P. Gay says that George, unlike Nietzsche, 'did not choose to be alone; it was the heart of his method to build a secret empire for the sake of the new Reich to come . . . It was an élitist programme pushed to the very limits of élitism; the secret Germany was a club to which new members were elected, and for which they were trained, one by one. Many called, few were chosen . . .'[10]

Through the circle's journal, through his own work and that of his disciples, George's vision evolved and came into ever sharper focus. There were echoes of Nietzsche and, paradoxically and despite George's distaste for 'decadence', Gabriele d'Annunzio, who was not only the arch 'decadent' of the age, but also perhaps its most flamboyantly (if self-appointedly) heroic figure. There were many echoes of H. P. Blavatsky and Theosophy. There were echoes of Wagner, even though George seems to have concurred with Musil's description of Wagner's music as 'a luggage van bound for the Infinite'. There were also many echoes of classical thought and mythology, such as characterised the work of George's most important Germanic precursor, Friedrich Hölderlin.

In many respects, George was unabashedly pagan, scathingly condemning Judaeo-Christian tradition and theology. Church teachings were for him 'a cycle of venerable fairy tales' and 'the last glowing embers of a creed which had had its time'. His paganism, while emphasising form and formal perfection, was never materialistic. It remained highly spiritualised, almost platonic. The fauns in George, like those in Mallarmé, are not crude embodiments of lust and 'unregenerate nature'. On the contrary, they are oracles; they are mythic incarnations of the sublime magic that sustains all life; and they are manifestations of a spirituality more intense and profound than that of any organised religion. In a poetic dialogue entitled 'Man and Faun', one of the horned, cloven-footed and goat-tailed creatures speaks thus to its human interlocutor:

Beasts are devoid of shame and men of thanks.
With all that you contrive you never learn
What most you need, but we in silence serve.
One thing: In slaying us you slay yourselves.
Where we have trailed our shag the milk will spurt,
Where we withhold our hooves no blade will grow.
If only mind of men had reigned, your kind
And all you do would long ago be done.
Your fields would be infertile, dry your brake . . .
Only by magic life is kept awake.[11]

In his paganism, George did not share Heine's fear of Wotan and
Thor re-emerging to demolish the cathedrals of Christendom.
'Each age', he felt, 'has only / One god, and only one proclaims his
throne'.[12] He warned that 'when its gods have died a people dies'.[13]
And future renewal resided, again, with the nation's young: 'Now
youth calls up the gods, both the eternal / And the returning when
their day is rounded.'[14] In consequence, George was quite prepared
to welcome new manifestations of the forces and principles
anthropomorphised as the gods of antiquity. Like Hölderlin,
however, he was less interested in the old Teutonic pantheon than he
was in that of the classical world. He sought in the soil of Germany,
in a uniquely and specifically Germanic context, certain forces,
certain principles, certain embodiments of energy, certain dynamics
or processes at work that might be ascribed, metaphorically, to the
agency of 'deities'. George denoted these incarnations, or what
might be called 'concentrations of godhood', as 'avatars', a term that
figured prominently in Theosophical thought. But the 'avatars' of
H. P. Blavatsky were intended to be taken literally – invisible 'secret
masters' in the Himalayas who periodically, as in the case of Jesus,
assumed human form and intervened in the world's affairs.
George's 'avatars', like the somewhat similar figures scattered
through the work of W. B. Yeats, were much more metaphorical
and symbolic.

One of the most important 'avatars' in George's work is a figure
invoked under the name of 'Maximin', implying all the associations
of the English words 'maximum' and 'minimum' – everything and
nothing, for example, or greatest and least, or macrocosm and

microcosm. As he functions in George's work, 'Maximin' is quite clearly a kind of artistic reincarnation of the dead youth Maximilian Kronberger. Resurrected and translated into literary immortality, 'Maximin' displays all the attributes of godhood – a godhood which constitutes George's own unique personal inspiration and presides over his relationship to the young who are Germany's future. Thus, in the fragment entitled 'Maximin':

> To some you are a child,
> To some a friend, to me
> The god whom I divined
> And tremble to adore.[15]

And in 'Incarnation':

> Now that you are strong and high,
> What you have prophesied was done:
> You have changed our pact, and I
> Am the child of my own son.[16]

In other words, the poet has been reborn through the agency of his own literary creation and the youth who inspired it. This becomes clearer from another poem, 'Introit':

> Resigned I face the riddle that he is
> My child, and I the child of my own child . . .[17]

> Who is your god? All that my dreams avowed,
> Kin to my vision, beautiful and proud.
> He is the force the lap of darkness vented,
> The sum of every greatness we were granted,
> The deepest source, the inmost blaze – he is
> Where I have found the purest form of these.
> He flooded every vein with richer teeming
> Who first for one was rescue and redeeming.
> He filled the gods of old with fresher breath,
> And all the words the world has done to death.
> The god is veiled in highest consecration,

With rays around he manifests his station,
Embodied in a son whom stars begot
And a new centre conjured out of thought.[18]

To the modern mind, much of this may seem bizarre. One must remember, however, that it is essentially a personal mythology transmuted into a symbolic poetic 'system'. As such, it is not significantly different, and certainly no more bizarre, than the elaborate system evolved by Yeats and outlined in that most daunting of all his works, *A Vision*. And indeed, there is one very specific antecedent for George's concept of 'avatars' in English literature: the short narratives such as 'Denys l'Auxerrois' and 'Apollo in Picardy' by Walter Pater in the collection *Imaginary Portraits*.

The 'avatars' that interested George were universal in their attributes, but also uniquely and specifically manifest in a Germanic context. Throughout his work, there is a preoccupation with German history, with sacred sites and topographical features such as the Rhine, and with illustrious figures of a semi-legendary heroic past. Among the most important of these figures were the Hohenstauffen emperors of the high Middle Ages, and especially the greatest of them, Friedrich II, who brazenly defied the pope, established a multi-cultural and multi-racial court in Sicily, provided a bridge to the West for Arabic and Judaic arts and sciences, and professed himself an adept in alchemy, astrology and other arcane disciplines. In 1927, Ernst Kantorowicz, one of the Jewish members of George's circle, published what was then regarded as the definitive biography of Friedrich. Three years previously, in May 1924, a number of members of the circle, including Berthold von Stauffenberg, made a special pilgrimage to Friedrich's tomb in Palermo. Once again, the phrase 'secret Germany' was invoked. On the sarcophagus of the Hohenstauffen ruler, a wreath was laid bearing the inscription:

SEINEN KAISERN UND HELDEN
DAS GEHEIME DEUTSCHLAND

['To their emperors and heroes
From the Secret Germany'][19]

It must be remembered that this designation, 'Secret Germany', was not only used to denote George's circle. It was also, later, to be the name Claus von Stauffenberg adopted for his cadre of conspirators. And '*Es lebe unser geheimes Deutschland!*' – 'Long live our Secret Germany!' – were to be his last words, flung back defiantly at the firing squad that took his life.[20]

Given George's characteristic themes – the glory and majesty of Germany's resonant past, the propensities of a sacred soil to nurture avatars of godhood, the formation of a new aristocracy of the spirit which evoked echoes of the Nietzschean 'superman' – it is not difficult to see why he should have endeared himself to the National Socialist hierarchy. Superficially, at least, his treatment of these themes seemed to harmonise perfectly with theirs, just as did many elements in Nietzsche and Wagner. And there were other motifs in George's work which also proved of considerable interest to the Nazis.

The swastika today has only one primary association. It immediately connotes, above anything and everything else, the Third Reich. During the first three decades of the twentieth century, however, the swastika was a familiar quasi-esoteric device – as familiar as, say, the phoenix. Even Rudyard Kipling had many of his books printed with a swastika embossed on the jacket. It had long been an ancient sun symbol in ancient Hinduism and certain schools of Tibetan Buddhism. H. P. Blavatsky's personal emblem consisted of an anti-clockwise swastika within a circle, surmounted by the interlocked triangles – or six-pointed star – of the mystical 'Seal of Solomon'. From 1892 until 1900, translations of Blavatsky's works were printed in a German periodical that bore a swastika on its cover. And the swastika was adopted, too, by certain of the Ariosophist sects, such as the Order of the New Templars and the Thule Society. It symbolised their self-arrogated connection with Indian thought, and their putative claim to a racial link with the ancient Aryans who colonised the Indian sub-continent.

George, too, adopted the swastika and used it as a personal device on his publications, as did certain members of his circle. Its associations for George were as private and idiosyncratic as those of the phoenix were for D. H. Lawrence, and he used it in much the same way. To outsiders, not surprisingly, it seemed to imply a shared *Weltanschauung*, perhaps even an identification, with the Ariosophists, and subsequently with National Socialism.

Even more important than his use of the swastika, however, were the connotations and implications George attached to the term '*Führer*'. It has now been virtually established that the significance Hitler attached to the term derived directly from George.[21] According to *Mein Kampf*, Hitler saw his first opera, Wagner's *Lohengrin*, as a boy of twelve in Linz. At the end of the last act of this opera, the title of '*Führer*', which means literally nothing more than 'leader', is conferred by Lohengrin on the Duke of Brabant. Undoubtedly, given Wagner's appeal to Hitler, the term's significance in *Lohengrin* cannot be overlooked, especially when one recalls Hitler's infatuation with the Grail romances, the later depiction of him as would-be 'Grail knight' and the attempt to exalt the SS as a latterday conflation of the Teutonic Knights with those of the Round Table. But it was George, not Wagner, who invested the title of '*Führer*' with the specific qualities that Hitler, in his use of it, arrogated to himself.

George had immersed himself in the arcane cosmological systems of Joachim de Fiore, a twelfth-century Cistercian esotericist whose subsequent influence was to be considerable – on Dante, for example, on Renaissance magi like Giordano Bruno, on such of George's own contemporaries as Joyce and Yeats, on such modern literary figures as Michel Tournier. If George's preoccupation with the number seven owed something to Theosophy, it owed much more to Joachim, whose own preoccupation with the number involved, among other things, the opening of the Book of the Seven Seals described in Revelation. Joachim also endeavoured to divide human history into three messianic ages – cycles of time presided over by God the Father, God the Son and God the Holy Spirit. The age of God the Father corresponded to the period of the Old Testament, the age of God the Son to the Christian era of the New. The age of the Holy Spirit, according to Joachim, would correspond to the dispensation of the future, which would supersede that of conventional Christendom and the established Church.

In the years just before and after Joachim's death in 1202, rumours and legends began to circulate of a great messianic emperor who would transform and redeem European civilisation. These came increasingly to focus on the Hohenstauffen emperor Friedrich II, who did nothing to dispel them. On the contrary, he and his propagandists actively encouraged them, and milked them for all they were worth. Friedrich proclaimed his own birthplace to be a second Bethlehem and declared himself to have been 'raised up by God in the spirit of Elijah' (whose mystical return had been one of Joachim's recurrent themes). 'To his supporters,' the historian M. Reeves has observed, 'Frederick was the ultimate *renovator mundi*', the ultimate renewer and redeemer of the world.[22] He took pains to identify himself quite specifically with the ruler ordained to preside over Joachim de Fiore's age of the Holy Spirit.

In describing this ruler, Joachim had used the Latin designation '*dux*'. He had cited Matthew 2:6, the earliest Latin versions of which read: '*Et tu Bethlehem terra Iuda . . . ex te enim exiet dux . . .*' A modern Bible will usually translate this as: 'And you, Bethlehem, in the land of Judah . . . for out of you will come a ruler . . .' But 'ruler' is not the only, nor even the most accurate, rendering of '*dux*'. Neither are such later derivations as the English 'duke', the French '*duc*', the Italian '*duce*' (as adopted by Mussolini) or the German '*Herzog*', which Luther used in his vernacular translation of the Bible. All of these denote a particular rank of nobility, which came into being only during the latter days of the Roman Empire. Prior to that, '*dux*' meant, quite simply, 'leader'. But its context in Matthew imbued it with specifically messianic connotations. A '*dux*', in other words, was not just a conventional leader, but a messianic leader – a messiah, a saviour, a redeemer, ordained and consecrated for his rôle by the active principle of divine grace, God's will made manifest.[23] Vestiges of this exalted significance persist even today. Thus, for example, a British duke or duchess is not a 'Majesty', nor a 'Highness', but a 'Grace'.

Luther's translation of the Bible may have used for '*dux*' the word '*Herzog*', the German equivalent of 'duke'. Later German Bibles use for '*dux*' a much more accurate word. They use '*Führer*', meaning a specifically messianic leader. It was precisely in this sense that George used the word in, for example, *The Seventh Ring*. It was precisely in this sense, too, that members of George's circle used the word, sometimes in reference to George himself. In 1928 one of his disciples, Max Kommerell, published *Der Dichter als Führer in der deutschen Klassik* (*The Poet as Leader in the German Classical Period*), a text extolling Hölderlin as 'the seer of the secret Germany' which would one day in the future awake. At the present time, Kommerell concluded, Stefan George 'is the *Führer*' – in, again, a specifically messianic sense.[24] It was precisely in this sense, with all its lofty and exalted religious connotations, that Hitler appropriated the designation for himself. The supposedly redemptive principles he advocated were, of course, rather different from poetry.

The Nazis were more than eager to acknowledge their debts to George and to do him homage. Certain of his poems were officially read out during celebrations of National Socialist Party Day in Nuremberg, as well as at Hitler Youth meetings. His last volume of poetry, *Das Neue Reich* (*The New Reich*) was hailed as heralding the National Socialist dispensation. George himself was acclaimed as a prophet who had anticipated the new era, in which the spheres of spirit and politics would merge. He was consistently lauded as an oracular custodian of German self-awareness and identity (which, under the new régime, would fully manifest itself through the German people). There were many invitations and appeals for him to join the National Socialist Party, which already included a few members of his own circle.

George was painfully aware of the ways in which Nietzsche had been appropriated, misinterpreted and exploited. He was scathing in his condemnation, while, at the same time, commiserating with the dead philosopher, whom he acknowledged as a '*Führer*' and explicitly linked with Jesus:

> The rule of fervent silence shall continue
> Until the brutes who soil him with their praise
> And fatten further on the reek of rotting
> Which helped to strangle him, at last are stifled.
> But you shall live in glory through the ages
> With crowned and bleeding brow like other leaders.[25]

That he himself would soon suffer a fate similar to Nietzsche's was becoming, to George, only too bitterly apparent.

In actual fact, he loathed and despised the Nazis, who represented 'ghastly caricatures of his elusive ideal'.[26] They gradually began to assume for him a status even more loathsome than his antipathies and 'pet peeves' of longer standing. Aloof, patrician, aristocratic and élitist as he was, George had always recoiled from 'the mob' and everything associated with it, including, of course, such mass movements as Communism – which, in seeking a lowest common denominator, reduced all humanity to the level of 'the mob'. He had always recoiled from '*das Leichte*', the 'Facile' – the ersatz, the shoddy, the spurious, the vulgar, the tacky, everything that resulted from spiritual and creative laziness and the quest for a 'short cut'. He had always recoiled from what he called 'Prussianism', by which he meant not just militarism, but also conformity, uniformity, regimentation, stodginess, bureaucracy, straight-laced complacency, philistinism, materialism and an arid lack of imagination.

The Nazis, for George, combined all of these things in a new nadir of human and spiritual degradation. National Socialism effectively fused mob mentality with both the 'Facile' and 'Prussianism'. And the Party's adherents were guilty, too, of an even more grievous transgression – of tramping into the sacred domain of George's own rarefied thought, appropriating it as their own and in the process, reducing it to a gauche and grotesque travesty. In Nazism, George saw elements of his own exalted and supernal vision reflected as in a trick mirror at a fun fair, warped and twisted perversely out of shape. To that extent, his grievance with National Socialism was more intensely personal than, say, Thomas Mann's, whose detached, Olympian yet unequivocal hostility was proof against any attempt to co-opt it. The Nazis, George felt, had plundered and sullied sacrosanct aspects of his most private self – the very inspiration and sense of mission that sustained him. And thus, though he was never threatened as Mann was, his only option was exile – exile dictated not by self-preservation, but by an overwhelming disgust.

If George's attitude towards Nazism was misunderstood – both by the Nazis themselves and by subsequent commentators – so, too, were certain of his other attitudes. He has sometimes been accused, for example, of anti-Semitism. Yet he spurned the so-called 'Cosmics' and the racial theoreticians associated with them precisely because he recoiled from anti-Semitism. His attitude towards anti-Semitism was one of lofty, almost weary, contempt:

A racial policy is no new thing: it is no more than an evil legacy from the nineteenth century. Only the spirit, not some breeding establishment, is capable of producing a good new race of men.[27]

George's grievance was not with Jews or with Judaism, but, like Lawrence's, with Judaeo-Christian thought and tradition, with values and attitudes rather than with people. So far as people were concerned, George made no distinction whatever between 'Jewish' and 'Aryan' Germans. There were a number of Jewish members in his circle, one of whom later joined the German resistance in Holland and died in a concentration camp. In the summer of 1933, shortly after the Nazi accession to power, another Jewish member of George's circle, a woman named Edith Landmann, wrote an essay entitled 'To the German Jews who belong to the Secret Germany'.[28] In this essay, Frau Landmann endeavoured to raise support for an ambitious scheme – an exodus of German Jews and the creation of ideal communities, based on George's thinking, abroad.

In his attitude towards Judaism as such, George characteristically sought deeper, more subterranean dynamics than were apparent to the naked eye. He took pains to discern latent connections between Germans and Jews. For George, the hatred and prejudice involved in German anti-Semitism displayed an intensity only possible in instances of blood kinship and self-recognition – the relationship, ultimately of Cain and Abel. If Jews were guilty of anything, it was of being too akin to the Germans.

> You, the extremes: the one from barren snow-drifts
> And wave-swept cliffs, the other from the glowing
> Wastes of a spectral god, are both at equal
> Remove from radiant seas and fields where mortals
> Live out their lives and shape themselves and gods.
> Fair-haired or dark, the selfsame womb begot you.
> Each hates and seeks and does not know his brother,
> And always roams and never is fulfilled.[29]

Behind these ostensibly straightforward lines, there is what the jargon of current literary criticism would label a complex 'sub-text'. The same sub-text was also being explored and developed by Thomas Mann, who addressed it in his massive tetralogy, *Joseph and*

*His Brothers*. Like Mann, George was aware of how extremes of climate encouraged altered states of consciousness and thereby religious experiences. The primary agent in the relationship between climate and consciousness was wind.

The Greek word '*pneuma*' combines a number of associated meanings. It denotes 'spirit', and 'breath' or 'exhalation', and also 'wind'. As George was aware, the association of these, as exemplified by the word '*pneuma*', had been a commonplace since biblical times, if not indeed before, and had figured prominently throughout esoteric thought. Wind was taken to be, quite literally, the breath of God, God's spirit, the closest approximation God ever assumed to physical manifestation. For Joachim de Fiore, wind functioned as symbolic herald for the coming age of the Holy Spirit; and the same theme has more recently been developed by Michel Tournier.

In Ecclesiastes 12:7, the '*Ruach*', the fiercely hot desert wind, is equated with the spirit that returns to God after the body has died and returned to dust. For the ancient Israelites, however, the '*Ruach*' was the literal breath of their god of wrath. Indeed, as Thomas Mann has argued, there are etymological grounds for believing that the very word '*Ruach*' evolved into 'Yahweh' and thence into 'Jehovah'. In much the same fashion, Wotan, whose name evolves from '*Wode*', an archaic Germanic word for 'rage', derived from the shrill Valkyrie-like shrieking of the Arctic wind sweeping through the ancient Germanic forests.

In their later development, both Wotan and Jehovah were essentially gods of wrath, of power, of majesty, of pageant and spectacle, of battle and conquest, of Cecil B. De Mille special effects and casts of thousands. Both trafficked in the particular kind of fear, or 'sacred awe', engendered by grandeur and sheer physical ferocity, yet in their origins both were gods of wind and, as such, essentially formless. For George, form was of paramount importance; and the sculpted, anthropomorphic divinities of the classical world were thus immeasurably more congenial to him than the abstraction of wind-born deities.

If allegations of pro-Nazi sympathies and anti-Semitism on George's part have been misplaced, so, too, have allegations of his homosexuality. His relationship with Maximilian Kronberger, despite assumptions to the contrary, was never homo-erotic in character or in practice; and the love expressed in the poems post-dating Maximilian's death could hardly be described as amorous idolatry. It is, rather, a paternal tenderness and solicitude fused with a rarefied platonic soul kinship. There is no evidence that any other relationships in George's life were homosexual. And although he displayed little interest in women, during the 1890s he maintained a lengthy affair with Ida Coblenz, who later married a member of his circle. Ultimately, it would seem, George was not so much either homosexual or heterosexual as simply 'sexless'. He appears to have sublimated his sexuality entirely into an exalted idealisation of 'pure' beauty and 'pure' form.

George's asexuality is illuminated by Gustave von Aschenbach, the protagonist of Thomas Mann's nouvelle *Death in Venice*. Contrary to the impression conveyed by Visconti's film, Mann's nouvelle is most emphatically not a psychological 'case study' of homosexuality, latent or of any other kind. The real theme in *Death in Venice* is the toll exacted on the personality by a life dedicated, with a single-minded and religious sense of vocation, to the spirit and to art. Such monomaniacal dedication inevitably involves a cost to other aspects of the personality, which, rigorously suppressed and denied all expression, fester in a neglected recess of the psyche, turn rancid and depraved.

In his monklike devotion to art, Aschenbach, Mann tells us, has lived his life like a perpetually clenched fist. The nouvelle depicts how, fatigued by the incessant pressure it has sustained, this fist, under the influence of almost any catalyst, can inadvertently relax – and how aspects of human experience, repudiated for so long and consequently corrupted, can then suddenly erupt with obsessive power and usurp the foreground of consciousness. Aschenbach has devoted his life religiously to beauty of form. When he is seduced, it is not by sexuality, nor by eroticism, but by a human embodiment of what he has always worshipped – a pure, classically Grecian beauty of form. The youth by whom he is besotted conforms precisely to George's concept of an 'avatar', but this youth could just as easily have been a girl, or an animal, or a tree, or a landscape. In human form, however, beauty becomes more seemingly attainable – and in masculine human form, more potent as a metaphor.

Homosexuality in *Death in Venice* is essentially a metaphor rather than a psychological phenomenon explored for its own sake. The real issue is Aschenbach's self-abandonment and the 'depravity' that follows. Homosexuality was simply the most shocking metaphor that Mann, writing in 1911, could find for self-abandonment and 'depravity', but Aschenbach could just as readily have succumbed to heterosexual dissipation, to gambling, to alcoholism, to drug addiction or to any of numerous possible manifestations of a hitherto rigorously controlled psyche losing control of itself and being overwhelmed by its own neglected aspects.

Aschenbach is often said to have been based, at least in part, on Gustav Mahler, a suggestion reinforced, obviously, by his Christian name. Yet there are reasons for suggesting that he was also based on Stefan George, whom Mann described as 'this proud and priestly temperament'. Certainly Aschenbach's life – lived like a clenched fist which makes him a 'culture hero', a beacon and 'rôle model' for generations of youth – has much in common with George's. It is clear that George recognised something of himself in Aschenbach and took umbrage. He pronounced *Death in Venice*, as Mann ruefully and sympathetically acknowledged, to be 'the highest drawn down into the realm of decadence'.[30] For George, then, writing in 1911, adoration of classical beauty in human form was commendably lofty and worthy, but homosexual attraction, even if never actualised in practice, was decadent and reprehensible. Like Aschenbach, George lived his life like a clenched fist. In George's case, however, the fist remained firmly clenched.

When asked what constituted his greatest work, George, in words now famous, replied: 'My friends.' His concept of friendship was rather different from what most people would associate with the word. For George, it entailed warmth, trust, intimacy and loyalty, but it also entailed aloofness, remoteness and detachment – the relation, again, of a magus or guru to his deferential disciples. He drew sustenance from their adulation and fidelity, but kept himself deliberately distant and mantled in mystery. Discussion in his circle revolved primarily around 'ideas' and 'issues'. If it ever became personal at all, it became so in connection with his protégés' lives rather than his own. George ultimately saw his 'friends' as sources of inspiration for himself, and as malleable raw material to be shaped and groomed, as if his relationship to them were itself a work of art.

Yet it is doubtful whether any of George's disciples would have seen that relationship as in any sense one-sided or selfish. Nor can one deny the element of altruism in his attitude. Although he himself was hardly a man of action – he conveys an impression of physical inertia worthy of the Buddha, if not, indeed, of full-fledged godhood – he insisted, emphatically and repeatedly, on the necessity for action by his disciples. They were to be the custodians of Germany's future, an exclusive and élite cadre meticulously nurtured and honed for the task of leadership. The training and refinement of this cadre was something George regarded as a mission, a sacred duty, a discharging of his own personal responsibility to Germany – and, beyond Germany, to humanity as a whole, to the life of the spirit, to the cosmos and whatever gods or governing principles presided over it.

There are, of course, illustrious classical precedents for the rôle George, perhaps arrogantly, assumed. In many respects his circle suggests an updated version of the ancient Platonic academy, with George himself playing the part of Socratic mentor, guide and sage. George himself would probably not have welcomed this comparison. For one thing, Platonic thought was rather too abstract for his taste; for another, the academy, as it appears in its Platonic manifestation, was too divorced from mundane practical reality, from the world of action.

For George, the real classical antecedents of his circle were the schools associated (at least according to esoteric tradition) with Pythagoras. Pythagorean teaching was, if anything, even more spiritual and mystical than Platonic thought, but it was also more concrete, emphasising a network of interlocking connections between the phenomenal world and the numinous. Most important of all, the prevailing image of the Pythagorean schools was not one of quietism and isolation from secular life. The schools were generally seen as mystically and magically oriented precursors of, say, Harrow and Eton, preparing and grooming hand-picked cadres of young men for active rôles of service in public life, in government, administration, the military and other spheres of civic responsibility.

Legislators of the World

Whatever the fine points of difference between the Platonic and the Pythagorean, the prototype for George's circle lay, so far as he was concerned, in ancient Greece. Such a classical point of reference was thoroughly in keeping with his classical sympathies in other respects, and with his paganism and antipathy towards Judaeo-Christian tradition. Yet despite his antipathy towards that tradition, George nevertheless grafted one supremely crucial aspect of it on to his own essentially pagan *Weltanschauung*. This was the necessity for self-sacrifice as a vehicle to spiritual salvation and redemption. However inimical George felt Judaeo-Christian tradition to be, his concept of sacrifice is recognisably, and emphatically, Judaeo-Christian. And in order to articulate his concept, he had no compunction about plundering Judaeo-Christian terminology, imagery and symbolism.

Referring to Claus and himself, Berthold von Stauffenberg stated that 'We are not really what are called Catholic believers in the proper sense. We did not go to church very often, nor to confession: my brother and I feel that Christianity is unlikely to produce anything creative.'[31] Yet the Stauffenbergs had been born and raised as Catholics. However tepid their faith, they also, all their lives, considered themselves to be Catholic. How did they accommodate their Christianity, nominal though it may have been, with George's unique hybrid of esotericism and paganism? One answer to this question would seem to be George's concept of sacrifice. For the Stauffenbergs, as well as for other members of George's circle, the concept of sacrifice appears to have been a connecting link between conventional established religion and the 'Master's' thought. Through the concept of sacrifice, Christian believers could draw from paganism a new energy and vitality for their faith. And through the concept of sacrifice, George's paganism acquired an element of acceptability, respectability and legitimacy. It could not be branded 'subversive', 'immoral' or 'anti-social', as, for example, D. H. Lawrence's was.

By July 1944, it had become apparent that Claus von Stauffenberg could no longer just direct and co-ordinate the conspiracy against the hierarchy of the Third Reich. He would have to act personally, taking upon himself the responsibility of assassinating Adolf Hitler – and this, needless to say, would in all likelihood mean an act of

275

self-sacrifice. Towards the beginning of July, Stauffenberg conceived the idea of an oath of mutual intent to bind the inner circle of the conspiracy together – quite possibly to ensure their cohesion and continued dedication of purpose in the event of his death. He discussed the matter with his brother, Berthold, and with Rudolf Farhner, and asked them to draft a preliminary text. This was accordingly drawn up, and Berthold's secretary typed it out. The original copy disappeared, having probably been destroyed in the aftermath of 20 July, but Rudolf Fahrner kept a photocopy, with hand-written amendments by Stauffenberg, which a woman friend hid until after the war. Parts of it were published in 1952, the whole of it in 1992. The document echoes much of Stefan George's teachings and many of his poems. One particularly central passage reads:

> We want a new order which makes all Germans responsible for the state and guarantees them law and justice; but we despise the lie that all are equal and we submit to rank ordained by nature. We want a people with roots in their native land, close to the powers of nature, finding happiness and contentment in the given environment, and overcoming, in freedom and pride, the base instincts of envy and jealousy. We want leaders who, coming from every section of the nation, are in harmony with the divine powers and set an example to others by their noble spirit, discipline and sacrifice.[32]

It is as an illumination of these tenets – noble spirit, discipline and sacrifice – that George's monumental poem 'Secret Germany' should here be quoted in its entirety (and with the reminder that no translation of a poem, and especially of a poem like this, can approximate to the effect of the original):

> Let me stand at your verge,
> Chasm, and not be dismayed!
>
> Where irrepressible greed has
> Trampled down every inch of
> Earth from equator to pole and

Shamelessly wielded relentless
Glare and mastery over
Every nook of the world,

Where in the smothering cells of
Hideous houses, madness
Just has found what will poison
All horizons tomorrow:
Even shepherds in yurtas,
Even nomads in wastes –

Where no more in a stony
Forest valley the she-wolf
– Rugged nurse! – suckles boy twins,
And neither untrodden islands,
Nor a garden of virgins
Dawn to foster the Great,

There in the sorest of trials
Powers below pondered gravely,
Gracious celestials gave their
Ultimate secret: They altered
Laws over matter and founded
Space – a new space in the old . . .

Once down by the southern
Sea I lay on a boulder,
Wrung as lately my kin
Spirit, when breaking through
Olives, the Spook of Noon
With goaten foot flicked me:

'Now that your eyes grew discerning,
Go and find in your sacred
Land primordial soil,
Slumbering lap of fill,
And regions as pathless and dark
As the densest of jungles.'

Pinions of sunny dream,
Carry me close to the depth!

They told me of one who from rock-ridden coast
An instant had seen the Olympian gods
In heavens which split with the light of the dawn,
Whereat his soul was flooded with dread.
He shunned the board where his friends were grouped
And plunged into riotous waters.

In the town where the trivia from everywhere
Are posted on pillars and patches of wall
For people to gape at and hasten on,
No one had eyes for the greater event:
Uncanny through tottering structures and streets
The dangerous prowl of the demon!

In winter he stood in the candle-lit hall,
His shimmering shoulder hidden in folds,
The flame on his cheek in the leaves of a wreath,
The god concealed from the stare of fools,
In clear-scented warmth of the winds of spring,
Set foot on flowering courses.

The Listener who knew every person and thing,
Played ball with the stars in a rapturous reel,
The hunter unhunted, yet here he avowed
With stammering lips, his apostle-like form
Transfixed in the gleam of the opaline globe:
'This passes my grasp, I am silenced.'

Then forth from the region of order and peace,
Through sulphurous night a tempest unloosed
The clash and the clamour of savage wars,
The smoulder of worlds in the throes of the end.
And crumbling terrains and shadows unleashed
The silver hooves of the chargers.

I came upon him of the pale-golden hair
Who smilingly lavished serene repose
Wherever he went. He was hailed by us all
The darling of Fortune, but late he confessed
His vigour was drained to give strength to a friend,
His life a sequence of offerings.

I loved him who – my blood in his veins –
Had sung the song only less than the best,
Who idly shattered his lute when he failed
To gain a treasure he once divined,
Who merged with anonymous throngs and bowed
A forehead destined for laurels.

Throughout the country, on roads and in squares,
Wherever I was on the watch, I asked
Omniscient Rumour with hundreds of eyes:
'Have you ever heard of the like?' And he
– Though loth to be startled – replied: 'I heard
Of much – but this is unheard-of!'

Let me mount to your height,
Summit, and not be destroyed!

Who then, who of you brothers
Doubts, unshocked by the warning,
That what you most acclaim, what
Most you value today is
Rank as leaves in the fall-wind,
Doomed to perdition and death!

Only what consecrate earth
Cradles in sheltering sleep
Long in the innermost grooves,
Far from acquisitive hands,
Marvels this day cannot grasp
Are rife with the fate of tomorrow.[33]

This poem was among the last George wrote. It was composed, and read aloud at a special meeting of his circle, in 1928. The book in which it appeared was published in the same year. During the five years of life remaining to him, George published nothing further. He had effectively said all he had to say; and 'Secret Germany', as its very title suggests, stands as his definitive valedictory pronouncement, a kind of testament. There have been suggestions, too, that, for certain members of his circle, the poem was regarded as a sort of coded programme for the future, a blueprint for how to carry on in the 'Master's' absence.

It is, of course, impossible to know whether Stauffenberg himself saw 'Secret Germany' in this way. Did he perhaps feel that, in some oblique, symbolic or even 'occult' fashion, it had been addressed to him personally? That he later considered it immensely relevant to his circumstances is apparent from his use of its title for his own network of conspirators. And from the perspective of hindsight, the modern reader can discern the poem as being, despite its opacity, eerily apposite.

It is clear that Stauffenberg felt George's spirit to be close to him during the spring and summer of 1944, and especially during the final days culminating with the explosion of 20 July. He would quote frequently from 'The Antichrist', and also from 'Verses for the Dead':

> When men of the future are purged of dishonour,
> Their shoulders released from the shackles of bondage[34]

He must surely, too, have had constantly in mind the stanzas of 'Templars', such as:

> And only one of ours can complete
> The needed change or do the iron feat
> To which they summon us when chaos reigns,
> Only to stone and curse us for our pains.[35]

In the early hours of the morning of 21 July, Stauffenberg and the three men shot with him were hastily buried. Later that day, the bodies were exhumed and cremated, and their ashes were scattered over the fields. There disappeared at the same time two pieces of personal jewellery which Stauffenberg always wore. One was an ancient cross that had come down to him through his wife's family. The other was a weighty gold ring which he wore on the remaining finger of his left hand. Engraved on it in raised letters were the words: 'FINIS INITIUM'. This ring represented for him his personal covenant with Stefan George. The inscription, which translates as 'The End and the Beginning', derives from the last line of a poem

George published in 1913, in the volume *Der Stern des Bundes* (*The Star of the Covenant*):

> I am the One, I am the Two,
> I am the womb, I am the sire,
> I am the shadow and the true,
> I am the faggot and the fire.
> I am the bow, I am the shaft,
> I am the seer and his prediction,
> I am the sheath, I am the haft,
> I am abundance and affliction,
> I am the victim and the slayer,
> I am the symbol and the meaning,
> I am the altar and the prayer,
> I am the end and a beginning.[36]

# Part Five

---

## HEROISM IN THE
## TWENTIETH CENTURY

# 13

# *In the Courtyard of the Bendlerstrasse*

In the end one returns to that moment just after midnight, a few minutes into 21 July 1944, in the courtyard of the War Office, in the Bendlerstrasse – the crack of rifle shots and those defiant words: '*Es lebe unser geheimes Deutschland!*' One returns, as well, to the three or four hours immediately preceding that moment.

By the early evening of 20 July, it was obvious that Hitler was alive, that the conspiracy had failed and that nothing could possibly be gained by further effort. Yet Stauffenberg continued to conduct himself as if success could still be achieved. Even when the situation was clearly hopeless, he proceeded as if it could still be salvaged. When he died, it was not with the disappointment, still less the despair, of a thwarted man. It was with a gesture of undiminished affirmation, even, paradoxically, of triumph. In a public execution, with an audience of spectators and witnesses, such a gesture might be explicable and understandable, but in the privacy of that nocturnal courtyard, for whose benefit was it made?

The so-called 'work ethic' introduced by Protestantism emphasises the act – the act that yields tangible results, that culminates in demonstrable and measurable accomplishment. Success is palpable proof of God's favour and, therefore, a testimony to virtue. The man who succeeds is the virtuous man, and vice versa. Success and virtue are synonymous.

Stauffenberg was raised, trained and shaped according to a different, more subtle, logic – the logic of Stefan George's syncretic thought with its emphasis on sacrifice, and, before that, the logic of Catholic tradition. If the logic of Protestantism is pragmatic, that of both George and the Church can be described as essentially poetic. According to poetic logic, the symbolic gesture weighs as heavily as the utilitarian act. Indeed, in the moral and spiritual balance, it may even count for more. It may even, in itself, constitute a redemptive principle, regardless of whether or not it accomplishes anything. Thus, for example, saints and martyrs are revered more often than not for pragmatically futile but poetically resonant gestures. They thereby conform to the figure who performed the supreme such gesture in Western tradition – Jesus himself.

This is not to suggest, of course, that Stauffenberg should be seen as a 'Christ figure', or that he ever saw himself as such. Nor is it to suggest that he sought nothing more than the symbolic significance of martyrdom. He was, above all else, a man of action, who wanted the conspiracy to achieve an actual, as well as a symbolic, success. Were that not the case, he could easily enough have ensured the Führer's death through his own self-immolation, as Axel von dem Bussche and Ewald von Kleist, their uniforms packed with explosive, had been prepared to do. Stauffenberg, however, felt it necessary to keep himself alive, not from a personal desire for self-preservation, but to ensure the conspiracy achieved its goals.

Yet it is clear that poetic logic still figured prominently in his, and in many of the other conspirators', thinking. According to this logic, the symbolic gesture might still salvage a measure of triumph when the utilitarian act had failed. In the pragmatic sphere of politics and mundane history, the conspiracy might prove futile and accomplish nothing, but in the moral and spiritual sphere, it might, as a symbolic gesture, constitute an accomplishment of an altogether different kind. On behalf of Germany as a whole, it could be an act of atonement, without which there could be no redemption. This calls to mind Henning von Tresckow's statement that 'Just as God once promised Abraham that he would spare Sodom if only ten just men could be found in the city, I also have reason to hope that, for our sake, he will not destroy Germany.'[1]

What, then, kept Stauffenberg functioning as he did until the very end? It was something much loftier than the prosaic propaganda purpose of 'letting the world know that there were good Germans'. It was the desire to make atonement for Germany, and so redeem everything most valid and laudable in Germanic history and culture – redeem the Hohenstauffen emperors and the achievements of the high Middle Ages, redeem Luther and the Reformation, redeem Goethe and Schiller, Hölderlin and Novalis, Gneisenau and Yorck von Wartenburg and, above all perhaps, redeem Stefan George, whose own work had inadvertently contributed to Germany's damnation. Like a number of the other conspirators, Stauffenberg viewed his own actions from the standpoint of posterity. He saw himself as taking Germany's sins upon his own shoulders and dying for them. We are the posterity for whose sake Stauffenberg offered himself in sacrifice. To the extent that we accept and acknowledge his sacrifice, the culmination of the drama in the courtyard of the Bendlerstrasse was not a failure, but an apotheosis.

\*

From one point of view, the events of 20 July and the circumstances surrounding them offer just another story of twentieth-century political conspiracy, and a failed conspiracy at that. It may have been well-intentioned, even noble and exalted, but it was also bungled. It did not significantly alter the course of events, and is therefore little more than a footnote to history. Yet what if one shifts one's perspective and points of emphasis? What if one transfers one's focus from the conspiracy itself to Stauffenburg and the men like him? What if one concentrates not on the plot of 20 July, nor even on the war as a whole, but on the vista stretching back at least to 1933? Such a vista would include Stauffenberg organising an honour guard at Stefan George's bier to prevent the dead poet's body from being taken back to Germany and used as a pretence for an official state ceremony. It would also include Stauffenberg daring to walk out in the middle of a lecture by Julius Streicher. It would include his humane efforts, during the invasion of Czechoslovakia, to keep the local population supplied with food and other vital resources. It would include his calling an officer to account for the indiscriminate shooting of two peasant women in Poland. It would include his ongoing personal crusade against the SS and everything they represented. It would include his rigorous adherence to a code of honour, chivalry and decency amid circumstances that militated violently against such virtues. It would include the recognition of responsibility implicit in his statement while convalescing in hospital from his wounds: 'Since the generals have so far done nothing, it is time for the colonels to act.'[2]

The story that then emerges from this book is not just the story of a failed conspiracy. It is the story of a unique, distinctive and extraordinary man who mirrored in himself Germany's collective identity crisis, and effected his own reconciliation between the martial nationalism of his ancestor, Gneisenau, and Goethe's ideal of dedication to culture and the spirit. It is the story of a figure who bridges the great modern gulf between 'the man of thought' and 'the man of action'. It is the story, in short, of an heroic figure – and, even more, of a specifically twentieth-century heroic figure. To that extent, his story transcends the historical context of the Third Reich. It applies equally to Germany, and to all of us, today.

*

Before the advent of self-awareness, self-consciousness and self-alienation, action alone was sufficient to determine and define heroism. Homer may single out Odysseus by virtue of his resourceful intelligence and capacity for 'strategic thought'. Thucydides may cite Pericles' funeral oration to the Athenians at the end of the first year of the Peloponnesian War:

> We were capable at the same time of taking risks and of estimating them beforehand. Others are brave out of ignorance; and, when they stop to think, they begin to fear. But the man who can most truly be accounted brave is he who best knows the meaning of what is sweet in life and of what is terrible, and then goes out undeterred to meet what is to come.[3]

Despite such homages to intelligence, however, the hero of antiquity was exemplified by such figures as Achilles in *The Iliad*, or Cuchulain in the Irish sagas of the Red Branch of Ulster. They are indeed 'brave out of ignorance'. Their bravery amounts to little more than an insensate berserker rage, an embarrassingly infantile temper tantrum. Except for a certain rudimentary tactical cunning, both Achilles and Cuchulain are consummate dolts. But in their own eras and milieux, bravery and martial prowess are alone sufficient to confer heroic status. They are, in effect, virtues in themselves, and even extolled as the highest virtues. They exist in a kind of vacuum, utterly divorced from any moral context or hierarchy of values. Even politics are of peripheral importance, and war is reduced to the level of two boxers in a ring.

As civilisation, culture and consciousness evolve, the intelligence informing Pericles' oration becomes more meaningful and relevant. There arises, too, the desire for what might be called a 'strategic' context, an acknowledgement not just of bravery alone and for its own sake, but also of its implications and ramifications, its repercussions, consequences and effects. Even more significantly, there arises, too, the desire for a moral context.

We recognise today, for example, that simple bravery is in itself a questionable virtue. It can often stem from, and be equated with, sheer arrant stupidity. It can also stem from, and be equated with, something manifestly reprehensible, wicked or evil. If bravery is a virtue at all, it can only too easily be negated by the absence of other virtues – by the absence of a moral context, or by the cynical expediency which allows ends to justify means. Many of the SS were unquestionably brave. So, too, no doubt, are certain members of today's Provisional IRA. But that does not render them any the less morally bankrupt, contemptible and repellent. To the modern mind, bravery in itself can no longer automatically validate, justify and redeem itself, the man who displays it or the cause on behalf of which he does so.

To the extent that we now demand (at least in theory) a moral context for action, humanity can probably be said to have progressed. Yet such progress has brought new problems in its wake; for the very awareness that demands a moral context for action is the same awareness that can question the purposes of any action whatever, and can lead ultimately to paralysis. In mobilising the United States for the Second World War, Roosevelt pointed out that all we have to fear is fear itself. Awareness can foster a greater fear of fear than of the circumstances that engender fear. We are all familiar – through books and films, if not through personal experience – with the soldier who is less afraid of the enemy guns than of something in himself, something which might, at the crucial moment, panic in the face of those guns. It is a tired but none the less valid truism that some price in efficiency will be paid by the soldier who thinks, who questions the cause for which he is fighting, who visualises the circumstances of his own death, who imagines what he will feel at the impact of bullet, bomb or mine. His morale may well flag. He may become utterly panic-stricken and freeze. Heroism in such circumstances is less a triumph over an external foe than over something within himself – a form of self-mastery.

The epic, 'larger-than-life' protagonists of nineteenth-century literature – Faust, for example, Prince Andrey Bolkonsky in *War and Peace* or Ivan Karamazov – perform precisely such an act of self-conquest. It is from this, in large part, that their heroic stature derives. But in the process, they also resolve the dichotomy between what Conrad, towards the end of the century, labelled 'the man of thought' and 'the man of action'.

The achievements of such fictional characters had their counterparts in history. Since the Lutheran Reformation, if not indeed before, the 'Renaissance man' – the man displaying audacity in both thought and action – had played a dominant rôle in Western civilisation. There were, for example, the figures of the Elizabethan age – soldier-poets like Sir Philip Sidney, explorers and adventurers like Sir Walter Raleigh. In the seventeenth century, there were figures like Rupert of the Rhine, Gustavus Adolphus and Wallenstein. In the eighteenth century, there was Frederick the Great himself who, between campaigns, consorted with Voltaire, composed music, wrote poetry and speculated in philosophy. In the nineteenth century, there were Nelson and Napoleon. There were some of the dashing yet still reflective commanders of the American Civil War, such as the 'Grey Ghost', John Singleton Mosby; there were adventurers like Sir Richard Burton, and explorers like Ludwig Leichart, the prototype for Patrick White's Voss. All of these individuals were men endowed with the capacity for thought and action. And it was largely from their aptitude for both that they derived their heroic status.

\*

It is by now a cliché that the twentieth century witnessed the decline of traditional concepts of heroism – not just the primitive heroism of Achilles and Cuchulain, but also the heroism of the 'Renaissance man'. There were, of course, many contributing factors to this decline. The First World War produced heroism on an inflationary scale, like that of German currency in its aftermath; and like German currency, the very concept of heroism became debased and devalued. In the prolonged stalemate of the Western Front, there was not much opportunity for distinctive or decisive heroic action. Anyone, with a bare minimum of effort, could become a hero. One did not even have to lead a localised charge or perform a deed of derring-do. One had only to poke one's head too far above the parapet of a trench – or, like Saki, according to the accepted story, light three cigarettes on a match – and one promptly became a dead hero. With heroism in itself so plentiful and so easily obtainable, the concept became discredited.

Then, too, there was the debasement of language by the burgeoning organs of the media. In *The Man Without Qualities*, the protagonist is known only as Ulrich, his surname having been suppressed 'in order not to embarrass his father'. Ulrich is a man without qualities because he is conscious of possessing, at least in potential, all qualities – which is tantamount to having no qualities because they cancel each other out. As a result, Ulrich is left with the agonising dilemma of what to do with his life – and, even more painful, of what simply to *be*. For a time he considers becoming 'a man of importance'. That seeming somewhat too vague, he then entertains the prospect of becoming a genius, which he is certainly sufficiently well equipped to do. But this alternative is also frustrated by what the media have done with language:

The time had already begun when it became a habit to speak of geniuses of the football-field or the boxing-ring, although to every ten or even more explorers, tenors and writers of genius that cropped up in the columns of the newspapers there were not, as yet, more than at the most one genius of a centre-half or one great tactician of the tennis-court. The new spirit of the times had not yet quite found its feet. But just then it happened that Ulrich read somewhere – and it came like a breath of too early summer ripeness blown down the wind – the phrase 'the race-horse of genius'. It occurred in a report of a spectacular success in a race, and it was quite possible that the writer was far from aware of the magnitude of the inspiration wafted into his pen by the spirit of contemporaneity. Ulrich, however, suddenly grasped the inevitable connection between his whole career and this genius among race-horses. For to the cavalry, of course, the horse has always been a sacred animal, and during his youthful days of life in the barracks Ulrich had hardly ever heard anything talked about except horses and women. That was what he had fled from to become a man of importance. And now, when, after varied exertions, he might almost have felt entitled to think himself near the summit of his ambitions, he was haled from on high by the horse, which had got there first.[4]

As Musil ironically demonstrates, both the term and the concept of 'genius' could easily be debased by media hacks. A similar debasement of such terms and concepts as 'hero', and 'heroism' had already, by Musil's time, begun to occur. If a sports journalist could speak of a 'race-horse of genius', he could – and often does – speak of, say, the horse's 'heroic effort in the final stretch'. And if comparison with a horse can deter one from wanting to be a genius, it can equally well deter one from wanting to be a hero.

The concept of heroism also implies that, in the fashionable American phrase, 'one man can make a difference'. Almost by definition, the hero is an individual whose action, to one or another degree, makes a difference. In Homer's *Iliad*, the outcome of the Trojan War rests entirely on the actions of the heroic figures Achilles and Odysseus. But as society grows more complex, as chains of command become more attenuated and complicated, as the decision-making process becomes more collectivised and bureaucratic, the opportunities to make a difference become more limited. By the twentieth century, the scope for heroic action of a decisive kind has become dramatically circumscribed. What, for instance, could anyone conceivably have done to make the difference – or even *a* difference, however modest – on the Western Front during the First World War? One could obviously rescue a comrade, eliminate an enemy machine-gun post, capture a sector of trench. But such feats could do nothing to alter or determine the course of events, unless they were performed in such quantity as to become routine.

In the world of the twentieth century, what scope remains for the kind of heroism that was still possible as recently as a century before – for a unity of thought and action that makes some sort of decisive difference? One can no longer play Wyatt Earp and single-handedly 'clean up' today's equivalents of Dodge City and Tombstone. Despite the impressions fostered by film and television, modern law enforcement is more often than not a bureaucratic 'team effort', which offers little latitude for the decisive individual initiative of 'mavericks'. In the sphere of exploration, there are precious few uncharted territories to discover, no lost cities to seek, no Northwest Passage to be found. Terrestrial exploration now more closely resembles sport than anything else; and even the vaunted 'conquest of space' is a bureaucratic 'team effort' which, like law enforcement, offers little latitude for decisive individual initiative. One cannot simply find a patron, recruit a crew, build or buy a ship and set off into the unknown as did the maritime adventurers of five centuries ago. Even war, the traditional arena for heroism, affords restricted opportunities for it today. One can no longer lead the flamboyantly colourful cavalry charge that determines the outcome of the battle. In modern warfare, the only opportunity for decisive individual heroism lies in covert operations, in guerrilla activity, in sabotage and missions behind enemy lines – the sort of thing associated with the Long Range Desert Groups, or with the SAS and other special forces of our own era. Even then the individual's actions may not necessarily be decisive. They may simply be contributing factors – and relatively minor contributing factors at that – to the eventual outcome.

It is difficult to imagine a sphere of today's world in which an individual's behaviour, combining thought and action, can make a significant difference – can qualify, in other words, as 'heroism', on something more than a circumscribed, parochial or localised level. During the peak of the Cold War, espionage represented one of the few such spheres remaining. Thus James Bond could become a hero of the sixties. Even then, most people recognised that Bond was more fantasy than anything else, and that the world of espionage was much more accurately portrayed by Len Deighton and John le

Carré; and today, the dashing spy whose derring-do saves 'civilisation as we know it' is little more than escapism, camp or farce. What remains? Perhaps the best answer to that question offers scant comfort. For if there is still one realm in which a semblance of 'heroism' is still possible, it is crime. Thus the criminal can become a romantic figure and a rôle model for a generation of youth unable to find heroes elsewhere. In reality, as opposed to Hollywood, Wyatt Earp may have been transformed into corporate man, a cog in the wheel of an ever more automated, ever more 'high-tech' police force, but Billy the Kid, Jesse James, Bonnie and Clyde, the Mafia 'hit man' of today and, in Northern Ireland, his terrorist paramilitary counterpart can still retain a spurious mystique of romantic individual glamour – can still become, according to the popular phrase, a 'contemporary folk hero'.

\*

The twentieth century has been an age of celluloid heroes, mass-produced by the film and television industry. Their sheer prevalance, and the appeal they exercise, attest to our perennial need for such figures; and our need is all the greater because current history and reality contains so few of them.

Although the First World War could accommodate innumerable localised heroic deeds, it allowed no sustained heroic activity, and certainly not an heroic life, except in peripheral theatres of operation, where a man like T. E. Lawrence could make his mark. The rhetoric of politics and the jargon of the media both indulge in a facile, indiscriminate hyperbole which debases language and renders such words as 'hero', 'heroism' and 'heroic' meaningless. The nature of modern society provides less scope for decisive heroic action, and our own pervasive awareness of implications, ramifications, repercussions and consequences often constitutes an inhibiting factor which dissociates the 'man of thought' from the 'man of action'. As a result, the dominant protagonist of twentieth-century literature is one or another variant of what critics call the 'anti-hero'. According to these same critics, the 'anti-hero' is the epitome, and most accurate reflection, of twentieth-century man.

Who or what precisely is the 'anti-hero'? Literary and cultural criticism has devoted endless pages of analysis to this question; for the 'anti-hero' can appear in as many guises as can the hero. Ultimately, however, he conforms to one of four basic patterns. He can be a 'man of action', who lacks the awareness and capacity for thought required to cope with his circumstances. Such is the dilemma of Franz Biberkopf, the protagonist of Alfred Döblin's influential novel *Berlin, Alexanderplatz*, and of Joe Christmas in Faulkner's *Light in August*. Alternatively, the 'anti-hero' can be a 'man of thought', whose hyperconscious awareness negates his capacity for action – Mann's Tonio Kröger, for instance, Joyce's Stephen Dedalus and all the other artist-protagonists of twentieth-century fiction. Third, the 'anti-hero' can be the kind of figure who populates Kafka's work, incapable of effective thought *or* effective action, a hapless victim at the mercy of an alien and inimical reality. Or he can be like Musil's Ulrich in *The Man Without Qualities*, potentially capable of both thought and action, but trapped in a milieu which allows the effective exercise of neither.

In whichever guise the twentieth-century 'anti-hero' appears, he differs from his heroic nineteenth-century predecessors precisely in his inability to bring thought and action together and exercise them in an effective manner. It is this which makes him appear ineffectual, 'small', impotent or even puerile in comparison with the likes of Faust, Ivan Karamazov or Prince Andrey – and with Patrick White's eponymous protagonist in *Voss*, the creation of a twentieth-century artistic imagination but placed in an earlier historical context.

The 'anti-hero' is not, of course, unique to Germany. He is a product of twentieth-century civilisation as a whole; and, as such, he can be found everywhere – in English, Irish and continental literature, in the literature of North and South America, from the dawn of the twentieth century to the present day. But it could be argued that he is accorded his fullest, most comprehensive, most exhaustive and obsessive treatment by Germanic artists of the first half of the century – by Mann, Musil, Broch, Rilke, Kafka, Döblin, Hesse and numerous lesser-known figures. What is more, he performs, in Germanic literature, a very particular function. The dissociation in Germanic literature between the 'man of thought' and the 'man of action' mirrors, in individual terms, the collective identity crisis – the dissociation between a political entity based on nationalism, and Goethe's ideal of a nation dedicated to culture and the spirit.

★

Is it coincidental that the two most monstrous totalitarian 'isms' of the twentieth century took root in Germany and Russia, the two nations most torn by a collective identity crisis, most in quest of a self-definition and therefore most vulnerable? Not if one again draws an analogy to the individual undergoing a personal identity crisis, whose quest for self-definition all too readily leads him into the hands of a petty Führer – the guru, or the cult leader. In both instances, the individual and the collective, the need for self-definition is accorded an ersatz fulfilment which conforms to what Stefan George called '*das Leichte*', 'the facile'. By means of '*das Leichte*', the Führer, whether great or petty, fosters more than just a sense of solidarity and belonging. He also fosters a sense of group identity, to compensate for the abdication of individual identity. And this group identity will invariably be that of an 'elect', a 'chosen few' – or a 'master race'. Each member of the collective entity is handed a ready-made and prefabricated identity. He is 'one of the saved', 'one of the enlightened', one of those entrusted with a destiny higher and more exalted than that of other people; and this complacent arrogation of superiority offsets the vacuum within. Identity and self-definition are no longer to be sought and found within oneself, but in the group as a whole. And through the group as a whole, one can acquire the qualities one lacks in oneself, including heroism.

The totalitarian 'isms' of our century, whether Left or Right on the political spectrum, propagate a kind of collective heroism. The 'People' as a whole become heroic, whether they be the German '*Volk*' of Nazism or the 'proletarian masses' of Marxism-Leninism. Again and again in the rhetoric of Nazi Germany and Soviet Russia, as well as in that of Mussolini's Italy and Mao's China, words like 'heroism' and 'heroic' are repeated like a drumbeat. It is not the individual that is heroic, however, but the collective. A grandiose collective ideal of heroism is proclaimed, while individual awareness is negated or eclipsed through a semi-hypnotic state induced by mindless chanting and incantatory rhythm, through an air-tight system of belief which requires only adherence and precludes any independence of mentality. And as an adhesive component for the collective-as-hero, a scapegoat will be put forward, which inspires even greater fear than that inspired by the unknown and unpredictable elements within man himself – a scapegoat who distracts one from the potential dangers of introspection, and focuses one's energy on a supposed external threat. In near-Manichaean conflict with this supposed threat, collective heroism is seemingly attained – or, at least, promised.

The meretricious character of such collective heroism should be self-evident enough. If it absolves – or, more accurately, deprives – the individual of responsibility, it also deprives him of his very individuality, of everything Western civilisation considers most uniquely sacred. And the putative collective heroism offered by twentieth-century totalitarianism is also profoundly retrograde – a return to the 'primitive'. It is, in effect, the mindless berserker bravery of Achilles again, divorced from a moral context and justified solely by an enforced unanimity and uniformity. It does nothing to fulfil the need for self-definition, either individual or collective. It offers no satisfactory solution to the individual or the collective identity crisis. It fails to re-integrate the dissociated spheres of thought and action. At best, it constitutes a form of psychological and spiritual anaesthesia.

Claus von Stauffenberg represents an alternative. Like T. E. Lawrence and perhaps a dozen or so others, he is a lineal successor to the epic, 'larger-than-life' heroic figures of nineteenth-century literature and nineteenth-century history – a 'real life' avatar, in a sense, of Prince Andrey Bolkonsky. He is also an heroic figure of particular relevance to our century: a man whose capacity for action is equalled, yet not inhibited, by his capacity for thought. In his own personality, he reconciles political commitment with moral vision, and with Goethe's ideal of dedication to culture and the spirit. To that extent, he embodies a resolution to Germany's collective identity crisis. To that extent, too, he exemplifies what the German people at their best can be – and not just the German people, but all of us, and our civilisation as a whole.

On 22 July 1944, two days after Stauffenberg's bomb exploded at Rastenburg, an article appeared on page 4 of *The Times* of London. In the small hours of that morning, the article reported, shortly after German radio stations had closed down for the night, a broadcast was picked up on Frankfurt's wavelength. Emanating mysteriously out of the war-torn darkness, the voice of an unknown and unidentified German officer issued a defiant proclamation:

Achtung, comrades. Achtung, soldiers. Achtung, listeners in Germany. Stand by for an announcement of the utmost importance.

My comrades, the death of Klaus [sic] von Stauffenberg sounds the clarion call to action, the call to battle with all means at our disposal, the call to us German officers to go on fighting until Hitler has been destroyed. Today Hitler has been forced to admit that sections of the German Officer Corps – those who are decent and honest – have taken their stand against him. He can no longer deny today that the German officers have gone over to organise resistance against him.

If he tries to paralyse this fight of resistance, and attempts to speak of 'a small clique of traitors and destroyers', let him know this much for certain – there is more than one Stauffenberg, there are more than a hundred, these Stauffenbergs are here in their thousands.

My comrades, the German officers with us are officers who have kept their uniforms clean and for whom honour and duty have remained fixed principles. These are our men. I call today on those officers who have not yet established contact with us, wherever they are stationed, at the front or in the reserves, no longer to obey the orders of Hitler and his henchmen.

Whose was that lost voice? For all one knows, it may simply have been a ploy of Anglo-American or Russian propaganda, though one would like to believe it genuine. In any case, and despite the voice's assertion, there were not, unfortunately, enough Stauffenbergs left in 1944 to make the decisive difference. But as the spectre of Nazism emerges to haunt Europe today, let us hope that this time there will indeed be enough Stauffenbergs to exorcise it.

# Notes and References

When not cited here, the full bibliographical details are to be found in the Bibliography.

*Introduction*

1  Kramarz, *Stauffenberg*, p.100.
2  Ibid., pp.101–2.
3  Leber, *Conscience in Revolt*, pp.260–1.
4  Herwarth, *Against Two Evils*, pp.215–16.
5  Zeller, *The Flame of Freedom*, p.175.
6  Ibid., p.274.
7  About twenty p-40 fighter-bombers from the US 33rd Fighter Group were attacking the German retreat. Two were shot down by ground fire. See Shores, *Fighters over Tunisia*, p.297; also Maurer, *Airforce Combat Units of World War II*, pp.86–7. The fullest account of this retreat and Stauffenberg's injuries is given in Hoffmann, *Claus Schenk Graf von Stauffenberg und seine Brüder*, pp.294–6.
8  Zeller, op.cit., p.183.
9  Ibid.
10  Kramarz, op.cit., p.105.
11  Ibid., p.104.
12  Zeller, E., *Geist der Freiheit*, German edition: München, 1965, p.361.
13  George, *Werke*, p.258.
14  Zeller, op.cit., p.277.

# Notes and References

## 1 The German Resistance

1 Hoffmann, *Hitler's Personal Security*, pp.268–9.
2 The most comprehensive account of German Resistance is Hoffmann's magnificent *The History of the German Resistance 1933–1945*.
3 Ibid., p.75.
4 Ibid., p.77.
5 Halder said during his interrogation after the war, on 25 February 1946:

'May I make a personal remark. I am the last male member of a family which for 300 years were soldiers. What the duty of a soldier is I know too. I know that in the dictionary of a German soldier the term treason and plot against the State does not exist. I was in the awful dilemma of one, the duty of a soldier, and another, the duty which I considered higher. Innumerable of my old comrades were in the same dilemma. I chose the solution for the duties I deemed higher. The majority of my comrades deemed the duty to the flag higher and essential. You may be assured that this is the worst dilemma that a soldier may be faced with.'

See *Nazi Conspiracy and Aggression*, Supplement B, p.1563.
6 Gisevius, *To the Bitter End*, p.312.
7 Hoffmann, *The History of the German Resistance 1933–1945*, pp.92–3. The members of this raiding party are given in ibid., p.561., n.101. A leading planner of this attempted execution of Hitler was Major-General (as he was later) Hans Oster, chief of Staff to Admiral Canaris, head of the *Abwehr* – Military Intelligence. See ibid., p.255. Oster was also co-ordinating various German contacts with the British Government before the outbreak of war. He fell under strong suspicion and was dismissed from the Abwehr in April 1943. He was arrested on 21 July 1944 and hanged for his part in the conspiracy against Hitler on 9 April 1945.

Oster said, 'One might say that I am a traitor but in reality I am not; I consider myself a better German than all those who run after Hitler. It is my plan and my duty to free Germany, and at the same time the world, of this plague.' See Klemperer, *German Resistance against Hitler*, p.196.
8 For a detailed exploration of the resistance's attempts to interest a wilfully ignorant British Government in their cause see Meehan, *The Unnecessary War*. See also Lamb, *The Ghosts of Peace*, pp.246–89, and Hoffmann, *The History of the German Resistance 1933–1945*, pp.54–68, 104–21, 153–72.
9 Hoffmann, *The History of the German Resistance 1933–1945*, p.93.
10 Ibid., pp.96 and 99.
11 *Nazi Conspiracy and Aggression*, Supplement B, pp.1557–8. For a detailed discussion see Meehan, op.cit., pp.170–86.
12 Wheeler-Bennett, *The Nemesis of Power*, p.459.
13 Ibid.
14 Extract from an interview with Colonel-General Hammerstein which was

# Notes and References

supplied to the authors by Axel von dem Bussche, December 1992.

15 John, *Twice through the lines*, p.44. Beck and Hammerstein both wanted a restoration of the monarchy. See Hoffmann, *The History of the German Resistance 1933–1945*, p.189, also p.220.
16 Hoffmann, *The History of the German Resistance 1933–1945* p.260.
17 Ibid., pp.278–9; see also Herwarth, *Against Two Evils*, p.249; Schlabrendorff, *The Secret War against Hitler*, pp.230–1.
18 Hoffmann, *The History of the German Resistance 1933–1945*, p.282.
19 Schlabrendorff, op.cit., p.236.
20 Ibid., p.237.
21 Ibid., pp.238–9. See also Hoffmann, *The History of the German Resistance 1933–1945*, pp.283–9; Zeller, *The Flame of Freedom*, pp.163–4.

## 2 Operation Valkyrie

1 Balfour, *Withstanding Hitler*, p.109. Professor Balfour adds: 'People whose motivating influences are patriotism and Christianity are not nowadays likely to wade through rivers of blood in the hope of reforming society.'
2 Ibid., p.109.
3 Kramarz, *Stauffenberg*, p.132.
4 Ibid., p.25; Hoffmann, 'Claus von Stauffenberg und Stefan George: Der Weg zur Tat', *Jahrbuch der deutschen Schillergesellschaft*, Bd.12, 1968, p.540.
5 Kramarz, op.cit., p.126.
6 Now Margarethe, Gräfin von Hardenberg. See Meding, *Mit dem Mut des Herzens*, p.103.
7 Hoffmann, in Large, *Contending with Hitler*, p.127.
8 Hoffmann, *Hitler's Personal Security*, pp.63, 74–5.
9 Bullock, *Hitler: A Study in Tyranny*, p.661.
10 Hoffmann, *The History of the German Resistance 1933–1945*, pp.323–8.
11 Ibid., pp.328–9.
12 Ibid., p.374.
13 Zeller, *The Flame of Freedom*, p.292.
14 Hoffmann, in Large, op.cit., p.126.
15 Ibid., p.127.
16 Zimmermann and Jacobsen, *Germans against Hitler*, p.156.
17 Zeller, op.cit., p.232.
18 Schlabrendorff, *The Secret War against Hitler*, p.277.
19 Kramarz, op.cit., p.110.
20 Hoffmann, *The History of the German Resistance 1933–1945*, p.374.
21 Zeller, op.cit., p.191.
22 George, *The Works of Stefan George*, trans. by Marx and Morwitz, p.398.
23 Galante, *Hitler Lives – And the Generals Die*, p.6.
24 Zeller, op.cit., p.292.
25 Ibid., p.432, n.31.

26  *Spiegelbild einer Verschwörung*, p.117.

3 In the Wolf's Lair

  1  *Spiegelbild einer Verschwörung*, p.399.
  2  Zeller, *The Flame of Freedom*, p.304.
  3  Hoffmann, *The History of the German Resistance 1933–1945*, p.409.
  4  Ibid., p.419 for the first sentence, which was crossed out – perhaps to protect the signals staff who would have been hard-pressed to explain why they dispatched it in the original form. The remainder of the message is in Zimmermann and Jacobsen, *Germans against Hitler*, pp.131–2. For a discussion regarding the alterations see Hoffmann, ibid., p.681, n.39.
  5  Hoffmann, ibid., p.422.
  6  Ibid.
  7  Ibid., p.422.
  8  Interview with Dr Otto John, Berlin, 8 October 1992.
  9  Schlabrendorff, *The Secret War against Hitler*, p.287.
 10  Zeller, op.cit., pp.307–8.
 11  Schlabrendorff, op.cit., p.288.
 12  Hoffmann, *The History of the German Resistance 1933–1945*, p.424.
 13  Gisevius, *To the Bitter End*, p.544.
 14  Ibid., p.545.
 15  Hoffmann, *German Resistance to Hitler*, p.128.
 16  John, *Twice through the Lines*, p.151.
 17  *The Times*, 21 July 1944, p.4.
 18  Interview with Ludwig von Hammerstein, Bonn, 7 December 1992, and further clarification 8 March 1993. Hammerstein said that the shooting was between Captain Klausing and Lt-Colonel Herber who was in the office of Olbricht's secretary. Herber also shot and wounded Stauffenberg.

Hammerstein served in the 9th Infantry Regiment of Potsdam. His father had been the Commander in Chief of the German army until 1933 and had known and despised Hitler since the late 1920s. The Hammerstein family lived in a private apartment in the Army Headquarters in the Bendlerstrasse.

On 20 July Hammerstein and other young officers were given duties in Stauffenberg's section at the Army Headquarters. Hammerstein had not made any preparations in case the coup should fail. However, a fellow officer told him to remember the Swedish diplomats, saying that they could perhaps get him out.

Late in the evening, when it was known that Hitler had survived and when the dispute broke out between Stauffenberg and other Staff officers that led to a brief exchange of gunfire, Hammerstein saw that it was over. As a soldier he knew that, if the battle was lost, it was better to flee rather than to give up. He knew the huge and complicated Headquarters building well because he had lived there as a child, and so was able to escape and go to his home. He told his mother that it was finished and that he had to go underground. Unfortunately he left his pistol and his maps in the Bendlerstrasse.

In the neighborhood lived an elderly couple and their daughter whose officer husband had died in Russia. Hammerstein knew that they opposed Nazism and had, at considerable risk to their lives, given refuge to fugitive Jews. He went to them and asked if they would hide him. They agreed and so he stayed, together with a Jewish woman who was already in the house.

Hammerstein remained there until April 1945. He recalled that during this time he was visited by a man who had been living for two years in the underground and had become very organised. He arrived with a box containing all the requisite tools to make a forged photo pass, food coupons and other vital documents. By this stage of the war, there were many people living underground in Berlin.

Hammerstein was present when the city fell to the Russians: as they entered, all the residents simply stood in their doorways quietly watching the army advance up the street. The Russian soldiers approached the civilians in a very friendly manner and took all their watches: in return they gave cigarettes and cigars.

At one time, when Hammerstein was arrested, he was taken to the local Russian commander. Hammerstein explained that he was an officer who had taken part in the 20 July plot. The Russian officer clearly knew about this and proceeded to mark it in Russian on Hammerstein's driving licence – the only document he had. From this time on, he had no trouble passing through any of the check-points.

19   Hoffmann, *The History of the German Resistance 1933–1945*, p. 507.
20   Ibid.
21   Wolf, 'Political and Moral Motives behind the Resistance', *The German Resistance to Hitler*, p. 195.
22   Zimmerman and Jacobsen, op. cit., p. 297.
23   *The Times*, 24 October 1992, p. 10.
24   For extracts from Himmler's speech at Posen on 3 August 1944, where this doctrine of *Sippenhaft* is explained, see Zimmermann and Jacobsen, op. cit., p. 195.

The doctrine of *Sippenhaft* was applied to all the families. We spoke to Gottliebe von Lehndorff during 17–18 September 1992. Her husband, Lt Heinrich von Lehndorff, owned a huge estate, Steinort, in East Prussia which had been in his family for 600 years. He had a substantial country house, one wing of which had been taken over by Ribbentrop and his SS guards as their field headquarters. The estate contained the OKH headquarters, Mauerwald, and was close to the OKW headquarters at the Wolfsschanze.

Lehndorff was serving with Tresckow in the Central Army Group on the eastern front and had been part of the conspiracy ever since he had seen an SS man kill a baby by beating it against a wall. This took place at the beginning of the invasion of Russia, 1941. On his next leave home he told his wife about the shocking murder he had witnessed and said that he was fully involved in opposition to Hitler. He asked if she was with him in this. The duty assigned to him by the conspirators was to find more members, to talk to people and draw them in.

Stauffenberg twice visited Lehndorff at his estate: in order to speak freely the two of them would drive about the estate in a horse-drawn coach, reasoning that the noise would make eavesdropping impossible.

Lehndorff's task in the coup was to act as OKH liaison officer in Königsberg – to make sure that the orders from Berlin Army headquarters were carried out and to report back on events.

On 20 July he had gone to Königsberg but, after the failure of the coup, had returned home. He was very depressed and talked of killing himself. The next day, at 9 a.m., two open Mercedes cars arrived bearing eight SS men. They asked for him at the door. Lehndorff, hearing this, jumped out of a first-floor window and ran away, bare-footed, into the forests on his estate, running through water when the SS started tracking him with German shepherd dogs.

Two days later Gottliebe von Lehndorff received a telephone call from him saying where he was and that she should come and collect him in a car. Suddenly black cars, bristling with guns and SS, swept up: they had been tapping her phone. They drove off and captured her husband, taking him to prison in Königsberg. He decided not to escape for fear of what might happen to his wife and children. They had three daughters, and Gottliebe von Lehndorff was pregnant with her fourth.

She had known that something was planned: Major-General Tresckow had told her on 10 July that 'it had to be done'. She had frequent contact with many of the conspirators and noticed on 18 and 19 July that everyone had become very nervous. In fact, she thought them too nervous to carry it through.

On 20 July, General Heusinger's aide had come to visit Steinort and take coffee with Gottliebe von Lehndorff. At 2 p.m. the telephone rang; it was OKH headquarters; he was to report immediately to the Wolfsschanze. He returned to Steinort at 4 p.m. saying, 'I saw Hitler and nothing happened to him. Everyone is completely crazy there.' Shortly before this, Ribbentrop's adjutant had come and informed her of the bomb and Hitler's survival.

Heinrich von Lehndorff was brought before the people's court: he stood his ground, saying, 'I have done this because I consider Hitler to be a murderer.'

Gottliebe von Lehndorff and her children were all arrested. The children, the eldest of whom was seven, were told to say goodbye to their mother: 'You will have to change your names and Hitler will educate you and you will never see your mother again.' The children were taken to a concentration camp where they were separated from each other. The eldest managed to find only her youngest sister, aged one.

Heavily pregnant, Gottliebe von Lehndorff was imprisoned in Torgau until the birth of her daughter. Four days later she was taken by two Gestapo women to another camp. After a train journey she was made to walk, carrying her child, from the station to the camp. She was very weak and was bleeding. The Gestapo women beat her each time she fell. When she arrived at the camp, she collapsed, unconscious.

Later she received her husband's last letter: he wrote that 'It was more important to do this, more important than our family.' He begged that she would understand this.

25  Zeller, op.cit., p.370.
26  Kramarz, op.cit., p.9.
27  Zeller, op.cit., p.370.
28  Leber, *Conscience in Revolt*, p.262.
29  On 15 October 1992, 2nd-Lt Ewald Heinrich von Kleist, of the 9th Infantry Regiment of Potsdam, spoke to us of 20 July 1944 as a day in which 'history was balancing on the edge of a knife'. He explained that such an atmosphere forms people, guides people: even the air, in some way, feels heavier.

Kleist was an aide in the Army Headquarters at the Bendlerstrasse. Late in the afternoon of 20 July he met, on the stairs, his friend Captain Friedrich Klausing, also of the 9th Infantry Regiment, who was acting as an aide to Stauffenberg. Kleist inquired where he was going. Klausing replied, 'To get a pistol.' 'Why?' asked Kleist. Klausing stopped and said, 'Now, you know we have been together in Russia. We have been in tight situations and I always said that we would get out of it. But this time it is over.' Nevertheless Klausing played his part and was executed for it.

As there were no troops at the Army headquarters Kleist was sent to the local Berlin Headquarters to see the commander, Lt-General Paul von Hase – a member of the conspiracy – and obtain some troops. All was in great confusion there and he was unable to achieve anything.

He returned to the Bendlerstrasse, walking cautiously through the Tiergarten, pondering the events of the day. In the distance he heard shooting which he thought did not bode well. He sat down to think about what to do. He had an escape route prepared: in wartime, to use any type of transportation one needed documents, the best being a 'white' paper which would cover every type of transport. Kleist had a number of these, all correctly stamped for use. He had discovered a German battalion in Norway, very near to the Swedish border, and he intended going there and then escaping into Sweden. While he was considering all this, he could hear the trains going by very close to him. He could easily have escaped at that moment. But he did not wish to leave until he knew the situation at Headquarters. So he carried on to the Bendlerstrasse, where he was later arrested and taken to a Gestapo prison.

On one occasion, between interrogations, he was pushed face first against a wall with his hands spread above his head. Another prisoner was brought in and also pushed against the wall. He glanced cautiously to the side and saw his

father. They could not speak but his father's eyes said, 'I hope you behave' –
that is, I hope you have refused to talk. Kleist never saw his father again.

His trial was set for December 1944, but unexpectedly he was set free. He
went home, had a good bath, a meal and a sleep, then, as he was curious about
why he had been released, he returned to the Gestapo HQ the next day to find
out.

He was interrogated in a curious fashion, the Gestapo officer asking leading
questions, hinting at how he should answer. For example: 'I said that on release
you would go to the front line right away.' To this, Kleist quickly agreed, and
although he realised that he was supposed to go to the east, he went instead to
see a friend in the High Command of the army fighting in Italy and obtained
papers to travel there. He was captured there by the Allies.

Long after the war he met up with an SS general who told him the reason
that he had been released was in order to try to find his friend Ludwig von
Hammerstein, who was still at large. They thought that Hammerstein might
break cover and try to contact Kleist.

30  Zimmermann and Jacobsen, op.cit., p.212.
31  Speer, *Inside the Third Reich*, p.395.
32  Zimmermann and Jacobsen, op.cit., p.201.
33  Ibid.
34  Ibid.
35  Ibid.
36  Klemperer, *German Resistance against Hitler*, p.385.
37  Schlabrendorff, op.cit., pp.294–5.
38  Leber, op.cit., p.259.
39  Zimmermann and Jacobsen, op.cit., p.254.
40  Leber, op.cit., p.186.
41  Zeller, op.cit., p.132.
42  Hoffmann, *The History of the German Resistance 1933–1945*, p.526.
43  Leber, op.cit., p.250.
44  For a discussion of the various recollections of Stauffenberg's last words see
    Hoffmann, *The History of the German Resistance 1933–1945*, p.710, n.12; *Claus
    Schenk Graf von Stauffenberg und seine Brüder*, p.598, n.318; 'Claus Graf
    Stauffenberg und Stefan George: Der Weg zur Tat' in *Jahbuch der deutschen
    Schillergesellschaft*, Bd.12, p.540.

*4 Blood and Iron*

1  Wunder, *Die Schenken von Stauffenberg*, p.71.
2  Ibid., p.101.
3  Ibid., p.100.
4  Ibid., p.105.
5  Ibid., p.80.

6  Ibid., p.462.
7  Ibid., p.321.


5 *The Cult of Stefan George*

1  Kramarz, *Stauffenberg*, p.19.
2  Pfizer, 'Die Brüder Stauffenberg', *Robert Boehringer. Eine Freundesgabe*, p.489.
3  Ibid., p.499.
4  Hoffmann, *Claus Schenk Graf von Stauffenberg und seine Brüder*, p.85.
5  Ibid.
6  Ibid., p.93.
7  Interview with Major-General Berthold von Stauffenberg, Stuttgart, 14 September 1992.
8  Interviewed in the television documentary 'The Restless Conscience' by Hava Kohav Beller, 1991.

We talked to Major Axel von dem Bussche on 6 and 7 December 1992. He told us of what he considered to be the profoundest moment of his life, when his eyes opened and he realised the full horror of the true situation in Germany. He used an odd word to describe this awakening which, he said, took place while he was serving in the Ukraine in October 1942.

'I was *privileged* to see hundreds of naked Jews shot at the airport of Dubno. I knew I had to do something. I said that we have to kill the Führer to destroy the power of the oath, for by this, he had captured the flower of the German Youth.'

Subsequently, through his friend and fellow officer in the 9th Infantry Regiment of Potsdam, Fritz-Dietlof von der Schulenburg, Bussche was drawn into the anti-Hitler conspiracy.

Bussche was much wounded and much decorated: he lost his thumb in France, where he was awarded the Knight's Cross, and was wounded in the lung near Moscow in the winter of 1941. During 1942 he served in the Ukraine and the Crimea as an officer in a Romanian regiment. He later took part in the siege of Leningrad.

During the siege, Bussche and his fellow officers, including Captain Friedrich Klausing and Lt Richard von Weizsäcker (later President of Germany) were sitting in the commander's dacha one evening drinking schnapps. Their commander was absent. On the wall in front of them was a photograph of Hitler. Suddenly one officer drew out his pistol and shot at Hitler's portrait, putting a hole through Hitler's forehead and the wall behind.

There was a dreadful moment of silence. Then Weizsäcker said, 'Before we discuss what to do we had better all shoot at it.' So the others drew their pistols and fired at the portrait: it then had six holes through it. Another silence followed. They decided to take the portrait down and replace it with another. This would also cover the bullet holes. Unfortunately they discovered that there was no other portrait: the one they had destroyed was the sole regimental allocation.

Again they stopped to consider what they had done. They all wondered how they might justify their actions to their commander, a former policeman. Then one recalled a German army regulation: that if a superior officer got into a fight with any of his subordinate officers then that superior would be transferred without further investigation.

Accordingly, later that evening, when they heard their commander returning over the snow, they all rushed outside and, acting drunk, gave him a resounding beating. Then they retired to their quarters. The next day, feeling rather nervous, they apologised to him. He said that he had been dealing on the black-market and thought that they had beaten him up for bringing the regiment into disrepute. He never talked about the incident again, neither did he ever report the reason for the bullet holes in his wall.

Later, in December 1943, Bussche was again badly wounded. He lost one leg and retained only partial use of the other. He was to spend almost a year in an SS hospital – for they had the best facilities, which he merited as a highly decorated officer.

While there, he became friendly with a nurse who told him, in horror, of the things she was witnessing: the chief surgeon was a fervent Nazi involved in medical experiments. She told him how, on one occasion, when a new shoulder blade was transplanted on to an SS officer, the replacement blade had come from a concentration camp inmate especially executed for the purpose.

Bussche was still in his hospital bed on 20 July 1944. He heard on the radio about Stauffenberg's bomb and that it had failed. A leading Nazi, Robert Ley, came on the radio to rant about 'blue-blooded swine and traitors'.

The next day one of Bussche's nurses returned from Berlin extremely angry. On the previous afternoon she had been in the office of her husband, an SS officer, when the telephone rang. Her husband listened, then turned to her and said, 'Now it has started.' He took out a steel helmet and grenades and took up a post by the window. He was expecting the building to be stormed by anti-Hitler troops that afternoon.

Bussche spent the night of 20 July eating his address book, page by page. Yet in his kit he still had the explosives from his own abortive attempt to assassinate Hitler during the showing of new uniforms. It was some time before a friend was able to get rid of them.

Three days before the coup attempt the extrovert Captain Klausing had visited Bussche in hospital and had made himself very popular among the SS there. He appeared on the first published list of those arrested. Some time later Bussche was invited to drink some wine with the wounded SS officers. They said, 'Well, your friend Klausing made such a good impression that we have sent a cable to the Führer asking that he not be hanged.' The Führer replied that all must hang. The day after Klausing was executed, his father, a convinced

Nazi and rector of the University of Prague, shot himself.

After his discharge from hospital Bussche was granted a small car, modified so that he could drive it despite his injuries. Late in March 1945 he travelled to Berlin to collect it. As he was leaving he was flagged down by a colonel in full battledress who said he was in command of that sector of Berlin and yet had no fuel for his own transport. Bussche gave him a lift.

During the journey they drove past a number of trams being filled with rubble. Bussche, in some astonishment, asked what this was for. The Colonel replied that it was to stop the Russian tanks. In disbelief Bussche inquired as to how long he thought such obstacles would stop them. 'About sixty seconds,' replied the Colonel dryly. 'Fifty-nine seconds for them to stop and laugh and one second to drive through.'

'But don't worry,' he added, 'we have a secret weapon.' Bussche looked at him. 'You have heard of the V-1 and the V-2 weapons? Well, we have the V-8 to end the war.' And what was that, Bussche inquired sceptically. 'Adolf with a club,' retorted the Colonel. Bussche then knew that it was all finished.

After the war Bussche met the pharmacist who had prepared the suicide pills for the Nazi leadership once they realised that they were probably going to lose the war. It was with one of these pills that Himmler and Goering took their own lives. Bussche asked at what date did the leadership request these. Early 1944, was the reply.

9  Interview with Ewald Heinrich von Kleist, Munich, 15 October 1992.
10  Ibid.
11  Ibid.
12  Ibid.
13  Kramarz, op.cit., pp.69–70.
14  Mann, 'Freud and the Future', *Essays*, p.319.
15  Ibid.
16  Ibid.
17  Ibid., pp.319–20.
18  Ibid., p.320.
19  Musil, *The Man Without Qualities*, I, p.45.
20  Schiller, *Wilhelm Tell*, p.55 (ll. 1274–8).
21  For a review of the Wandervögel groups, see Rudolph Raasch, *Deutsche Jugendbewegung 1900–1933*, German edition: Frankfurt, 1991; George L. Mosse, 'The Youth Movement', *The Crisis of German Ideology*, pp.171ff.
22  Kramarz, op.cit., p.23 and p.186, n.16.
23  J. Kramarz, *Claus Graf Stauffenberg*, German edition: Frankfurt, 1965, p.20.
24  Thormaehlen, 'Die Grafen Stauffenberg freunde von Stefan George', *Robert Boehringer. Eine Freundesgabe*, p.693.
25  Ibid., p.694 and p.695.
26  Hoffmann, *Claus Schenk Graf von Stauffenberg und seine Brüder*, p.83.
27  Thormaehlen, op.cit., p.695.

28  Goldsmith, *Stefan George: A Study of his Early Work*, p.1.

29  Bennett, *Stefan George*, p.18.

30  Scott, *Bone of Contention*, p.111.

31  George, *Werke*, p.295.

32  Kramarz, *Stauffenberg*, pp.26–7.

33  Pfizer, op.cit., p.492.

34  Hoffmann, 'Claus Graf Stauffenberg und Stefan George: Der Weg zur Tat', *Jahrbuch der deutschen Schillergesellschaft*, Bd.12, p.528.

35  Thormaehlen, op.cit., p.695.

36  Hoffmann, *Claus Schenk Graf von Stauffenberg und seine Brüder*, p.76.

37  Ibid., p.78.

38  Thormaehlen, op.cit., p.693.

39  Kramarz, *Stauffenberg*, p.25.

40  All the letters from Claus von Stauffenberg to Stefan George quoted are held in the Stefan George-Archiv in the Württembergischen Landesbibliothek, Stuttgart. This letter has been published in Hoffmann, *Claus Schenk Graf von Stauffenberg und seine Brüder*, p.80.

41  George, *The Works of Stefan George*, trans. Marx and Morwitz, p.343.

42  Pfizer, op.cit., p.501.

43  George, op.cit., trans. Marx and Morwitz, p.307.

## 6 The New Reich

1   Hoffmann, *Claus Schenk Graf von Stauffenberg und seine Brüder*, p.84.

2   Zeller, *The Flame of Freedom*, p.174.

3   Kramarz, *Stauffenberg*, p.35.

4   Ibid., p.33.

5   Ibid., p.35.

6   Hoffmann, op. cit., p.97.

7   Ibid.

8   Craig, *Germany 1866–1945*, p.568.

9   Grunberger, *A Social History of the Third Reich*, p.427.

10  Kramarz, op.cit., p.25.

11  George, *Werke*, p.258.

12  Hoffmann, op. cit., p.118.

13  Ibid., p.117.

14  Ibid.

15  Boehringer, *Mein bild von Stefan George*, p.202.

16  Hoffmann, op. cit. p.128.

17  Pfizer, *Die Brüder Stauffenberg*, p.490.

18  This information was first published in H. Foertsch, *Schuld und Verhangnis*, Stuttgart, 1951, p.22. It is discussed critically by Kramarz, op. cit., pp.37–40 and p.191, n.2–6; Hoffmann, *Claus Schenk Graf von Stauffenberg und seine*

*Brüder*, p.123 and at considerable length on pp.507–9, n.115.

19 Kramarz, op.cit., p.41.
20 Ibid.
21 Zeller, op.cit., p.184.
22 Herwarth, *Against Two Evils*, p.216.
23 Kramarz, op.cit., p.42.
24 Grunberger, op.cit., p.424.
25 Craig, op.cit., p.589.
26 Ibid., p.590.
27 Shirer, *The Rise and Fall of the Third Reich*, p.283.
28 Interview with Axel von dem Bussche, Bonn, 6–7 December 1992.
29 Interview with Ewald Heinrich von Kleist, Munich, 15 October 1992.
30 Interview with Axel von dem Bussche, Bonn, 6–7 December 1992.
31 Hoffmann, op. cit. p.121.
32 Ibid., p.132; Kramarz, op.cit., p.41.
33 Kramarz, op.cit., p.44.

7 *The Path of Aggression*

1 Kramarz, *Stauffenberg*, pp.45–6.
2 Ibid., p.46.
3 Ibid.
4 Ibid., p.47.
5 Ibid., p.48.
6 Zeller, *The Flame of Freedom*, p.175.
7 Kramarz, op.cit., p.48.
8 Ibid.
9 Zeller, op.cit., p.178.
10 Ibid., p.177.
11 Ibid.
12 Kramarz, op.cit., pp. 50–1.
13 Ibid., p.51.
14 J. Kramarz, *Claus Graf Stauffenberg*, German edition: Frankfurt, 1965, p.58.
15 Kramarz, op.cit., pp.54–5.
16 Meehan, *The Unnecessary War*, p.115.
17 Kramarz, op.cit., p.59.
18 Gisevius, *To the Bitter End*, p.334.
19 Kramarz, op.cit., p.58.
20 Zeller, op.cit., p.186.
21 Kramarz, op.cit., p.61.
22 Mann, *Doctor Faustus*, p.291.
23 Kramarz, op.cit., p.57.
24 Ibid.

25  Hitler had ordered mass killings. He informed the High Command of this at a meeting at the Berghof, 22 August 1939. He said:

'Our strength lies in our quickness and in our brutality; Genghis Khan has sent millions of women and children into death knowingly and with a light heart. History sees in him only the great founder of States. As to what the weak Western European civilisation asserts about me, that is of no account. I have given the command and I shall shoot everyone who utters one word of criticism, for the goal to be obtained in the war is not that of reaching certain lines but of physically demolishing the opponent. And so for the present only in the East I have put my death-head formations in place with the command relentlessly and without compassion to send into death many women and children of Polish origin and language. Only thus can we gain the living space that we need . . . Be hard, be without mercy, act more quickly and brutally than the others. The citizens of Western Europe must tremble with horror.'

Following this speech, Goering, enthused, 'jumped on a table . . . [and] danced like a wild man'. See: *Documents on British Foreign Policy*, 3rd Series, Vol. VII, pp.258–9.

26  Kramarz, op.cit., p.61.
27  Ibid., p.72.
28  Ibid.

*8 Operation Barbarossa*

1   Kramarz, *Stauffenberg*, p.75.
2   Herwarth, *Against Two Evils*, p.217.
3   Kramarz, op.cit., pp.74–5.
4   Zeller, *The Flame of Freedom*, p.187.
5   Ibid.
6   Herwarth, op.cit., p.210.
7   Van Roon, *German Resistance to Hitler*, p.269.
8   Kramarz, op.cit., pp.66–7.
9   Herwarth, op.cit., pp.215–16.
10  Kramarz, op.cit., pp.67–8.
11  Ibid. p.69.
12  Ibid.
13  Ibid., p.73.
14  Ibid., p.74.
15  Schlabrendorff, *The Secret War against Hitler*, pp.245–8.
16  Kramarz, op.cit., p.78.
17  Parker, *Struggle for Survival*, p.267.
18  Ibid.
19  Zeller, op.cit., p.188.
20  Kramarz, op.cit., p.91.

# Notes and References

21  Ibid.
22  Hoffmann, *Claus Schenk Graf von Stauffenberg und seine Brüder*, p.251.
23  Hitler, *Table Talk 1941–1944*, p.617, 6 August 1942.
24  Herwarth, op.cit., p.216.
25  Goebbels, *The Goebbels Diaries*, p.135, 25 April 1942.
26  Ibid., p.169, 22 May 1942.
27  Ibid., p.254, 14 April 1943.
28  The history of these organisations is given in Andreyev, *Vlasov and the Russian Liberation Movement*.
29  Kramarz, op.cit., p.83.
30  Herwarth, op.cit., p.221.
31  Ibid., p.216.
32  Zeller, op.cit., p.181.
33  Graber, *Stauffenberg*, p.105.
34  Kramarz, op.cit., p.96.
35  Ibid., pp.92–3.
36  Hoffmann, op. cit., p.268.
37  Zeller, op.cit., pp.189–90.
38  Ibid., p.190.
39  Kramarz, op.cit., p.97.
40  Zeller, op.cit., p.191.
41  Hoffmann, op. cit., p.259.

## 9 After the War of Liberation

1  Koch, *A History of Prussia*, p.196.
2  Introduction by R. J. Hollingdale to Fontane, *Before the Storm*, p.xx.
3  Wykes, *Himmler*, pp.121–2.

## 10 Culture and Conquest

1  Goethe, *Conversations and Encounters*, p.92.
2  Ibid., pp.92–3.
3  Heine, 'Concerning the History of Religion and Philosophy in Germany' in *Selected Works*, p.417.
4  Ibid.
5  Ibid., pp.417–18.
6  Ibid., p.418.
7  Mosse, *The Crisis of German Ideology*, p.15.
8  Ibid.
9  Mosse, *Toward the Final Solution*, p.47.
10  Copleston, *Fichte to Nietzsche*, p.162.
11  Ibid., p.220.
12  Ibid., p.223.

# Notes and References

13 Ibid., p.220.
14 Ibid., p.213.
15 Ibid., p.218.

## 11 Myth and Might

1 Broch, *The Sleepwalkers*, p.373.
2 Ibid., p.647.
3 Jung, 'The Role of the Unconscious', *Civilisation in Transition* (Collected Works, vol. 10), p.13.
4 Jung, 'Wotan', op.cit., p.184.
5 Brod, *Heinrich Heine*, p.21.
6 Scholder, *The Churches and the Third Reich*, vol. 1, p.417.
7 Ibid., vol. 1, p.420.
8 Ibid.
9 Ibid., vol. 1, p.531.
10 Robertson, *Christians against Hitler*, p.25.
11 Ibid., p.18.
12 Rosenberg, *The Myth of the Twentieth Century*, p.387.
13 Jung, *Civilisation in Transition*, p.190, n.16.
14 Tournier, *The Erl-King*, p.228.
15 For a discussion of the religious aspects of National Socialism see M. Baigent, R. Leigh and H. Lincoln, *The Messianic Legacy*, London, 1986, pp.135ff.
16 Seward, *The Monks of War*, p.135.
17 Heine, 'Concerning the History of Religion and Philosophy in Germany' in *Selected Works*, p.417.
18 Mosse, *The Crisis of German Ideology*, p.184.
19 Tournier, op.cit., p.231.
20 Siemsen, *Hitler Youth*, p.65.
21 Much of this information was given in the trial of Baldur von Schirach at Nuremberg, see: *Trials of the Major War Criminals, Proceedings . . .* Part 14, pp.360–408, especially pp.396–400; See also ibid., Part 15, pp.1–30. The following song was sung by members of the Hitler Youth at the Party Rally, 1934:

> We are the rollicking Hitler Youth:
> We have no need of Christian truth;
> For Adolf Hitler is our Leader
> And our Interceder.
>
> No evil old priest these ties can sever;
> We're Hitler's children now and ever.

This was presented as evidence for the prosecution. See ibid., Part 14, p.397.

22 Bentine, *The Door Marked Summer*, p.291.

23 Goodrick-Clarke, *The Occult Roots of Nazism*, p.2.

24 Ibid.

25 Ibid., p.195.

26 Ibid., p.33.

27 For the Thule Gesellschaft see: Phelps, 'Before Hitler Came', *Journal of Modern History*, xxxv, 1963, pp.251ff; and Goodrick-Clarke, op.cit., pp.144ff.

28 A list of Thule members and sympathisers is given in Sebottendorf, *Bevor Hitler Kam*, pp.221ff.


*12 Legislators of the World*

1 George, *The Works of Stefan George*, Marx and Morwitz, p.363.

2 Ibid., p.365.

3 Bennett, *Stefan George*, p.12.

4 Goldsmith, *Stefan George: A Study of his Early Work*, p.120.

5 George, op.cit., pp.238–9.

6 Ibid., p.338.

7 Hoffmann, *Claus Schenk Graf von Stauffenberg und seine Brüder*, p.65.

8 Ibid.

9 Landmann, *Erinnerungen an Stefan George seine Freundschaft mit Julius und Edith Landmann*, p.137.

10 Gay, *Weimar Culture*, p.50.

11 George, op.cit., p.378.

12 Ibid., p.309.

13 Ibid., p.362.

14 Ibid., p.363.

15 Ibid., p.257.

16 Ibid., p.267.

17 Ibid., p.318.

18 Ibid., p.319.

19 Kantorowicz, *Kaiser Friedrich der Zweite*, Vorbemerkung.

20 An alternative translation of the words into English is: 'It lives, our Secret Germany!'

21 Bowra, *The Heritage of Symbolism*, p.140.

22 Reeves, *Joachim of Fiore and the Prophetic Future*, p.62.

23 Interview with Hans-Dietrich Fuhlendorf, Keil, 11 October 1992. For a discussion of this point, see his *Rückkehr zum Paradies oder Erbauen dies Neuen Jerusalem?*, pp., 192–3.

24 Hoffmann, op. cit., p.66.

25 George, op.cit., p.219.

26 Gay, op.cit., p.49.

27 Kramarz, *Stauffenberg*, p.28.

28  Landmann, op.cit., p.136.
29  George, op.cit., p.326.
30  Mann, *Letters*, p.96.
31  Zeller, *The Flame of Freedom*, p.448, n.14, quoting *Spiegelbild einer Verschwöring*, p.455.
32  Zeller, op.cit., p.395. For the complete oath see Hoffmann, op. cit., pp.396-7.
33  George, op.cit., pp.371-4.
34  Ibid., p.398.
35  Ibid., p.239.
36  Ibid., p.322.

*13 In the Courtyard of the Bendlerstrasse*

1  Schlabrendorff, *The Secret War Against Hitler*, pp.294-5
2  Kramarz, *Stauffenberg*, p.104.
3  Thucydides, *History of the Peloponnesian War*, p.147.
4  Musil, *The Man Without Qualities*, p.46.

# Bibliography

Andreyev, C. *Vlasov and the Russian Liberation Movement* (Cambridge, 1987)

Astor, D. 'Why the Revolt against Hitler Was Ignored', *Encounter*, vol. xxxii, No. 6 (June, 1969), pp. 3ff.

Balfour, M. *Withstanding Hitler* (London, 1988)

Bender, R. J. and Law, R. D. *Uniforms, Organization and History of the Afrikakorps* (Mountain View, 1973)

Bennett, E. K. *Stefan George* (Cambridge, 1954)

Bentine, M. *The Door Marked Summer* (St Albans, 1982)

Bielenberg, C. *The Past Is Myself* (London, 1970)

Boehringer, R. *Mein Bild von Stefan George* (München, 1951)

Bowra, C. M. *The Heritage of Symbolism* (London, 1947)

Broch, H. *The Sleepwalkers*, trans. Willa and Edwin Muir (London, 1986)

Brod, M., *Heinrich Heine*, trans. Joseph Witriol, (London, 1956)

Bullock, A. *Hitler: A Study in Tyranny* (London, 1952)

Carsten, F. L. *A History of the Prussian Junkers* (Aldershot, 1989)

Christiansen, E. *The Northern Crusades* (London, 1980)

Copleston, F. 'Fichte to Nietzsche'. Volume VII of *A History of Philosophy* (London 1971).

Craig, G. A. *Germany 1866–1945* (Oxford, 1978)

Crankshaw, E. *Bismarck* (London, 1981)

Denslow, W. R. *10,000 Famous Freemasons*, 4 vols (Richmond, 1961)

Deutsch, H. C. *The Conspiracy against Hitler in the Twilight War* (Minneapolis, 1968)

Deutsch, H. C. 'German Soldiers in the 1938 Munich Crisis' in *Germans Against Nazism*, ed. Francis R. Nicosia and Lawrence D. Stokes (Oxford, 1990)

*Directory of Wheeled Vehicles of the Wehrmacht 1933–45*, ed. Chris Ellis (London, 1974)

Dulles, A. W. *Germany's Underground* (New York, 1947)

FitzGibbon, C. *To Kill Hitler* (London, 1972). First published as *The Shirt of Nessus* (London, 1956)

# Bibliography

Fontane, T. *Before the Storm,* trans. R. J. Hollingdale, (Oxford, 1985)

Frey, A. *Cross and Swastika,* trans. J Strathearn McNab (London, 1938)

Fuhlendorf, H-D. *Rückkehr zum Paradies oder Erbauen dies Neuen Jerusalem?* (Flensburg, 1992)

Galante, P. *Hitler Lives – and the Generals Die* (London, 1982)

Gay, P. *Weimar Culture* (Harmondsworth, 1992)

George, S. *Werke* (Stuttgart, 1984)

George, S. *The Works of Stefan George,* trans. Olga Marx and Ernst Morwitz, 2nd, rev.ed. (Chapel Hill, 1974)

Gisevius, H. B. *To the Bitter End,* trans. Richard and Clare Winstone (London, 1948)

Goebbels, J., *The Goebbels Diaries,* trans. and ed. Louis P. Lochner (London, 1948)

Goethe, J. W. von *Conversations and Encounters,* ed. and trans. David Luke and Robert Pick (London, 1966)

Goldsmith, U. K. *Stefan George: A Study of his Early Work* (Boulder, 1959)

Goodrick-Clarke, N. *The Occult Roots of Nazism* (Wellingborough, 1985)

Gordon, H. J. *Hitler and the Beer Hall Putsch* (Princeton, 1972)

Graber, G. *Stauffenberg* (New York, 1973)

Grunberger, R. *A Social History of the Third Reich* (London, 1974)

Gundolf, E. 'Stefan George und der Nationalsozialismus' in *Castrum Peregrini,* lxix, (1965), pp.52ff.

Hassell, U. von *The Von Hassell Diaries 1938–1944* (London, 1948)

Heiden, K. *Hitler. A Biography* (London, 1936)

Heine, H. *Selected Works,* trans. Helen M. Mustard (New York, 1973)

Herwarth, J. von. *Against Two Evils* (London, 1981)

Heston, L. L. and R. *The Medical Casebook of Adolf Hitler* (London, 1979)

Himmler, H. 'Nachlass Himmler', typescript, Bundesarchiv, Koblenz, 1966

Hitler, A. *Mein Kampf,* trans., James Murphy (London, 1939)

Hitler, A. *Hitler's Table Talk 1941–1944,* trans. Norman Cameron and R. H. Stevens (London, 1953)

Hoffmann, P. 'Claus Graf Stauffenberg und Stefan George: Der Weg zur Tat' in *Jahrbuch der deutschen Schillergesellschaft,* Bd.12, 1968, pp.520ff.

Hoffmann, P. *Hitler's Personal Security* (London, 1979)

Hoffmann, P. *The History of the German Resistance 1933–1945,* trans. Richard Barry (Cambridge, Mass., 1979)

Hoffmann, P. 'Peace through Coup d'Etat: The foreign contacts of the German Resistance 1933–1944' in *Central European History,* vol. xix, No.1 (March 1986) pp.3ff.

Hoffmann, P. *German Resistance to Hitler* (Cambridge, Mass., 1988)

Hoffmann, P. 'Internal Resistance in Germany', in Large, D. C. *Contending with Hitler* (Cambridge, 1991), pp.127ff.

Hoffmann, P. *Claus Schenk Graf von Stauffenberg und seine Brüder* (Stuttgart, 1992)

# Bibliography

Höhne, H. and Zolling, H. *The General Was a Spy*, trans. Richard Barry (London, 1971)

Höhne, H. *Canaris*, trans. J Maxwell Brownjohn (London, 1979)

Höhne, H. *The Order of the Death's Head*, trans. Richard Barry (London, 1981)

Holborn, H. *Ulrich von Hutten and the German Reformation* (New Haven, 1937)

Howe, E. *The Magicians of the Golden Dawn* (London, 1972)

Jackson, W. G. F. *The North African Campaign* (London, 1975)

John, O. *Twice through the Lines*, trans. Richard Barry (London, 1972)

Jung, C. G. *Civilisation in Transition* (Collected Works, vol. 10), 2nd ed., trans. R. F. C. Hull (London, 1974)

Kantorowicz, E. *Kaiser Friedrich der Zweite*, 2 vols (Berlin, 1927)

Kershaw, I. *The Hitler Myth* (Oxford, 1991)

King, F. *The Secret Rituals of the O.T.O.* (London, 1973)

Klemperer, K. von *German Resistance against Hitler* (Oxford, 1992)

Klessmann, C. and Pingel, F. (eds) *Gegner des Nationalsozialismus* (Frankfurt, 1980)

Koch, H. W. *A History of Prussia* (New York, 1978)

Kramarz, J. *Stauffenberg: The Life and Death of an Officer*, trans. Richard Barry (London, 1967)

Krausnick, H. and Broszat, M. *Anatomy of the SS State*, trans. Dorothy Long and Marian Jackson (London, 1979)

Lamb, R. *The Ghosts of Peace 1935–1945* (Wilton, 1987)

Landmann, M. *Erinnerungen an Stefan George seine Freundschaft mit Julius und Edith Landmann* (Amsterdam, 1970)

Large, D. C. (ed.) *Contending with Hitler* (Cambridge, 1991)

Leber, A. *Conscience in Revolt*, trans. Rosemary O'Neill (London, 1957)

Lennhoff, E. *The Freemasons*, trans. Einar Frame (Shepperton, 1978)

Lewes, G. H. *The Life and Works of Goethe* (London, 1965)

Liddell Hart, B. H. *History of the Second World War* (London, 1973)

Mann, G. *The History of Germany since 1789*, trans. Marion Jackson (Harmondsworth, 1990)

Mann, T. *Essays*, trans. H. T. Lowe-Porter (New York, 1957)

Mann, T. *Doctor Faustus*, trans. H. T. Lowe-Porter (Harmondsworth, 1968)

Mann, T. *The Letters of Thomas Mann*, selected and trans. Richard and Clare Winston (London, 1970)

Manvell, R. and Fraenkel, H. *The July Plot* (London, 1964)

Maurer, M. *Airforce Combat Units of World War II* (Washington, 1980)

Mead, G. R. S. *Simon Magus* (London, 1892)

Meding, D. von *Mit dem Mut des Herzens. Die Frauen des 20. Juli* (Berlin, 1992)

Meehan, P. *The Unnecessary War* (London, 1992)

Mosse, G. L. *The Crisis of German Ideology* (London, 1966)

Mosse, G. L. *Toward the Final Solution* (London, 1978)

Mund, R. J. *Jörg Lanz von Liebenfels und der Neue Templer Orden* (Stuttgart, 1976)

# Bibliography

Musil, R. *The Man without Qualities,* trans. Eithne Wilkins and Ernst Kaiser, 3 vols (London, 1954)

*Nazi Conspiracy and Aggression,* United States Office of Chief Counsel for Prosecution of Axis Criminality, ed. R. W. Barrett and W. E. Jackson, 8 vols, 2 supplements (Washington, 1946–1948)

Nicosia, F. R. and Stokes, L. D. (eds) *Germans against Nazism* (Oxford, 1990)

O'Leary, M. *USAF Fighters of World War Two* (Poole, 1986)

Orlow, D. *The History of the Nazi Party,* 2 vols (Newton Abbot, 1971)

Padfield, P. *Himmler: Reichsführer-SS* (London, 1991)

Paret, P. *Yorck and the Era of Prussian Reform 1807–1815* (Princeton, 1966)

Parker, R. A. C. *Struggle for Survival* (Oxford, 1989)

Peterson, C. *Stefan George* (Berlin, 1980)

Pfizer, T. 'Die Brüder Stauffenberg' in *Robert Boehringer. Eine Freundesgabe* (Tübingen, 1957) pp.487ff

Phelps. R. H. 'Before Hitler Came: Thule Society and Germanen Orden' in *Journal of Modern History,* vol. xxxv, No.3 (Sept. 1963) pp.245f.

Preussen, L. F. von *Im Strom der Geschichte* (München, 1989)

Reeves, M. *Joachim of Fiore and the Prophetic Future* (London, 1976)

Reitlinger, G. *The SS: Alibi of a Nation, 1922–1945* (London, 1981)

Reynolds, N. *Treason Was No Crime* (London, 1976)

Riess, C. *Joseph Goebbels* (London, 1949)

Robertson E. H. *Christians against Hitler* (London, 1962)

Rosenberg, A. *The Myth of the Twentieth Century,* trans. Vivian Bird (Torrance, Calif., 1982)

Schacht, H. *Account Settled,* trans. Edward Fitzgerald (London, 1949)

Scheibert, H. *Deutsche Panzergrenadiere 1939–1945* (Dorheim, 1968)

Schellenberg, W. *The Schellenberg Memoirs,* trans. Louis Hagen (London, 1956)

Schiller, F. von., *Wilhelm Tell,* trans. William F. Mainland, (Chicago, 1972)

Schlabrendorff, F. von *The Secret War against Hitler,* trans. Hilda Simon (London, 1966)

Scholder, K. *The Churches and the Third Reich,* trans. John Bowden, 2 vols (London, 1987)

Schonauer, F. *Stefan George* (Hamburg, 1986)

Scott, C. *My Years of Indiscretion* (London, 1924)

Scott, C. *Bone of Contention* (London, 1969)

Sebottendorf, R. von *Bevor Hitler Kam* (München, 1933)

Seward, D. *The Monks of War,* (St Albans, 1974)

Shirer, W. L. *The Rise and Fall of the Third Reich* (London, 1981)

Shores, C., Ring. H., Hess, W. N. *Fighters over Tunisia* (London, 1975)

Siemoneit, M. A. *Politische Interpretationen von Stefan Georges Dichtung* (Frankfurt, 1978)

Siemsen, H. *Hitler Youth,* trans. Trevor and Phyllis Blewitt (London, 1940)

Speer, A. *Inside the Third Reich,* trans. Richard and Clara Winston (London, 1970)

# Bibliography

*Spiegelbild einer Verschwörung: Die Kaltenbrunner-Berichte an Bormann und Hitler über das Attentat vom 20. Juli 1944* (Stuttgart, 1961)

Tennant, P. *Touchlines of War* (Hull, 1992)

Terraine, J. *The Right of the Line* (London, 1985)

Thormaehlen, L. 'Die Grafen Stauffenberg freunde von Stefan George' in *Robert Boehringer. Eine Freundesgabe* (Tübingen, 1957) pp.685ff

Thucydides *History of the Peloponnesian War*, trans. Rex Warner (Harmondsworth, 1972)

Tournier, M. *The Erl-King*, trans. Barbara Bray (London, 1972)

Trevor-Roper, H. R. *The Last Days of Hitler*, 4th ed. (London, 1971)

*Trial of the Major War Criminals before the International Military Tribunal. Proceedings of the International Military Tribunal Sitting at Nuremberg Germany*, 22 Parts, (London, 1946–1950)

Uxküll-Gyllenband, W. von *Das Revolutionäre Ethos bei Stefan George* (Tübingen, 1933)

Webb, J. *The Occult Establishment* (Glasgow, 1981)

Wheeler-Bennett, J. W. *The Nemesis of Power*, 2nd ed. (London, 1967)

Wistrich, R. *Who's Who in Nazi Germany* (London, 1982)

Wolf, E. 'Political and Moral Motives behind the Resistance' in *The German Resistance to Hitler*, ed. Walter Schmitthenner and Hans Bucheim, trans. Peter and Betty Ross (London, 1970)

Wunder, G. *Die Schenken von Stauffenberg* (Stuttgart, 1972)

Wykes, A. *Himmler* (London, 1972)

Zeller, E. *The Flame of Freedom*, trans. R. P. Heller and D. R. Masters (London, 1967)

Zimmermann, E. and Jacobsen, H-A. *Germans against Hitler. July 20, 1944*, 5th ed. trans. Allan and Lieselotte Yahraes (Bonn, 1969)

# Index

# Index

# Index

# Index

Hohenzollern family/dynasty, 74, 80, 88

Hölderlin, Friedrich, 98, 99, 100, 108, 206, 212, 215, 230, 242, 243, 261, 262, 268, 287

Holland/Netherlands, 15, 121, 270; Hitler's Blitzkrieg in (1940), 27, 162–3

Holy Land (Palestine), 72, 78, 80

Holy Roman Empire, 76–9

Homer, 99, 208, 288; *Iliad*, 288, 291, 292

homosexuality, 271–3; in *Death in Venice*, 272–3; Ernst Röhm's, 141; Stefan George's alleged, 112, 114, 256, 271–2, 273

Hugo, Victor, 194, 195

Humboldt, Alexander von, 195, 239

Hungary, 77, 78, 190, 222

Hutten, Hans von, 84

Hutten, Ulrich von, 84

Huysmans, Joris-Karl, 254

identity crisis, collective, 187–8, 196, 202, 205, 210, 214, 215, 223, 224, 245, 288, 296

industrialisation, 94, 214, 215, 245

Isabella, Queen (Friedrich II's second wife), 79

Israel, 244

Italy, Italians, 5, 15, 76–7, 78, 94, 167, 189, 218, 224, 253, 296

Japan, 1

Jena, Battle of (1806), 86, 189, 207

Jerusalem, Frederick the Great crowned king of (1229), 78

Jesus Christ, 104, 227–8, 268, 286

Jewish-Masonic conspiracy, alleged, 250

Jews, anti-Semitism, 62, 101, 130, 144, 172, 173, 230, 236, 244, 247, 248, 256, 269–70; *Kristallnacht* (1938), 157–9; and *Volkische* ideology, 210

Joachim de Fiore, 266, 267, 271

John, King of England, 79

John, Otto, 51, 54–5

Johnson, Lionel, 254

Jones, Jim, in Guiana, 224

Joyce, James, 254, 266, 295

Jung, C. G., 135, 136, 226, 238

Jünger, Ernst, 233–4, 235; *Storm of Steel*, 234

'Junker' class, 66, 71, 72–3, 74, 191

Kafka, Franz, 295

Kaltenbrunner, Ernest, 61, 63

Kant, Immanuel, 198, 199

Kantorowicz, Ernest, 264

Kassel, 32, 54

Kasserine Pass, Battle of (1943), 3

Keitel, Field Marshal Wilhelm, 42–3, 44, 45, 49, 50, 51

Kennedy, President John F., 28, 104

Kennedy, Robert, 28

Keynes, J. M., 149

Khyber Pass, 231

Kierkegaard, Søren, 198

Kiesel, Dr Georg, 61–2

King, Martin Luther, 28

Kipling, Rudyard, 230, 265

Klages, Ludwig, 256

Kleist, Field Marshal Erwin von, 162

Kleist, Lieutenant Ewald Heinrich von, 22, 36–7, 52, 53, 62, 101–2, 143, 286; escapes execution 305–6n

Kleist, Heinrich von, 230

Kluge, Field Marshal Gunther von, 23

Knights Hospitaller, 72

Knights of St John, 80, 85

Knights' Revolt (1552), 81, 84

Knights Templar, 72

Kommerell, Max, *Der Dichter als Führer in der deutschen Klassik*, 267–8

Königsberg (now Kaliningrad), 32, 34, 54

Koresh, David, 224

Kramarz, Joachim, 171

'Kreisau Circle', 16, 28, 169

*Kristallnacht* (1938), 157–9

Kronberger, Maximilian, 256–7, 258, 263, 271–2

L'Amour, Louis, 232

Landmann, Edith, 270

Langermann, Doctor, 228

Lanz, Adolf Josef *see* Liebenfels

Latin America, 239, 241

Latvia, Latvians, 72, 74, 176

laudanum, 238

329

# Index

Sédan, German breaththrough at (1940), 163
Seward, D., 232
Sfax, Tunisia, 5, 6
Shakespeare, William, 98, 99, 194, 208; *Julius Caesar*, 107
Shelley, Mary, 204
Shelley, Percy Bysshe, 194, 254
Shirer, William, 142
Sicily, 78, 79, 264; Allied invasion of, 5
Sickingen, Franz von, 84
Sidi Bou Zid, Battle of (1943), 3
Sidney, Sir Philip, 290
Signorelli, Luca, 127
Silesia, 78, 159, 161
Simon Magus, 128–9, 130, 229
Sinclair of Roslin, Henry, 73
*Sippenhaft* ('blood guilt'), Nazi doctrine of, 60
Smolensk, Russia, 23, 169
Sobibor concentration camp, 35
Socialist Reich Party (SRP), Neo-Nazi, 58
Solovyov, Vladimir, 211
Somme, Battle of the (1916), 218, 220
South-West Africa, 230
Soviet Union, 1, 15, 25, 29, 66, 135, 155, 190, 197, 240, 296; Battle of Stalingrad (1942–3), 1–2, 33, 179–82; German Army Group Centre in, 23; Nazi invasion of (Op. Barbarossa), 166, 167, 168–9, 172–3, 174–82; SS atrocities in, 172–3; Tresckow's plan to assassinate Hitler in (1943), 23; *see also* Russia
Spain, 76, 190, 192, 224–5
Special Operations Executive (SOE), 23
Speer, Albert, 11, 63
Spengler, Oswald, *The Decline of the West*, 230
Spinoza, Baruch, 198
SS (*Schützstaffeln*), 9, 18, 21, 23, 28, 31–2, 33, 52–3, 54, 55, 60, 61, 63, 101, 125, 144, 160, 162, 165, 172–3, 175, 177, 183, 200, 228, 232, 234, 248, 266, 287, 289; atrocities committed by, 172–3; *Einsatzkommandos* ('rapid reaction'

death squads), 160, 172; shooting of SA by, 140–2; Waffen-SS, 50, 172
Staedke, Helmut, 162
Stalin, Josef, 29, 135, 168, 174, 175, 176, 178, 198
Stalingrad, Battle of (1942–3), 1–2, 33, 179–82
State, Hegel's concept of the, 213, 214, 216, 230
Stauffenberg family, 75, 79–80, 84, 85, 97, 101, 105
Stauffenberg, Alexander von (brother), 60, 85, 87, 97, 99, 100, 106, 107, 109, 112–13, 114, 115, 121, 133, 158, 235; 'The Warrior', 117–18
Stauffenberg, Alfred Schenk, Graf von (father), 85, 97–8, 107, 110
Stauffenberg, Berthold Schenk von, 80
Stauffenberg, Berthold von (brother), 9, 18, 39, 41, 52, 60, 61, 85, 87, 97, 99, 100, 106, 107, 109, 113, 114, 115, 121, 133, 160, 235, 275
Stauffenberg, Major-General Berthold von (son), 101, 124, 264
Stauffenberg, Burkhard Schenk von, 80
Stauffenberg, Lieutenant-Colonel Claus Philipp Maria Schenk, Graf von: Stefan George's influence on, 40, 65, 66–7, 77, 99, 105, 107–8, 109, 110–19, 127–33, 136, 144, 150, 215, 225, 247, 251–2; personality/character, 4, 7–8, 60–1, 108–9, 122, 133–4, 151–2, 170–1; family, 79–80, 84, 85, 86–7; birth (1807), 97; early years and education, 97–100, 106–19; ill-health of, 99, 106, 122, 151; aristocratic service ideal of, 100–3, 105, 110, 116, 134, 138, 150–1; 'mythic consciousness' of, 103–5; and cult of willpower, 106; joins 'New Pathfinders', 107; passes his *Abitur* (1926), 109; military career, 110, 116, 117, 120–3, 127; his oath of allegiance to Stefan George, 114–15, 144, 280; significance of 'Der Bamberger Reiter' to, 118–19, 120; joins 17th Bavarian Cavalry (1926), 120–1;

# Index